T0214937

Communications in Computer and Information Science 1214

Commenced Publication in 2007
Founding and Former Series Editors:
Simone Diniz Junqueira Barbosa, Phoebe Chen, Alfredo Cuzzocrea,
Xiaoyong Du, Orhun Kara, Ting Liu, Krishna M. Sivalingam,
Dominik Ślęzak, Takashi Washio, Xiaokang Yang, and Junsong Yuan

Shilpi Gupta · Jignesh N. Sarvaiya (Eds.)

Emerging Technology Trends in Electronics, Communication and Networking

Third International Conference, ET2ECN 2020
Surat, India, February 7–8, 2020
Revised Selected Papers

 Springer

Editors
Shilpi Gupta 🆔
Sardar Vallabhbhai National Institute
of Technology
Surat, India

Jignesh N. Sarvaiya
Sardar Vallabhbhai National Institute
of Technology
Surat, India

ISSN 1865-0929   ISSN 1865-0937 (electronic)
Communications in Computer and Information Science
ISBN 978-981-15-7218-0   ISBN 978-981-15-7219-7 (eBook)
https://doi.org/10.1007/978-981-15-7219-7

This Springer imprint is published by the registered company Springer Nature Singapore Pte Ltd.
The registered company address is: 152 Beach Road, #21-01/04 Gateway East, Singapore 189721, Singapore

Preface

It is a matter of great privilege to have been tasked with the writing of this preface for the proceedings of Third International Conference on Emerging Technology Trends in Electronics, Communication and Networking (ET2ECN 2020), organized by the Electronics Engineering Department of Sardar Vallabhbhai National Institute of Technology, Surat, India, during February 7–8, 2020. This conference was followed by a great success of the previous two international conferences organized in 2012 and 2014.

Changing trends in society expect the value orientation of its youth; hence knowledge acquisition followed by appropriate implementation should be the focus. Being an academician, it is our moral responsibility to fulfil the need of society by providing technological developments and innovative ideas. This demands a platform where the eminent engineers, scientists, educators, and research scholars get to share their views. This conference was intended to provide a common platform for an interactive exchange of ideas and latest developments in the field of engineering especially electronics, communication, and networking. The noted features of the conference included invited talks and paper presentation sessions covering a wide range of topics, including electronic devices, VLSI design and fabrication, photo electronics, microwave circuits: systems and applications, integrated optics, embedded systems, wireless communication, optical communication, free space optics, signal processing, image/audio/video processing, wireless sensor networks, next generation networks, optical networks network security, and many others.

The Program Committee of ET2ECN 2020 is extremely grateful to authors who showed an overwhelming response to the call for papers, submitting over 80 papers in three tracks. The entire review team (Technical Program Committee members along with external experts as reviewers) expanded tremendous efforts to ensure fairness and consistency during the selection process, resulting in the best quality papers being selected for presentation and publication. It was ensured to have at least three reviews for each paper. Checking of similarities and overlapping was also done based on international norms and standards. We are very thankful to our reviewers for their efforts in finalizing the high-quality papers, and based on the recommendations, this present book contains 23 papers accepted for publication. The proceedings of the conference are published as one volume in the *Communications in Computer and Information Sciences* (CCIS) series by Springer. We place our gratitude as the chairs to the Organizing Committee members and students, whose constant involvement and dedication supported us at every stage of this great task.

We, in our capacity as volume editors, convey our sincere gratitude to Springer for providing the opportunity to publish the proceedings of ET2ECN 2020 in their CCIS series.

The conference program was enriched by a series of keynote presentations and the keynote speakers included: Prof. Girish Kumar (IIT Bombay, India); Dr. Nirupam S. D.

(Senior Scientist, Head of IOT and AI, Energy Research Institute at NTU, Singapore); Mombasawala Mohmedsaeed (General Manager, Keysight Technologies, India); Dr. Chetan Singh Thakur (IISC Bangalore, India); and Dr. Vishwas Patil (Senior Research Scientist, IIT Bombay, India). We are grateful to them for sharing their insights on their latest research with us.

We find ourselves fortunate to have received generous support from the SVNIT authorities and financial support from TEQIP- III. We are also thankful to the other sponsoring agencies for joining their hands with us to make this conference a great success.

It is expected that the delegates and the participants have been enriched by the experience of this conference and the legacy of knowledge dissemination will continue.

February 2020

Shilpi Gupta
Jignesh N. Sarvaiya

Organization

General Chairs

Shilpi Gupta   Sardar Vallabhbhai National Institute of Technology, India

Shweta Shah   Sardar Vallabhbhai National Institute of Technology, India

Jignesh N. Sarvaiya   Sardar Vallabhbhai National Institute of Technology, India

Piyush N. Patel   Sardar Vallabhbhai National Institute of Technology, India

Program Committee Chair

Upena D. Dalal   Sardar Vallabhbhai National Institute of Technology, India

Local Chairs

Rasika N. Dhavse   Sardar Vallabhbhai National Institute of Technology, India

K. P. Upla   Sardar Vallabhbhai National Institute of Technology, India

Publicity Chairs

Sanjay Soni   Sardar Vallabhbhai National Institute of Technology, India

N. B. Kanirkar   Sardar Vallabhbhai National Institute of Technology, India

Abhilash Mandloi   Sardar Vallabhbhai National Institute of Technology, India

Sponsorship Chair

A. D. Darji   Sardar Vallabhbhai National Institute of Technology, India

Publication Chairs

P. K. Shah   Sardar Vallabhbhai National Institute of Technology, India

Z. M. Patel   Sardar Vallabhbhai National Institute of Technology, India

Web Chair

M. C. Patel   Sardar Vallabhbhai National Institute of Technology, India

Technical Program Committee

Abhay Gandhi	VNIT Nagpur, India
D. Sriramkumar	NIT Trichy, India
U. Shripathi Acharya	NIT Surathkal, India
R. P. Yadav	MNIT Jaipur, India
Rajoo Pandey	NIT Kurukshetra, India
Sarat Kumar Patra	IIIT Vadodara, India
Ghanshyam Singh	MNIT Jaipur, India
Vipul Rastogi	IIT Roorkee, India
Yogendra Prajapati	MNNIT Allahabad, India
Dhaval Pujara	Nirma University, India
Tanish Zaveri	Nirma University, India
Chirag Paunwala	SCET Surat, India
Arvind Sharma	NIT Kurukshetra, India
Vandana Rohokale	Singhad Institute of Technology, India
S. K. Dixit	RRCAT Indore, India
Om Prakash	RRCAT Indore, India
Viraj P. Bhanage	RRCAT Indore, India
Hitesh Pandya	IPR Gandhinagar, India
Vineet Sahula	MNIT Jaipur, India

Advisory Committee

Pavel Loskot	Swansea University, UK
Ivan G. Petrovski	Arkansas State University, USA
Shubhalaxmi Kher	Arkansas State University, USA
Marcin Paprzycki	Systems Research Institute, Polish Academy of Sciences, Poland
Miroslav Skoric	SRV, Serbia
M. Borgarino	Università di Modena e Reggio Emilia, Italy
Milind Mahajan	ISRO Ahmedabad, India
Monia Najjar	High Institute of Computer Sciences, Tunisia
Vijay Janyani	MNIT Jaipur, India

S. Patnaik   St. Xavier College of Engineering, India
Y. P. Kosta   Marwadi University, India
K. M. Bhurchandi   VNIT Nagpur, India
Alok Verma   Sameer Lab, IIT Powai, India

Additional Reviewers

C. M. Negi   K. N. Pathak
Pooja Lohia   Satyasai Nanda
Subhashish Tiwari   Ashish Phopalia
Dipali Kast   Falgun Thakkar
Manik Sharma   Captain Kamal
Jitendra Kumar   Suman Deb
Vipul Kheraj   Nitin Sharma
Neeta Chapatwala   Rajoo Pandey
Yogesh Trivedi   Niteen Patel
Utpal Pandya   Nitin Gupta
Prakash Pareek   A. K. Panchal
Niket Shastri   Suman Deb
Vishnu Awasthi   Maulin Joshi
Jignesh Bhatt   Hiren Mevada
Tanish Zaveri   Ravi Kumar Maddila
Rahul Kumar Chausasiya   Subhshish Tiwari
Ruchi Gajjar   Jagdish Rathod
J. N. Patel   Joydeepsen Gupta
Hemant Goklani   Kirti Inamdar
Idris Bholebawa   Deepak Joshi
A. Acharya   Prabhat Kumar Sharma
C. Periasamy   Amit Joshi
Dharmendra Kumar

Sponsoring Institutions

 Royal Electronics
Sales & Services

TEQIP-Ⅲ

Cell Phone/Tower Radiation Hazards
and Solutions
(Plenary Speaker)

Girish Kumar

IIT Bombay, Powai, Mumbai, India

Cell phone technology has grown rapidly in India, and currently there are more than 100 crores cell phone subscribers and nearly 6.0 lakhs cell phone towers. Cell operators are allowed to transmit 20W of power per carrier from individual cell tower antenna. One operator may have 4 to 6 carrier frequencies and there may be 2 to 4 operators on the same roof top or tower. Thus, total transmitted power may be 100 to 400W. From September 1, 2012, India has adopted 1/10 of ICNIRP Guidelines, which implies safe power density of 450 milliWatt/m^2 for GSM900 and 920 milliWatt/m^2 for GSM1800 after Inter-Ministerial Committee (IMC) report came out in January 2011, which mentioned several health hazards due to radiation.

Interphone study report in May 2010 mentioned that excessive users of mobile phones (i.e., 1/2 hour/day over 8 to 10 years) have doubled to quadrupled brain tumor risk. On May 31, 2011, WHO reported, "The electromagnetic fields produced by mobile phones are classified by the International Agency for Research on Cancer as possibly carcinogenic to humans."

A large number of scientists prepared Bio-Initiative Report in 2007 and gave 2000 references and they proposed safe radiation density of 1.0 milliWatt/m^2 for outdoor, cumulative RF exposure, and 0.1 milliWatt/m^2 for indoor, cumulative RF exposure. Again, 29 scientists from 10 countries prepared Bio-Initiative Report 2012 and gave additional references of 1,800 scientific/technical papers. We have also carried out radiation measurements at thousands of places and can say with certainty that adverse health effects occur over a few years of continuous exposure at 1.0 milliWatt/m^2. The most common complaints are: sleep disorder, headache, irritability, concentration problems, memory loss, depression, hearing loss, joint problems, etc. More severe reactions include seizures, paralysis, miscarriage, irreversible infertility, and cancer. Children and pregnant ladies are more vulnerable.

Expert Group formed by Environment Ministry, India, submitted their report in October 2011 on "Impacts of communication towers on Wildlife including Birds and Bees." They gave 919 scientific/technical references and mentioned that 593 papers reported adverse effect, 130 papers reported no effect, and 196 papers reported inconclusive/neutral effect. Thus, apart from humans, cell tower radiations also affect birds, animals, plants, and environment. Yield of fruit bearing trees near the cell towers and in the main beam is going down significantly.

Cell phone industry may not admit that there are harmful effects just like cigarette industry. People of India must unite to convince policy makers to adopt stricter radiation norm of less than 1 milliWatt/m^2, which will compel cell operators to transmit less power from each antenna mounted on the tower.

Keynote Speakers

The How Industrial IoT - Setting Yourself Up for Success

S. D. Nirupam

Senior Scientist, Head of IoT and Artificial Intelligence
Energy Research Institute at NTU, Singapore

Internet of things (IoT) is a smart technology that connects anything anywhere at any time. Such ubiquitous nature of IoT is responsible for draining out energy from its resources. Therefore, the energy efficiency of IoT resources has emerged as a major research and development issue.

In this talk, sharing an information on implementation effort of our proposed energy-efficient architecture for IoT, which consists of several layers, namely, sensing and control, information processing, and presentation. The architectural design allows the system to integrate energy harvesting/self-powered battery, ultra-low power sensors, robust radio's, etc. This mechanism allows the energy-efficient utilization of all the IoT resources. The experimental and deployment results show a significant amount of energy saving in the case of sensor nodes and improved resource utilization of cloud resources.

Highlights on how AI provides new solutions by centralized or distributed intelligence to analyze and extract meaningful data insight and provide autonomous decision support. Also, present information on our successful spinoff company funded by Singapore National Research Foundation (SG NRF) and few of our next generation connected intelligent IoT solutions integration with AI/ML and successful deployment of our multisense wireless sensors, multiprotocol communication gateways, AI/ML based data fusion platform and security, and data analytics engine.

In this talk, I will outline the challenges related to features of connected intelligent systems, design metrics with layered architectures, edge computing, connectivity, data visualization, modeling, and deployment of IoT applications that will benefit from wireless technologies, AI, blockchain, and potential research directions in resolving these challenges.

Understanding 5G NR REL 15,16 Standards

Mombasawala Mohmedsaeed

General Manager – Applications
Keysight Technologies India Pvt. Ltd., India

The wireless communication landscape has been ever changing with the advent of modern technologies to meet the needs of a connected world. The last two and half decades of wireless communication was focused on connecting human beings with the network. The next wave in this domain has multiple facets: connecting machines and things to the network, servicing mission critical applications with commercial wireless technologies, and spreading augmented reality to masses.

This lecture briefly discusses the three base 5G objectives which are enhanced mobile broadband (eMBB), massive machine type communication (mMTC) and ultra-reliability, and low latency communication (uRLLC). These three visionary objectives demand novel innovations in the technology and therefore make innovative test methodologies and platforms an imperative.

3GPP Release 15 defines eMBB and uRLLC services in mmWave bands specifically 24 GHz, 28 GHz, 37 GHz, and 45 GHz. eMBB is also pushing the communication bandwidth requirements to go as wide as 2 GHz. With current 3GPP 5G NR specifications, the cellular industry is developing a 5G-NR chipsets and gNB. The details of 3GPP 5G NR and upcoming specs in Release 16 like V2X, non-terrestrial 5G networks, released towards the end of 2019 will be explained in this lecture.

To achieve 5G objectives, a massive revamp of the stack is required which encompasses physical layer, protocol layer, and a layer above these. This lecture will briefly cover the proposed architectures of new physical layer and their corresponding test methodologies. 5G features such as beamforming at mm-Wave and spectrum sharing increase test complexity considerably. It is critical to emulate all the 5G system elements flexibly, make accurate measurements, and make informed decisions during the prototyping phase.

In this lecture, Keysight will introduce 5G Protocol R&D Toolset to help engineers streamline current and future 5G device workflow and efficiently prototype advanced 5G protocol features for 3GPP 5G NR, SDAP, beamforming at mm-Wave frequencies, and non-standalone use cases.

Low-Power Neuromorphic Computing Architectures for Edge-Computing

Chetan Singh Thakur

IISC Bangalore, India

Neurobiological processing systems are remarkable computational devices. Their basic computing elements, the neurons, are slow, heterogeneous, and stochastic in nature, and yet they outperform today's most powerful computers at real-world tasks such as vision, audition, and motor control. When compared with digital computers, the brain consumes much less power ($\sim$20W) and is highly adaptive. The loss of merely one transistor can wreck a microprocessor, but brains lose neurons all the time without losing functionality.

Neuromorphic engineering is an interdisciplinary approach to the design of information processing electronic systems that are inspired by the function, structural organization, and physical foundations of biological neural systems. We will demonstrate our novel low-power CMOS-Memristor based neuromorphic architectures, which utilizes promising features from the neuromorphic analog architecture, memristor synaptic memory, and the hardware-friendly learning algorithm. We will also discuss another novel computational framework, which is scalable and enables its implementation for low-power, high-density, and memory constrained embedded application.

The Platform Economies and Privacy as Their Currency

Vishwas Patil

Senior Research Scientist at IIT Bombay, India
PhD in Information Security, La Sapienza
Bachelor of Computer Engineering, SVNIT Surat, India

In the recent past, graphs have become a preferred way to store, annotate, and retrieve data. There are several compelling reasons for online services to do so. Graphical databases provide a flexible way to represent and access data by the nodes in the graph. This flexibility in accessing data comes with certain challenges. In this talk, we shall take help from Facebook's social graph to understand how this graph type of new data platform operates in terms of access control. We shall discuss Facebook's business model built around this dynamic graph, how the advertisement campaigns are designed, and the privacy implications to the users. We shall also discuss and correlate the reasons behind some of the challenges the platform is facing, the solutions (including Libra currency) being devised, and their limitations. The talk will help the system architects to understand the notions necessary to build systems that provide "privacy-by-design."

Contents

Networking

Electronics

QR Code Scanner Enabled Smart Car Parking System Using Raspberry Pi with Android App Access

Yesha Patel[✉], Preksha Gandhi, Swapnil Shah, Shital Soman, and Arpan Desai

Charotar University of Science and Technology, Changa, India
patelyesha2722@gmail.com

Abstract. A smart parking system using Raspberry Pi and android app access is proposed in this article. An automated smart parking system which provides the user to pre-book along with on the spot booking facility of parking spaces available around the area is implemented. The system also helps to store the user's information in database which enables for fast parking access thus reducing the traffic congestion. The hardware is realized using Raspberry Pi and IR sensor. In addition, the system is controlled through an app which is made using Kodular App Development tool, that helps the user to keep track of the updates about available parking spaces. The scalable and precise database can be created on firebase and host it on an application in real-time which is useful to store data in a json format (bucket format). The system is a perfect partner for people to book the parking spaces at their ease from remote locations without wasting time and avoiding traffic congestion.

Keywords: QR code scanning · Real-time database · Slot booking · Admin management

1 Introduction

Internet of things (IoT), a topic most discussed nowadays is a concept that connects billions of devices with the internet at any time and any place. The increasing traffic congestion has also led to increase in pollution. The number of vehicles is skyrocketing in India which causes imbalance in the ratio of vehicle and available parking spaces. In metropolitan areas, the traffic has also caused increase in anxiety level of drivers [1]. One of the most common problems today is less availability of parking spaces. Vehicles continue to outnumber existing parking spaces, thus clogging roads. Incidences of violence due to occupancy, deformed cars due to a space crunch, and overcharging for parking are some of the problems. The families are getting smaller but the total number of motor vehicles is exceeding the total number of heads per family which worsens the current parking scenario in the country. The situation is such that on any given working day approximately 40% of the roads in urban regions are taken up just for parking the cars. The problem has been further exacerbated by the fact that people from low-income groups are also able to own cars. Most cities propose

S. Gupta and J. N. Sarvaiya (Eds.): ET2ECN 2020, CCIS 1214, pp. 3–18, 2020.
https://doi.org/10.1007/978-981-15-7219-7_1

increasing parking spaces to combat the problem. Parks and vacant plots are used as potential parking spaces. Multi-level facilities are being built, irrespective of the limited land space and resources [2]. The other major problem is that the organizations do not have a secured and updated data of the drivers parking in their area. There is a huge proliferation in the population along with the number of vehicles in the country. This has led to mismanagement of parking spaces which has further created some problems like traffic congestion [3]. Thus, an automated smart parking system is required to be developed. It would help driver to locate the parking slot easily and also help in decreasing air pollution. According to a survey, 60% of driver's on-road feel anxious and stressed due to the road concession [4]. Barcodes were first invented but the storage capacity for barcode was less as it can store only 20 alphanumeric characters of information and the demand of users was to have more storage capacity and so new type of code was introduced called QR code. QR stands for Quick Response which was termed by Denso Wave Company. QR is used to take a piece of information from a temporary media and put it in the mobile [5, 6]. QR codes are two-dimensional matrix barcode that has to be scanned. QR code can hold up to 7089 characters. Nowadays QR code is used by users in mobile phones itself to scan anything or to purchase any product [7]. The QR code is combination of white and black square patterns and is having encoding and functioning region. Alternative to QR codes is implementation of devices with antennas which has higher range and directivity. There are many antennas proposed for smart applications which can be used for such applications [8–11]. The devices can be made smaller if the antenna sizes are reduced [12, 13]. However in the current application as the distance between user and system is not far, QR code will suffice the purpose.

In this article, the above problems are taken care of by deploying a smart parking system which helps to reduce the traffic congestion while providing easy access to available parking spaces through a touch on the phone. The application installed on the phone helps the user to find exact location of the free slots. The user can preregister in the app to reduce the time while arriving at the parking facility. QR code which is installed on the vehicle is scanned at the entrance which gathers the user information and checks the booking data with database thus allowing fast access to the parking slots. The user is directed to the available parking spots according to the data gathered using raspberry pie and sensors employed in the parking lot. It reduces time consumption and also parking issues [14].

2   Methodology

The successful implementation of the proposed smart car parking system includes Raspberry Pi, IR Sensor, Servo motors, Firebase Database, Android application all combined together where the real-time database management is done. A database is a collection of information that is structured in a systematic way so it is easily accessed, updated and available. Firebase is "NoSQL" database which is useful for data stored in more than one computer which is located in the same physical location or over network of linked computers. "NoSQL" stands for "not only SQL" and is useful for big data carrying out problems [15]. The aim behind creating a database is to store data in a minute way and to get the data whenever needed [16]. We consider firebase as web application platform. It stores data in JavaScript object notation (JSON) format which doesn't use any question for updating, deleting or adding any data to it. It is used to store the data and hence it is backend of a system [15]. To create the mobile app and web application firebase provides a particular platform and also can update it immediately [17]. The main features of firebase are real-time database, Authentication, storage, and cloud messaging. The real-time database is accessed through cloud platform and allows users to host it without having its dedicated hardware. Data is stored as JSON and is occurred at the same time to each related client. The user demand is more based on Real-time data example and when the new data is updated the instance gets change or updated. Firebase authentication gives backend services. For proving the identity of the user firebase uses password, email-id, or user name, phone number. The transferred documents can be easily stored and also can be downloaded. The message can be transferred through Cloud messaging without any expense.

The IR sensor and servo motor are interfaced with Raspberry Pi, which combinedly makes the network of hardware. This proposed system is divided into three parts: User, Developer and Staff Manager of the particular Building. The programming of the Raspberry Pi is done in such a manner that whenever any IR sensor senses a car, it will reflect as the change in status of the spot on the firebase database as soon as IR sensor detects (on based of delay given in the code and internet connectivity). The servo motor is interfaced with Raspberry Pi for entry and exit barrier, which will be enabled due to the entry IR sensor and exit IR sensor. If the parking is full or there will be no slots available, in this situation entry servo motor will not open the barrier. The entry IR sensor will count the total number of cars visited the parking area.

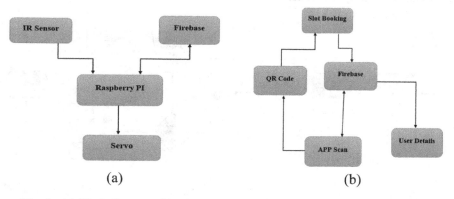

(a)   (b)

Fig. 1. (a) Block diagram of hardware set-up (b) Block diagram of software set-up

As depicted in Fig. 1, the Real-Time Database is created on the firebase. The database contains the status of all the parking spots, app-user details, details of QR code. The proposed system helps the user to find an appropriate parking slot to park the car. It also provides the direction on google maps so that the user can find the path easily. The proposed system also allows the user to pre-book the parking slots. The User app and Super admin app are created using Kodular App editor.

ADMIN SOFTWARE (DEVELOPER)

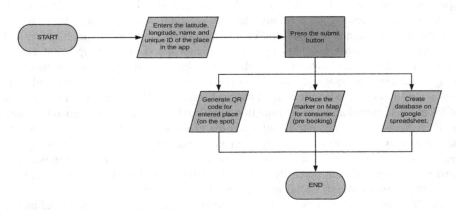

Fig. 2. Flowchart for developing the application

The admin app as illustrated in Fig. 2 is designed in such a way that the admin can add as many locations as per the requirement. Only the admin has the authority to add locations of the parking spaces and make them available to the users. As the admin opens the Parkspot App, the information about entering the latitude, longitude and unique ID of the place to be generated is asked. Once the submit button is pressed, the next step comprises of QR generation for the same location, place marker on the map and creating the database. Once this is done, new location can be added in the app which can be used by the users.

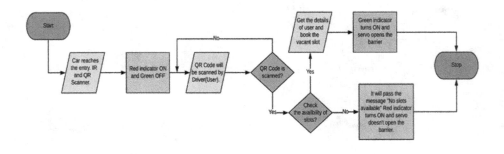

On the Spot Booking - Hardware

Fig. 3. Flowchart of hardware for on the spot booking

Figure 3 illustrates the user app which is designed in such a way so that the people can book the parking slot on the spot or pre-book the parking slot at their convenience. Once the user logged in to the app, the user uses the app for parking reservations. Once the QR code is scanned, the app prompts to confirm the details such as verifying the mobile number and vehicle number. The user can select the slot from the list of available slots through the android app. After the QR code is scanned, the servo motor will open the parking barrier. Scanning the QR code assures the user's database has been stored and gets updated once again when the user exits the parking area. The user app is developed in such a way that the user can easily understand the functionality.

USER APP (ON THE SPOT BOOKING)

START → User will scan the QR code → Pop-up window to verify mobile and vehicle number. → Click on the submit button.

loading

Data stored in the databae? — No

Yes

Specific parking slot alloted and car can enter the parking area.

END

Fig. 4. Flowchart for user interface using app-on the spot booking

Figure 4 shows the steps to be followed by the user using app for on the spot booking. When the user reach at Parkspot Parking area, the QR code needs to be scanned placed near the entrance. After scanning the QR code there will be one pop-up window to confirm the details and select the parking slot from the available spots. After clicking on confirm button, the selected slot will be allocated to the user.

PRE BOOKING (USERSIDE APP)

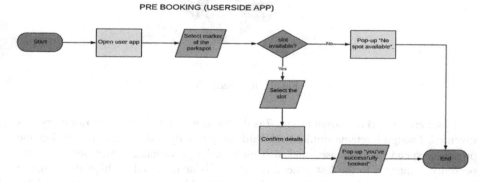

Start → Open user app → Select marker of the parkspot → slot available? —No→ Pop-up "No spot available".

Yes

Select the slot

Confirm details

Pop-up "you've successfully booked" → End

Fig. 5. Flowchart (user app-pre booking)

The pre-booking facility as shown in Fig. 5 is designed to control the chaos and traffic around the metropolitan areas. Once the user enters their details, they are asked to move the marker of Parkspot to the location they want to park their car. Once the location is selected, the available slots will be shown on the screen. If the slots aren't available the pop-up reads "No slot available", else the available slots can be selected. The pop up further reads "you've successfully booked".

3   Experimental Setup

The block diagram of the system is as shown in Fig. 6. Various hardware's used in the experimental setup are Raspberry pi 4 B, Servo motor, IR Sensor and Led.

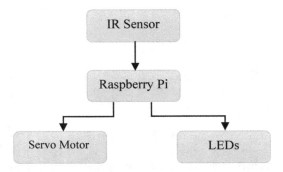

Fig. 6. Block diagram of experimental setup

Fig. 7. Raspberry Pi

Raspberry pi 4 B as shown in Fig. 7 is the latest module of the entire raspberry pi's invented. Though it retains similar backward compatibility and power consumption, the processor speed has increased and also multimedia performance, memory, and connectivity compared to the last generation. Pi B 4 is ameliorated by high-Performance Quad-core 4-bit Broadcom 2711. It also has a cortex A72 processor clocked at 1.5 GHz speed. The memory has been upgraded by 1 GB-4 GB LPDDR4 SDRAM. It has built-in cypress BLE chip for Bluetooth 5.0. It gives high-speed gigabit ethernet over USB 3.0. There are 40 GPIO header pins and 2 micro HDMI ports. For storage both micro SD card slot and data storage is available. Additionally for multimedia it has H 265 Decode (4Kp60), H.264, MPEG-4 decode (1080p60). H.264 encode (1080p30). OpenGL ES 1.1, 2.0, and 3.0 graphics.

Fig. 8. Servo motor (Color figure online)

The servo motor as shown in Fig. 8 is high-quality servo used for the mechanical needs like in our project needed as parking barriers. It has three pins which include +Vcc (connected to red wire), GND (brown wire connected to ground) and control pin (orange wire which drives the motor). The operating voltage of a servo motor is 4.8 V to 6 V. It is categorized as an analog servo. The rotary angle of the servo motor is 180°. The most important factor that is torque, the motor operates here. SG90 has torque of 2.5 kg/cm. This means that 2.5 kg of weight can be loaded on the servo when it is suspended at a distance of 1 cm.

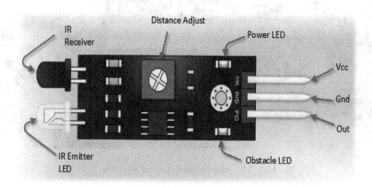

Fig. 9. IR sensor

IR sensor as shown in Fig. 9 is used to sense the infrared radiations and give the output based on it. An IR sensor consist of both IR LED and IR Photodiode. It has built-in IR transmitter and IR receiver. The infrared transmitter is LED which emits infrared radiations and Infrared receivers detect radiations from IR sensor. Though the

Led looks like a normal LED but the radiations emitted are invisible to human eye. When the radiations are emitted, they reach the object and some of the radiations reflect back to the receiver thus giving us the output.

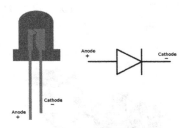

Fig. 10. LED

An LED as illustrated in Fig. 10 is a semiconductor light source, which emits radiations when it is activated. When the appropriate voltage is passed the electrons and holes recombine within the device and energy is released in the form of photons. The colour depends on the energy band-gap of the semiconductor. 30 mA is the continuous forward current and 100 mA is the peak forward current of this device. The reverse voltage is 5 V. The hardware setup of the proposed system is shown in Fig. 11.

Fig. 11. Hardware setup of system

Here, the IR sensor senses the car at a particular slot and reflects the change in firebase database with the help of Raspberry Pi. The entry IR sensor will count the number of cars entering a day and refreshes the counter after every 24 h (or any required time limit). If the parking area is full, the entry servo will not allow the car to enter the parking area. Other duties like maintaining slots data management of the particular parking area is done by the staff manager who collects the data from firebase.

4   Results and Discussion

The user-friendly mobile app is developed for the users through which they are able to book the parking slot as per the occupancy. As the IR sensor, led and servo are interfaced with raspberry pi the state of occupancy can be known that is, if the car parked is detected then the user will not be able to book that particular slot. The admin side has only the authority to add a new location and also the total number of car entries can be known through admin app.

Case 1: On the Spot Booking
As shown in Fig. 12, B2 and B3 are pre-booked by users. The available slots are B1, B4, and B5. For booking the parking slot, the user has to log in into the app.

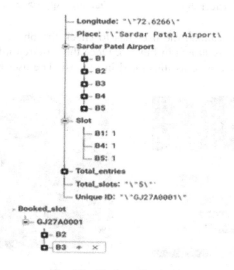

Fig. 12. Firebase database

As the user opens the app, the following symbol is shown in the app screen as shown in Fig. 13. The user has to click on the scan option. So, the QR code appears on the app which is to be scanned when the user enters the parking area as depicted in Fig. 14.

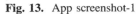

Fig. 13. App screenshot-1

Fig. 14. App screenshot-2

As the QR code is scanned the user has to check the phone number and vehicle number for verification as shown in Fig. 15. Once the required information is entered, the available slots gets visible as illustrated in Fig. 16. The user has to choose one of the slots available.

Fig. 15. App screenshot-3

Fig. 16. App screenshot-4

As soon as the user completes all the previous steps, a pop up shows up as shown in Fig. 17 which indicates that the slot is booked and the same will be updated in the firebase as shown in Fig. 18. As the user booked the slot B5 the firebase shows only B1 and B4 as available thus updating it in the app.

Fig. 17. App screenshot-5

Fig. 18. Firebase database

Case 2: Power of Admin

As the admin opens the application, 3 choices are available as shown in the Fig. 19. Once the admin clicks on the location services, the screen as shown in Fig. 20 show up. The admin further has 3 options-adding location, deleting location and checking updated database.

Fig. 19. Admin app screenshot-1   **Fig. 20.** Admin app screenshot-2

As the admin clicks on the first option for adding location, the following details are to be filled as shown in Fig. 21.

As the details are filled up, the admin is taken to the next step where the confirmed details are shown and further admin can generate QR code as shown in Fig. 22. The QR code is generated in the browser thus adding a location which is illustrated in Fig. 23.

Fig. 21. Admin app screenshot-3

Fig. 22. Admin app screenshot-4

Fig. 23. Admin app screenshot-5

The admin is taken back to the main menu as shown in Fig. 24 where if the admin clicks on the "delete location", admin is taken to the next page as shown in Fig. 25. The admin will be asked to choose an ID that needs to be deleted as shown in Fig. 26. A confirmation page shows up and on clicking continue the location selected is deleted as depicted in Figs. 27 and 28.

Fig. 24. Admin app screenshot-5

Fig. 25. Admin app screenshot-6

Fig. 26. Admin app screenshot-7

Fig. 27. Admin app screenshot-8   **Fig. 28.** Admin app screenshot-9

The admin is further taken to the main menu. The next case is if the admin wants to see the updated database, the admin can click on the database option as shown in Fig. 29. On clicking the database option there are 2 choices wherein the admin can choose the firebase as depicted in Fig. 30. Thus, the admin is taken to a firebase webpage where the admin is shown the updated list of parking spaces available and occupied. The admin can also see the locations available as shown in Fig. 31.

Fig. 29. Admin app screenshot-10

Fig. 30. Admin app screenshot-11

Fig. 31. Admin app screenshot-12

Case 3: Hardware Implementation

Fig. 32. B2 and B3 slots are booked (case-1)   **Fig. 33.** B5 slot is occupied (case-1)

As shown in Fig. 32, when one car enters the parking slot, B3 and B2 are already booked and the car has scanned the QR code and book the slot. Then the car moves forward where the entry IR sensor senses the car, thus the servo motor opens and it can occupy the booked parking space. The other car scans the QR code while first car is parking in B5 as depicted in Fig. 33 which helps in decreasing traffic congestion.

Fig. 34. No slots available (U-turn)   **Fig. 35.** Parking area full

When the car enters the parking space and scans the QR code as illustrated in Fig. 34, a message pops up saying all the parking slots are full, thus not passing the command to the servo. This doesn't allow the servo to open the barrier and the car takes a U-turn from the gate itself as shown in Fig. 35 which is an indication of parking full. This decreases the time consumption in finding spaces and also decreases the fuel consumption.

5 Conclusion

This paper presents a smart parking system. The struggle of finding a parking space in the metropolitan areas will be eliminated through the proposed system. Consumers will save time through this system and the organizations will be able to keep updated and secured information of the consumers parking in their area. The proposed online booking system will also alleviate traffic congestion and pollution in the cities.

References

1. Jain, V., Sharma, A., Subramanian, L.: Road traffic congestion in the developing world. In: Proceedings of the 2nd ACM Symposium on Computing for Development, p. 11. ACM, March 2012
2. Alsafery, W., Alturki, B., Reiff-Marganiec, S., Jambi, K.: Smart car parking system solution for the internet of things in smart cities. In: 2018 1st International Conference on Computer Applications & Information Security (ICCAIS), pp. 1–5. IEEE, April 2018
3. Idris, M.Y.I., Leng, Y.Y., Tamil, E.M., Noor, N.M., Razak, Z.: Car park system: a review of smart parking system and its technology. Inf. Technol. J. 8(2), 101–113 (2009)
4. Mejri, N., Ayari, M., Langar, R., Kamoun, F., Pujolle, G., Saidane, L.: Cooperation versus competition towards an efficient parking assignment solution. In: 2014 IEEE International Conference on Communications (ICC), pp. 2915–2920. IEEE, June 2014
5. Tarjan, L., Šenk, I., Tegeltija, S., Stankovski, S., Ostojic, G.: A readability analysis for QR code application in a traceability system. Comput. Electron. Agric. 109, 1–11 (2014)
6. Zainuddin, M., Baswaraj, D., Riyazoddin, S.M.: Generating SMS (short message service) in the form of quick response code (QR-code). J. Comput. Sci. Inf. Technol. 1(1), 10–14 (2012)
7. Pandya, K.H., Galiyawala, H.J.: A survey on QR codes: in context of research and application. Int. J. Emerg. Technol. Adv. Eng. 4(3), 258–262 (2014)
8. Desai, A., Upadhyaya, T., Palandoken, M., Patel, R., Patel, U.: Dual band optically transparent antenna for wireless applications. In: 2017 IEEE Asia Pacific Microwave Conference (APMC), pp. 960–963. IEEE, November 2017
9. Desai, A., Upadhyaya, T.K., Patel, R.H., Bhatt, S., Mankodi, P.: Wideband high gain fractal antenna for wireless applications. Progr. Electromagn. Res. 74, 125–130 (2018)
10. Desai, A., Upadhyaya, T., Patel, R.: Compact wideband transparent antenna for 5G communication systems. Microwave Opt. Technol. Lett. 61(3), 781–786 (2019)
11. Desai, A., Upadhyaya, T., Palandoken, M.: Dual band slotted transparent resonator for wireless local area network applications. Microwave Opt. Technol. Lett. 60(12), 3034–3039 (2018)
12. Patel, R.H., Desai, A.H., Upadhyaya, T.: Design of H-shape X-band application electrically small antenna. Int. J. Electr. Electron. Data Commun. (IJEEDC) 3, 1–4 (2015)
13. Patel, R.H., Desai, A., Upadhyaya, T.: A discussion on electrically small antenna property. Microwave Opt. Technol. Lett. 57(10), 2386–2388 (2015)
14. Goyal, S., Yadav, S., Mathuria, M.: Exploring concept of QR code and its benefits in digital education system. In: 2016 International Conference on Advances in Computing, Communications and Informatics (ICACCI), pp. 1141–1147. IEEE, September 2016

15. Chatterjee, N., Chakraborty, S., Decosta, A., Nath, A.: Real-time communication application based on android using Google firebase. Int. J. Adv. Res. Comput. Sci. Manag. Stud. (2018)
16. Yu, P.S., Wu, K.L., Lin, K.J., Son, S.H.: On real-time databases: concurrency control and scheduling. Proc. IEEE **82**(1), 140–157 (1994)
17. Srivastava, N., Shree, U., Chauhan, N.R., Tiwari, D.K.: Firebase cloud messaging (Android). Int. J. Innov. Res. Sci. Eng. Technol. **6** (2017). (An ISO 3297: 2007 Certified Organization)

Smart Automated Energy Meter

R. Subhash[(✉)], Venkatachalam Rajarajan Balaji[(✉)], K. E. Sanjana,
Nikhil Madhavan, and T. Siva

Department of Electronics and Communication Engineering, St. Joseph's
Institute of Technology, Chennai 600119, Tamil Nadu, India
Suburenu0408@gmail.com

Abstract. Electricity is one of the invaluable resources for ages. It is the most fundamental entity for each and every technical process in today's life. In almost all the developed countries, governments have implemented automated and smart energy meters to monitor and assess the usage of electricity in every house and industry. But in developing countries like India, these systems are yet to be initialized because the proper methodology and cost-efficient energy meter systems are yet to be introduced. Also, the assessor visits each house to read the meter readings, which makes the assessment inaccurate and prone to many other complications. So we propose a system that is intended to monitor Domestic Energy Meters remotely i.e. to automate the domestic energy meters. This methodology employs an Arduino microcontroller module and a GSM900 module without the use of any peripherals such as LDR's and optocouplers like other automated energy meters do. Thus the system enables automatic reading of the power consumed in an efficient and reliable fashion than the others. The project aimed is expected to receive monthly energy consumption from a remote location to a centralized EB office.

Keywords: Domestic energy meters · Arduino Nano · GSM900 · Automatic reading of power · Remote monitoring · Automatic billing

1 Introduction

About 1075 kWh of electricity produced in India are utilized by several companies, industries and households. Since it is a developing nation, the current methodology to monitor and read the usage of energy in each industry and household is done manually which employs human efforts to undergo the energy usage analysis process. Automation of this manual methodology helps in saving the long hours spent and provides details regarding average consumption of energy. Though most of the localities in our country have a surplus furnish of electricity some lag behind in this fundamental need. Our policies of its distribution are also partially responsible for this because we are still not in a position to correctly estimate our exact requirements and still power theft is prevailing. On the other hand, consumers are also not satisfied with the services of power companies. Most of the time they have complaints regarding statistical errors in their monthly bills. To solve these issues, we propose an Automated Energy Meter which automatically reports the consumption of power and the respective cost through wireless communication.

© Springer Nature Singapore Pte Ltd. 2020
S. Gupta and J. N. Sarvaiya (Eds.): ET2ECN 2020, CCIS 1214, pp. 19–28, 2020.
https://doi.org/10.1007/978-981-15-7219-7_2

All the previously introduced systems make use of basic components such as a microcontroller system, a GSM module and peripherals such as LDRs, optocouplers or metering IC's. The system we propose eliminates all these additional peripherals and employs only a microcontroller system and a wireless communication module. This makes our system to be much more cost-efficient, compact and reliable than others and in fact more accurate, because of the unique programming algorithm we use.

1.1 Literature Survey and Related Work

The basal objective for automating any analog or digital device is the acquisition of its parameters such as the output in a digital format in order to make the further processing of these parameters plausible for a microcontroller system. Probing the previous works and implementations done by the researchers and scholars in automating the energy meter, it can be inferred that the cardinal source for the acquisition of the output from a domestic energy meter is the pulse of the LED embedded in it.

The frequency of the pulse of the LED is directly proportional to the monitored amount of power consumed through that meter. Each pulse of the LED corresponds to a definite unit of power consumed which is 0.000625 Kwh and the number of pulses is determined by the use of an LDR which actually detects the light or an optocoupler whose output will be high or low according to the pulse of the LED in the energy meter [1, 2]. Raspberry Pi modules can also be used along with a light sensor module to detect the pulses and the data can be processed in a separate smartphone application using Google API [3].

Another technique, other than LDRs and optocouplers, is the usage of the metering IC (integrated circuits) ADE7757. The usage of ADE7757 provides instantaneous real power information which deploys only low-frequency outputs. The output frequency of ADE7757 will be directly proportional to the average real power consumed [4]. ARM 7 microcontroller, which is operated using Embedded C programming language, can also be used. Methodologies involving postpaid and prepaid schemes to pay the energy consumption bills can also be implemented for better convenience. One of the ways to transmit the energy consumption report is by using the RF link to a web server through GSM [5]. Energy management operation, as well as power quality monitoring for a smart building, can also be implemented by integrating an Advanced Metering Infrastructure (AMI) with a microgrid [6].

From this survey, it is evident that all the previously proposed and implemented technology incorporated at least one peripheral to determine the count of the pulse of the LED embedded in the energy meter. This can be overcome by the methodology we propose through this paper. Besides that, different types of microcontroller systems such as Arduino, Raspberry Pi and Intel 8051 were used. Among them, the Arduino microcontroller system is the most preferred because of the ease of implementation of codes and peripherals and also its compact design and reliability.

2 System Overview

The complete setup of the system is shown in Fig. 1. The basic components of this system include a domestic energy meter from which the usage of power can be derived, a 100 W bulb which acts as a load for this experiment and the necessary components for automating the reporting of energy usage are an Arduino Nano module, which is actually a microcontroller system and a GSM900 module for the transmission of the report to the desired commuter via SMS.

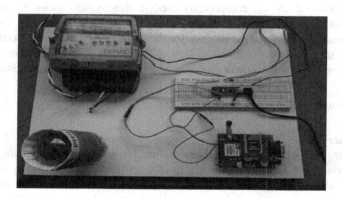

Fig. 1. Complete setup of the automated energy meter with load.

As soon as the connections are made and the system is turned on, the load starts to consume energy and this consumption is monitored simultaneously by the energy meter. As stated earlier, the pulse of the LED portrays the consumption of energy by the devices connected though the meter. So the operation of the bulb, which consumes energy, makes the LED to pulse at definite intervals with respect to the amount of energy drawn by it.

The frequency of pulse of the LED is analysed by the Analog Input of the Arduino module. A separate variable is used to store the numerical value derived from the analog input pin. Because of the input, which is analog in nature, each pulse of the LED causes a considerable number of iterations of a loop in the program and thus results in a definite value of the variable. The variable is then compared with a Threshold and then it is considered as one successful pulse. This results in the conversion of the pulses of the LED into a digital value which is stored in the Arduino. After a desired time, interval is reached, say a minute, the value stored in the counter variable of the Arduino will be equal to number of pulses of the LED in that interval.

Finally, the counter variable is used to obtain the amount of power consumed in that particular interval of time as follows.

Units consumed = Power factor * Count/1000;

The term 'Power factor' is a constant which denotes the average power consumed for a single pulse of the LED and it can be easily calculated from the energy meter specifications.

Once the Units of power consumed for a particular interval of time is calculated, the report is sent to the mobile or another GSM module of the commuter as well as the EB domain through the GSM900 module.

3   Design of Automated Energy Meter

A lucid explanation of the system can be given if it is expounded into two separate categories i.e. the hardware and the software design. The hardware design gives requisite explanation of all the components used in this system including their input, output and pin configuration. The software design frames the working of the program code incorporated in the Arduino module for the extraction of the pulse from the LED, converting it into digital format, calculation of the power Factor and units consumed and the transmission of the power consumption report through the GSM900 module.

3.1   Hardware Implementation

Energy Meter
Energy meter, also known as Watt Hour meter, is an instrument that measures the amount of electrical energy consumed by the commuters [7]. Energy meters are employed in all households, industries and organizations to measure the energy consumption by the loads such as lights, fans, refrigerators, televisions and other electrical appliances. Basic unit of power is watts. One thousand watts corresponds to one kilowatt. If we use one kilowatt in one hour, it is considered as one unit of energy consumed. These meters measure the instantaneous voltage and currents to give the instantaneous power. The power consumed is measured over a period of time, usually a month.

Fig. 2. Digital energy meter.

There are both single and three-phase energy meters depending on the supply utilized by domestic or commercial regions. For small service measurements like domestic customers, the meters can be directly connected between line and load. But for larger loads, step down current transformers must be placed to isolate energy meters from higher currents.

Every modern domestic energy meter, shown in the Fig. 2, has an LED embedded in it whose purpose is to indicate the consumption of electricity in the form of frequent pulse. Whenever the load consumes electricity, it makes the LED to pulse at a definite time intervals which is proportional to the amount of energy consumed. If multiple loads are connected i.e. the consumption of electricity is high, the LED pulses more frequently and vice versa. Each energy meter has its own power specification which gives the per unit LED impulse rate from which the powerFactor for that energy meter can be easily calculated. Thus the total consumption of electricity in a definite interval of time is directly proportional to the power factor and the number of pulses at that interval. For example, if the load makes the LED to pulse 25 times per minute, then the amount of energy consumed will be directly proportional to 25 times the power factor.

Arduino Nano

Arduino Nano shown in the Fig. 3 is a small and compact microcontroller module that provides a wide range of embedded, automation and IOT applications [8, 9] Arduino Nano contains 30 pins which provide all the necessary functions such as I/O, PWM, Serial Communication, ADC, power supply and ground. It employs an ATmega328 microcontroller including all the necessary peripherals such as voltage regulators, capacitors, reset buttons, status indicators, etc. Among the 30 pins in the module, 14 are Digital I/O pins (1, 2, 5–16) and 8 are Analog Input pins (19–26).

Fig. 3. Arduino Nano module.

In an Arduino module serial communication is used for printing the desired statements and outputs in the serial monitor window and for the transmission of data between the module and externally connected peripherals, in this case the GSM900 module. In Arduino Nano, the pins 1(Tx) and 2(Rx) are the default serial communication pins. These pins cannot be utilised for any external connection because the usage of the predefined serial communication function in the program code will hinder them from any other utilisations. Hence in this case the predefined serial communication function is used only to print the output in the serial monitor of the Arduino IDE. Arduino also enables the flexibility of declaring user defined serial communication functions through any digital I/O pins other than 1 and 2. So in addition to the default one, here, the pins 9 and 10 were declared as user defined serial communication pins which can be used for transmission of data to and from the GSM900 module.

GSM900

GSM (Global System for Mobile Communications, originally Group Special Mobile) is a standard developed by the European Telecommunications Standards Institute (ETSI) to describe the protocols for second-generation (2G) digital cellular networks used by mobile phones. The term GSM900 is used for a GSM system which operates in any 900 MHz [10]. The 900 MHz band defined in the ETSI standard includes the primary GSM band (GSM-P), the extension (E-GSM) and the remaining reserved for railways (R-GSM). The total GSM900 band defined in the standard ranges from 876–915 MHz paired with 921–960 MHz. Mobiles transmit in the lower band and base stations transmit in the upper band. A typical GSM900 module is shown in the Fig. 4.

Fig. 4. GSM900 module.

A GSM module can be a dedicated modem device with a serial, USB or Bluetooth connection, in this case serial communication since it can be employed in both the Arduino Nano and the GSM900 modules. The flowchart of the hardware design implemented in this system is shown in the Fig. 5.

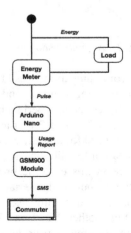

Fig. 5. Flowchart representing the hardware implementation.

3.2   Software Implementation

All the Arduino modules employ a unique form of programming language for the execution of desired tasks. The program code implemented in the Arduino module follows a hierarchical structure in which all the processes are executed in a step by step fashion. The algorithm for the calculation of energy consumed by the load for the desired time interval is shown in the Fig. 6.

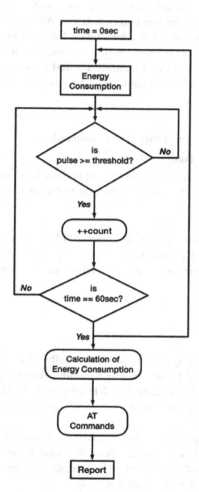

Fig. 6. Algorithm for determining the energy consumption and reporting.

The initial approach is to determine the number of pulses of the LED for a definite time interval. This is done by a separate looping statement and this produces a variable with the total number of pulses at that time interval. The desired time period is determined by a special function known as millis() which returns the total run time since the system started to consume energy.

Once the total number of pulse is determined, we can calculate the total amount of power consumed at that interval. This power is expressed in terms of Units consumed. Usually, power consumption by a household or industry is assessed for a time period of one month. The respective amount to be charged from the commuter is also calculated.

As soon as the data to be reported are calculated, the program statements for the operation of GSM900 module gets executed. Each specific functionality of the GSM900 module is accessed and operated by a special set of commands known as AT Commands which are transferred through the user defined serial communication port of the Arduino. AT Commands are run commands that run directly on the GSM module and are responsible for controlling the interaction between the GSM module and the cellular tower as well as some functionality on the phone such as storing phone numbers, reading SMS messages and calling desired contact, ending calls and much more. Table 1 shows the AT commands used in this system to send an SMS to the desired number.

Table 1. AT commands.

Commands	Function
AT + CMGF = 1	Sets the GSM modem in SMS Text mode or SMS PDU mode
AT + CMGS = <number>	Sends an SMS message to the GSM phone

The energy usage report can be sent to multiple number of users as desired by simply using the AT + CMGS command for the respective number of times. The SMS cost for each reporting message vary according to the norms established by the respective service provider.

4   Result

The load employed in this system is a 100 W bulb. The energy usage statistics is sampled for a time period of 1 min (usually a month). According to the specification of the energy meter used in this system, 1 KWH tally with 3200 pulses. Figure 7 shows the final report of the energy consumed by the load for 1 min in the form of SMS in the commuter's mobile phone.

Rounding off the energy usage value to the desired decimal point is also possible in Arduino programming. Multiple iterations of this system are done with a variety of time intervals and the results are found to be precise, thus ensuring the reliability and accuracy of this automated energy meter system.

Fig. 7. Report of energy usage in the form of SMS.

5 Conclusion

Since the emergence of technologies on automations and their implementations are in a much faster pace, it is a mandatory and much efficient idea to automate all the peripherals and devices we use in our daily life and making them smart. The management and monitoring of the electricity usage, in today's time, is performed through human efforts which is not advisory. Though we have many methodologies on automating the energy monitoring systems, most of them lag behind in one or some other ways such as usage of additional components, reliability, stranded technologies, etc. The system proposed though this paper effectively overcomes the hassles of peripheral components such as LDR's, optocouplers and metering IC's and the problems that arises due to their malfunctions because of the lack of timely maintenance. The usage of Arduino Nano provides much comfort in terms of cost, space and reliability. The transmission of the energy usage statistics is through GSM i.e. via Short Message Service (SMS). This enables us to report the data at a much lower price irrespective of the total time taken for the transmission. This system, as aspired, provides timely and more accurate energy usage statistics of the industries or the households upon a desired period such as monthly basis without human efforts. Thus, this methodology tends to be a much cheaper, efficient and error-free automated energy monitoring system.

References

1. Mir, S.H., Sahreen Ashruf, S., Bhat, Y., Beigh, N.: Review on smart electric metering system based on GSM/IOT. Asian J. Electr. Sci. **8**, 1–6 (2019)
2. Islam, M.S., Bhuiyan, M.S.R.: Design and implementation of remotely located energy meter monitoring with load control and mobile billing system through GSM. In: International Conference on Electrical, Computer and Communication Engineering 2017, pp. 158–163 (2017)
3. Chandra, P.A., Vamsi, G.M., Manoj, Y.S., Mary, G.I.: Automated energy meter using WiFi enabled raspberry Pi. In: IEEE International Conference on Recent Trends in Electronics, Information & Communication Technology 2016, pp. 1992–1994 (2016)
4. Bharath, P., Ananth, N., Vijetha, S., Prakash, K.J.: Wireless automated digital energy meter. In: IEEE International Conference on Sustainable Energy Technologies 2008, pp. 564–567 (2008)
5. Gupta, N., Shukla, D.: Design of embedded based automated meter reading system for real time processing. In: IEEE Students' Conference on Electrical, Electronics and Computer Science 2016, pp. 1–6 (2016)
6. Palacios-Garcia, E.J., et al.: Using smart meters data for energy management operations and power quality monitoring in a microgrid. In: IEEE 26th International Symposium on Industrial Electronics 2017, pp. 1725–1731 (2017)
7. Koay, B.S., et al.: Design and implementation of Bluetooth energy meter. In: Proceedings of the 2003 Joint Fourth International Conference on Information, Communications and Signal Processing, 2003 and the Fourth Pacific Rim Conference on Multimedia, pp. 1474–1477 (2003)
8. Deshmukh, A.D., Shinde, U.B.: A low cost environment monitoring system using raspberry Pi and arduino with Zigbee. In: International Conference on Inventive Computation Technologies, pp. 1–6 (2016)
9. Lee, I., Lee, K.: The Internet of Things (IoT): applications, investments, and challenges for enterprises. Bus. Horiz. **58**, 431–440 (2015)
10. Nittby, H., et al.: Cognitive impairment in rats after long-term exposure to GSM-900 mobile phone radiation. Bioelectromagn. J. Bioelectromagn. Soc. **29**(3), 219–232 (2008)

A High Efficiency Six Phase Voltage Doubler Cell Using 180 nm CMOS Process

K. Krishna Reddy$^{(\boxtimes)}$ and P. Sreehari Rao

ECE Department, National Institute of Technology, Warangal, Telangana, India
kkr281@gmail.com, patri@nitw.ac.in

Abstract. This work presents a fully integrated six-phase voltage doubler (SPVD) circuit with both NMOS driver circuit and PMOS driver circuit for modern smart electronic systems and verified in a 180 nm CMOS process. An optimized gate control technique is applied for charge transfer switches (CTS) using driver circuits to reduce reversion losses thereby increasing voltage conversion ratio and pumping efficiency effectively. For 1.8 V supply, the proposed circuit offers better performance relative to similar work reported in literature in terms of good voltage conversion ratio of 1.98 with an output voltage 3.58 V. Further, it can drive loads upto 0 to 1.1 mA.

Keywords: Charge pump · Charge transfer switches · Voltage doubler

1 Introduction

Advances in VLSI technology have empowered the development of low power devices and circuits in modern smart electronic systems including environment monitoring, Internet Of Things (IOT) sensors, health care systems, that seeks for a near endless operation with low maintenance. Energy scavenging is one of the promising Solutions that fulfil the requirements of such applications [1–7]. Since the scavenged energy relies on the availability of several sources such as photovoltaic (PV), piezoelectric, thermoelectric, and RF. Those sources are typically harvested by inductive or capacitive dc–dc power converters. Compared with inductive dc–dc boost converters, the charge pump features no off-chip inductors and is suitable for monolithic low power energy harvesting applications. Capacitor based DC-DC converters are referred as voltage multipliers or charge pumps that can generate various dc output voltages by transferring electric charge in a capacitor network using charge transfer switches (CTS) managed by clock phases [8]. The first monolithic integrated charge pump using two out of phase clocks was introduced by Dickson [9] but it suffers from the threshold voltage drop across the source and the drain at each stage. In later stages, large threshold voltage degrades the voltage gain and pumping efficiency when number of stages increases. To address these issues in Dickson charge pump, complicated structure charge pumps were developed [10]. One sort of charge pump with an effective two-phase scheme uses improved charge transfer switches (CTS) [11] that gives better pumping voltage gain than Dickson's charge pump. The charge redistribution loss is not negligible when charge is transferred to one branch of the CTS. So minimize this

© Springer Nature Singapore Pte Ltd. 2020
S. Gupta and J. N. Sarvaiya (Eds.): ET2ECN 2020, CCIS 1214, pp. 29–36, 2020.
https://doi.org/10.1007/978-981-15-7219-7_3

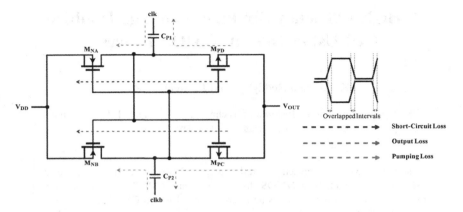

Fig. 1. Basic CCVD with its reversion losses and over lapped clock signals

effect [12] has proposed a linear charge pump architecture which comprises of inverter based controlled mechanism to drive CTS. As supply voltage is less than threshold voltage this architecture did not work effectively. The cross coupled voltage doubler (CCVD) proposed [13] with two branch charge transfer switches (CTS) shown in Fig. 1 employs only two control clock phases. CCVD has several benefits than a conventional charge pump. First, if output buffer capacitor has same capacitance it reduces output voltage drop and output voltage ripple. Second, the voltage drop equal to *Vds* which is less than threshold voltage of diode connected MOSFET in Dickson charge pump. However CCVD inevitably has a significant amount of reversion loss caused due to charge transfers from high voltage node to lower voltage node. The reversion loss comprises of an output loss (a transfer of backward charge from the output node to a booster node), a short circuit loss (a backward charge directly moving from output node to input supply node), a pumping loss (a backward transfer of charge from a booster node to input node) indicating in six power-loss paths as depicted Fig. 1. All of these power losses occur during clock transitions due to timing mismatch or overlapped clock signals, as depicted in Fig. 1. Previously, several techniques have been proposed [14–16], to eliminate or decrease reversion losses. In reported techniques, either level shifters or additional blocking transistors are used. As a consequence, additional power consumed or circuit stability reduces. Furthermore, due to use of level shifters, most of the previous designs cannot scale to multiple stages. In this paper, a fully integrated six-phase voltage doubler (SPVD) is proposed. It consists of charge transfer switches and NMOS driver and PMOS driver circuit. The proposed charge pump structure works with internally generated gating clocks. To minimize reversion loss, a cross coupled NMOS driver and PMOS driver circuit connected to charge transfer switches (CTS).

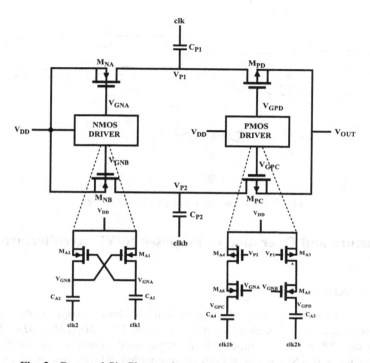

Fig. 2. Proposed Six-Phase voltage doubler with its driver circuits

- Compared to conventional charge pump, the proposed Six-phase voltage doubler structure demonstrates following advantages.
  - The proposed charge pump structure can scale to multiple stages.
  - Voltage doubler and Clock Generator circuit work with same supply.
  - Improvement in voltage conversion ratio, pumping efficiency is achieved.
  - All pumping and auxiliary capacitors were used as Metal-Insulator-Metal (MIM) CAP to decrease bottom plate parasitic capacitance.
  - Reversion losses eliminated using internally generated boosted gate drive voltages.

The validation of proposed Six-phase voltage doubler architecture is done by using UMC180 technology to quantify the advantage of the proposed SPVD compare to previous architectures. The paper is organized as follows: Sect. 2 presents structure and operation of proposed charge pump architecture cell, simulation results are discussed in Sect. 3, while conclusion is given in Sect. 4.

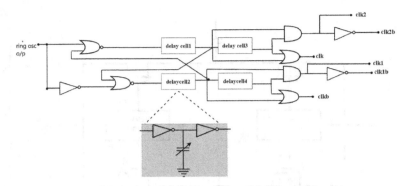

Fig. 3. Non overlapped clock generator circuit

2 Structure and Operation of Proposed SPVD Architecture Cell

2.1 Architecture

Figure 2 shows the architecture of the proposed six-phase voltage doubler (SPVD). The circuit comprises of four charge transfer switches (CTS) M_{NA}, M_{NB}, M_{PC}, M_{PD} and driver circuits. There are two types driver circuits used mainly to control the charge transfer switches (CTS), one is simple cross coupled NMOS pair with its outputs connected to switches M_{NA}, M_{NB} and the other is cross coupled NMOS pair along with two additional PMOS transistors M_{A3}, M_{A4}. PMOS transistors acting as buffer, are introduced to isolate V_{GPD} from V_{DD}.

2.2 Operation

A bootstrapping technique [19] is applied via driver circuits to enhance the gate driving voltage for MOSFET switches. The operation of the six-phase voltage doubler cell is explained. A non-over lapped clocks generated by a clock generator as shown in Fig. 3. The corresponded timing diagram is depicted in Fig. 4. Non overlapping clocks clk1, clk1b, clk, clkb, clk2, clk2b are used to drive driver circuits appropriately. The operation under stable conditions can be described as follows. Here, the operation is described with respect to pumping capacitor C_{P2}, and the similar operation can be observed in C_{P1}. The charge transfer switch (CTS) M_{NB} is controlled by clocks clk1 and clk2. As clk1 goes high and M_{NB} is turned on, V_{GNB} is precharged to VDD, as clk2 is rises, C_{A2} boosts the pre charged V_{GNB} to 2VDD, turning on M_{NB}. During dead time, clk1, clk2 go low, turning off both M_{NB}, M_{A2}, consequently charge loss from C_{P2} to VDD is prevented. For charge transfer M_{PC}, as clk2b goes low, V_{GPD} charges to VDD and as clk2b is rises, C_{A3} boosts the pre charged V_{GPD} to 2VDD. Therefore V_{GPD} and V_{GPC} swings from VDD and 2VDD.

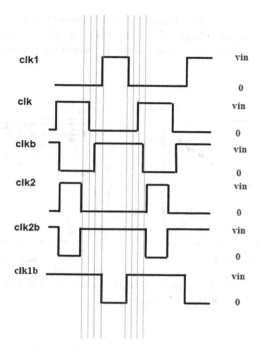

Fig. 4. Timing diagram of non overlapped clock signals

3 Results and Comparison

To verify the implementation of the proposed SPVD, three single stage voltage doublers were implemented in a 180 nm CMOS process. As implemented, the pumping capacitors C_{P1} and C_{P2} were sized as 48pf and additional capacitors C_{A1}–C_{A4} each of 1pf, requiring a total of 100pf for a single six phase voltage doubler stage. All capacitors were used as Metal-Insulator-Metal (MIM) devices to decrease bottom plate parasitic capacitor. A ring oscillator is used to generate prerequisite pumping clock frequency of 10 MHz. The input voltage amplitude VDD and control clock amplitude are same. Driver circuit transistors M_{A1}–M_{A6} were sized as 1◇m/180 nm. The main charge transfer switches M_{NA}, M_{NB}, M_{PC}, M_{PD} were sized 9◇m/180um and 20◇m/180 nm. The output voltage of the proposed six phase voltage doubler with respect to similar work reported in the literature is shown in Fig. 5(a) with supply voltage range from 0.7 V to 3 V. It was observed that, the proposed design output voltage values are very close to ideal values. The pumping efficiency of different voltage doublers in [15–17] reach around 78.5%–92.6% and 98.6%–99.3% and 97.8%–98% of ideal. The pumping efficiency of proposed design reach around 96.6%–99.8% of ideal value as shown in Fig. 5(b). The output voltage of voltage doublers with the load current ranging from 0 to 1.1 mA is shown in Fig. 6(a). The proposed six phase voltage doubler has better driving capability compare to voltage doublers in [15, 17]. The relative performance of the proposed SPVD circuit with respect to similar work reported in the literature is summarized and compared in Table 1. Our proposed SPVD achieved high output voltage 3.58, better efficiency 99.4%) and it can drive wide range load upto 0 to 1.1 mA. The layout of the proposed six phase voltage doubler as shown in Fig. 6(b).

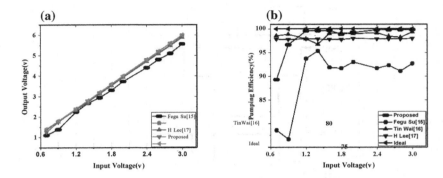

Fig. 5. a) Simulation result of six phase voltage doubler for different supply voltages b) Pumping efficiency for different supply voltages

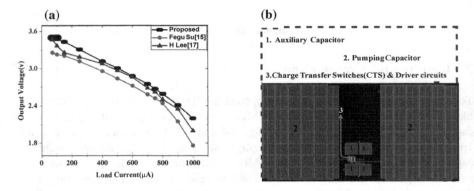

Fig. 6. a) Output Voltage for different load currents b) Layout of the proposed six phase voltage doubler

Table 1. Performance comparison and summary with the prior works

Reference	[18]	[13]	[14]	Proposed
CMOS process (nm)	40	350	46	180
No of stages	2	3	1	1
Input voltage (v)	1	1.8	2	1.8
Flying capacitor (pf)	20	2	20	48
Max voltage conversion ratio	2.53	3.75	1.96	1.98
Load range (mA)	0–10	0–0.1	0–1	0–1.1
Switching frequency (MHz)	60	10	10	10

4 Conclusion

A six phase voltage doubler (SPVD) is presented which nullifies reversion losses while operating only from mono supply VDD for both voltage doubler and clock generator. A bootstrapping technique is applied via driver circuits to enhance the gate driving voltage for MOSFET switches thereby increasing voltage conversion ratio and pumping efficiency effectively. The proposed circuit improves voltage gain and pumping efficiency and also driving capability compared to the prior works. The proposed six phase voltage doubler can also scale to multiple stages.

Acknowledgement. This research was supported by Chip design centre, National institute of Technology, Warangal under SMDP-C2SD sponsored by Ministry of Electronics and Information Technology (MeitY) Grant, Govt of India.

References

1. Calhoun, B.H., et al.: Design considerations for ultra-low energy wireless microsensor nodes. IEEE Trans. Comput. **54**(6), 727–740 (2005)
2. Lu, C., Raghunathan, V., Roy, K.: Efficient design of micro-scale energy harvesting systems. IEEE J. Emerg. Sel. Top. Circ. Syst. **1**, 254–266 (2011). https://doi.org/10.1109/JETCAS.2011.2162161
3. Hameed, Z., Moez, K.: A 3.2 V–15 dBm adaptive threshold-voltage compensated RF energy harvester in 130 nm CMOS. IEEE Trans. Circ. Syst. I: Regul. Pap. **62**(4), 948–956 (2015)
4. Ramadass, Y.K., Chandrakasan, A.P.: A battery-less thermoelectric energy harvesting interface circuit with 35 mV startup voltage. IEEE J. Solid-State Circ. **46**(1), 333–341 (2010)
5. Richelli, A., Mensi, L., Colalongo, L., Rolandi, P.L., Kovacs-Vajna, Z.M.: A 1.2-to-8 V charge-pump with improved power efficiency for non-volatile memories. In: 2007 IEEE International Solid-State Circuits Conference. Digest of Technical Papers, San Francisco, CA, pp. 522–619 (2007)
6. Ying, T.R., Ki, W.-H., Chan, M.: Area-efficient CMOS charge pumps for LCD drivers. IEEE J. Solid-State Circ. **38**(10), 1721–1725 (2003)
7. Breussegem, T.V., Steyaert, M.: CMOS Integrated Capacitive DC-DC Converters. Springer, New York (2013). https://doi.org/10.1007/978-1-4614-4280-6
8. Wong, O., Tam, W., Kok, C., Wong, H.: A novel gate boosting circuit for 2-phase high voltage CMOS charge pump. In: 2009 IEEE International Conference of Electron Devices and Solid-State Circuits (EDSSC), Xi'an, pp. 250–253 (2009)
9. Dickson, J.F.: On-chip high-voltage generation in MNOS integrated circuits using an improved voltage multiplier technique. IEEE J. Solid-State Circ. **11**(3), 374–378 (1976)
10. Hwang, Y.S., Wu, D.S., Lin, H.C., Chen, J.J., Yu, C.C.: A new inverter-based charge pump circuit with high conversion ratio and high power efficiency. Microelectron. J. **42**(8), 982–987 (2011)
11. Wu, J.-T., Chang, K.-L.: MOS charge pumps for low-voltage operation. IEEE J. Solid-State Circ. **33**(4), 592–597 (1998)

12. Su, F., Ki, W.-H., Tsui, C.-Y.: Gate control strategies for high efficiency charge pumps. In: 2005 IEEE International Symposium on Circuits and Systems, Kobe, vol. 2, pp. 1907–1910 (2005)
13. Ker, M.-D., Chen, S.-L., Tsai, C.-S.: Design of charge pump circuit with consideration of gate-oxide reliability in low-voltage CMOS processes. IEEE J. Solid-State Circ. **41**(5), 1100–1107 (2006)
14. Kim, J.Y., Park, S.J., Kwon, K.W., Kong, B.S., Choi, J.S., Jun, Y.H.: CMOS charge pump with no reversion loss and enhanced drivability. IEEE Trans. Very Large Scale Integr. (VLSI) Syst. **22**(6), 1441–1445 (2013)
15. Su, F., Ki, W.-H., Tsui, C.-Y.: High efficiency cross-coupled doubler with no reversion loss. In: 2006 IEEE International Symposium on Circuits and Systems (ISCAS), Island of Kos, pp. 4–2764 (2006)
16. Mui, T.W., Ho, M., Mak, K.H., Guo, J., Chen, H., Leung, K.N.: An area-efficient 96.5%-peak-efficiency cross-coupled voltage doubler with minimum supply of 0.8 V. IEEE Trans. Circ. Syst. II: Express Briefs **61**(9), 656–660 (2014)
17. Lee, H., Mok, P.K.T.: Switching noise and shoot-through current reduction techniques for switched-capacitor voltage doubler. IEEE J. Solid-State Circ. **40**(5), 1136–1146 (2005)
18. New, L.F., bin Abdul Aziz, Z.A., Leong, M.F.: A low ripple CMOS charge pump for low-voltage application. In: 2012 4th International Conference on Intelligent and Advanced Systems (ICIAS2012), Kuala Lumpur, pp. 784–789 (2012)
19. Kim, J.Y., Jun, Y.H., Kong, B.S.: CMOS charge pump with transfer blocking technique for no reversion loss and relaxed clock timing restriction. IEEE Trans. Circ. Syst. II, Express Briefs **56**(1), 11–15 (2009)

Long Period Fiber Grating Sensors Design Optimization Using Jaya Algorithm

Monika Gambhir[✉]

Panipat Institute of Engineering and Technology, Samalkha, Panipat, India
monika.ece@piet.co.in

Abstract. This article presents an approach to optimize the design parameters of Long period fiber gratings (LPFG) using Jaya optimization algorithm is presented. Long period gratings are passive optical fiber sensors. Transmission spectrum of these gratings contain a number of loss bands at resonance wavelengths. Strength of attenuation peaks at resonant wavelengths and sensitivity of the resonance bands are strong functions of the period of gratings, grating length, peak induced-index change, cladding mode order and fiber composition and core and cladding parameters. We have obtained transmission peak loss of $\approx$45 dB for 194 µm period, 40 mm length LPFG with peak induced-index change of 5×10^{-4}. Ultra high sensitivity of 3000 nm/RIU for liquids and biochemicals refractive index range is obtained using the LPFG.

Keywords: Long period gratings · Jaya algorithm · Optimization

1 Introduction

Turn around LPFGs have great potential in refractive index sensing. The ultrahigh sensitivity of LPFG that operate at or near turn around point has been reported in literature in a number of applications that include physical parameter sensing [1, 2], chemical sensing [3], adulteration detection [4–6], radiation dose [7] etc. True potential of TAP LPFGs can be investigated if we have techniques for optimizing grating and fabrication parameters.

True potential of TAP LPFGs can be investigated if we have techniques for optimizing grating and there are a number of design parameters of LPFGs, and each has its own effects on the sensitivity of these gratings. A systematic review of TAP LPFGs has been given in [8]. Optimization of these parameters therefore can help researchers in fabrication and experimentation of these gratings. This study presents the simple and best possible method to help optimizing the grating parameters. The focus of optimization is to maximize the wavelength shift and the transmission peak in order to facilitate both wavelength and amplitude based demodulations.

Undoubtedly significantly high sensitivities of LPFGs have been reported for physical parameter sensing. Sensitivity enhancement of these gratings for particularly SRI sensing applications such as chemical, biochemical applications, for which it can prove to be boon, is an ongoing research [9–11].

In this paper, parameters of long period gratings have been optimized using Jaya algorithm to maximize the sensitivity and transmission loss of these gratings. Section 2

S. Gupta and J. N. Sarvaiya (Eds.): ET2ECN 2020, CCIS 1214, pp. 37–43, 2020.
https://doi.org/10.1007/978-981-15-7219-7_4

provides the mathematical modeling of LPFGs using weakly guiding regime solved by coupled mode theory. Procedure of Jaya optimization algorithm has been discussed in Sect. 3. Section 4 includes the results obtained by varying the constraints and finally optimized parameters.

2 LPFG Mathematical Model

Coupled mode theory describes the mutual light wave interactions occurring between either counter propagating or co-propagating modes in presence of dielectric perturbation. Ideally, modes do not exchange any energy amongst each other in the absence of perturbation [12, 13].

Fundamental core and cladding modes coupling in LPFG take place in standard optical communication window. Rest coupling may show their effect in transmission or reflection spectrum outside the optical communication window.

Area of overlap of the transverse fields of the resonant modes E_i and average index of the grating Δn_i, determines that coupling of core and cladding modes

$$K_{ij} = \frac{\omega \varepsilon_0 n}{4} \int \Delta n_i E_i(r) E_j^*(r) dr \tag{1}$$

Grating transmission is a function of coupling coefficient K and is given by

$$T_{dB} = \cos^2(L\sqrt{K^2 + \delta^2}) + \delta^2 \left[\frac{\sin^2(L\sqrt{K^2 + \delta^2})}{K^2 + \delta^2} \right] \tag{2}$$

3 Jaya Optimization Algorithm

This algorithm is a meta-heuristic algorithm. Algorithm specific parameters are not required in Jaya algorithm thus making it easy to implement in comparison to well known optimization algorithms. The algorithm has been used in several constrained and unconstrained benchmark problems and other engineering problems [14–16]. The expression for variable updation in successive iterations is given as

$$X'_{j,k,i} = X_{j,k,i} + r_{1,j,i}(X_{j,best,i} - |X_{j,k,i}|) - r_{2,j,i}(X_{j,worst,i} - |X_{j,k,i}|) \tag{3}$$

where r_1 and r_2 are the random variables in the interval $[0,1]$, i is the no. of iterations, j = 1,2,…,m is the no. of design parameters and k = 1,2,…,n is the no. of candidate solutions. For any iteration i, $X_{j,best,i}$ provides the best solution out of the candidate solutions and $X_{j,worst,i}$ provides the worst solution out of the candidate solutions. Flowchart of Jaya algorithm has been shown in Fig. 1.

4   Results

Step index SMF-28 fiber has been considered for optimization using Jaya algorithm. Two layers geometry has been assumed for solving characteristic equation. Table 1 shows the parameters taken for simulation.

Table 1. Parameters for simulation

Parameter	Value
Core radius	4.61 μm
Cladding radius	62.5 μm
Core composition	3.1% GeO$_2$ doped silica
Cladding composition	Fused silica

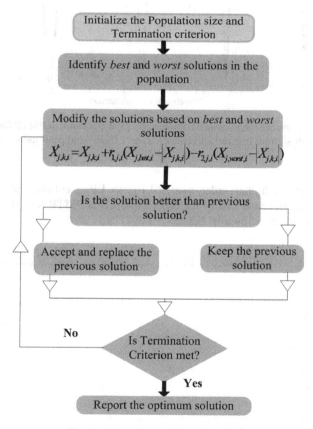

Fig. 1. Flowchart of Jaya algorithm

Wavelength dependent core and cladding indices have been calculated using Sellmeier equation. Solution to coupled mode theory for first fourteen circularly symmetric cladding modes has been obtained to compute propagation loss at resonance wavelengths.

Maximum number of functional evaluations is set to 5000 as a termination criterion. Simulation has been carried out with population size of 25. Grating parameters - period of grating, grating length, peak induced-index change and SRI have great impact on performance of LPFGs as sensors. Boundary conditions for constraints have been set to restrict the search of optimization algorithm at phase matched turning points being ultrahigh sensitive points.

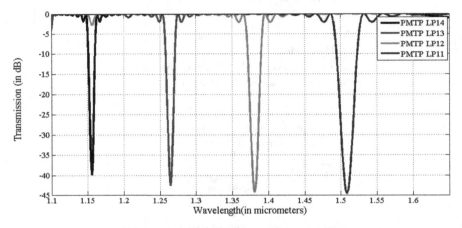

Fig. 2. Maximum transmission peak (dB) obtained by Jaya algorithm at PMTP for LP_{11} to LP_{14} cladding modes with surrounding refractive index n_3 as 1.0 (air) and peak induced-index change of 5×10^{-4} .

Linearly polarized higher order modes LP_{11} to LP_{14}, couple with fundamental mode and yield transmission loss of the order of 45 dB at PMTP $\approx$ 194, 173, 154 and 139 μm respectively as shown in Fig. 2.

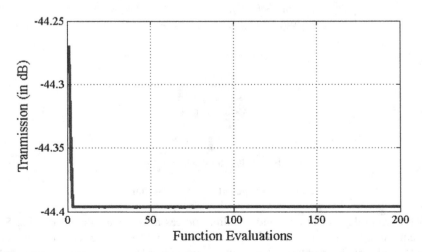

Fig. 3. Convergence of optimization function at grating period 194 μm

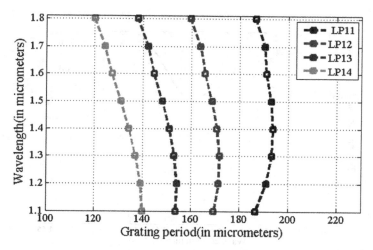

Fig. 4. Phase matching curves for higher order cladding modes

Figure 3 shows the convergence of the optimization function using 5000 function evaluation and 25 population size using Jaya algorithm. Figure 4 shows the phase matching curves for LP_{11} to LP_{14} higher order cladding modes Phase Matching curves drawn in figure for higher order cladding modes LP_{11} to LP_{14} between grating period and resonance wavelength for standard single mode fiber indicate the presence of turn around points in range $125 \leq \Lambda \leq 145$, $145 \leq \Lambda \leq 165$, $165 \leq \Lambda \leq 185$, $185 \leq \Lambda \leq 205$ μm.

Grating periods have been varied in these range to obtain maximum transmission loss peaks at phase matched turning around points. Grating length has been varied in $10000 \leq L \leq 40000$ μm for all simulations. Optimized parameters by considering surrounding refractive index as 1.0 has been given in Table 1.

Dissimilar coupling coefficients result in different loss of attenuation peaks at resonance bands. Fig. 5(a) shows the highest transmission loss of the order of 45 dB is obtained for strong grating with peak induced-index change of 5×10^{-4}. Figure 5(b) shows the SRI vs wavelength graph obtained by varying SRI and calculating the resonance wavelength.

Transmission peak loss of 45 dB has been observed after optimizing the parameters of LPFG. It enhances the sensitivity range for amplitude based demodulation. Highly sensitive LPFG with 3000 nm/RIU sensitivity enables LPFGs to be used for wavelength based demodulation schemes.

Surrounding refractive index response of a long-period grating over index range 1.3–1.4 has been modeled. Peak index change of $0.5 \times 10^{-4} - 10^{-4}$ leads to inscription of weak gratings [17]. Strong gratings having peak induced index change of 5×10^{-4} can be inscribed by either enhancing the photosensitivity of fiber or by tuning initial conditions e.g. etching the cladding or coating fiber with high refractive index materials.

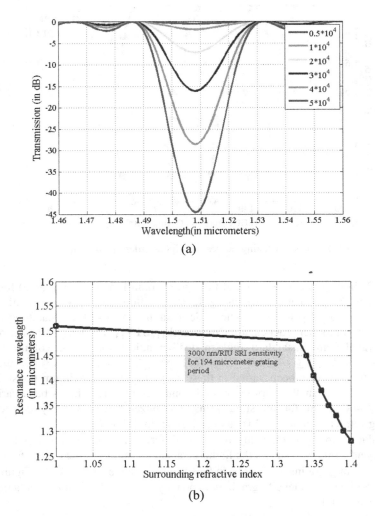

Fig. 5. (a) Variation of transmission loss (dB) with Peak induced-index change for 194 μm LPFG (b) Analysis of sensitivity of 194 μm LPFG with SRI in range 1.3–1.4.

5 Conclusion

Optimization of parameters to maximize the sensitivity and transmission loss of long period fiber grating sensors have been reported. SRI sensitivity analysis for higher order cladding modes PMTP LPFGs is accomplished by varying surrounding refractive index in 1.3–1.4 range which corresponds to liquids and most biochemicals. Ultra high sensitivity of 3000 nm per refractive index unit (3000 nm/RIU) has been obtained which is, according to our best knowledge, the highest ever reported in this range. The significance of the proposed work lies in the fact that a lot of work in finding suitable parameters for ultra high sensitivity can be reduced by applying evolutionary optimization algorithms.

References

1. Bhatia, V.: Applications of long-period gratings to single and multi-parameter sensing. Opt. Express **4**(11), 457–466 (1999)
2. Shu, X., Allsop, T., Gwandu, B., Zhang, L., Bennion, I.: High-temperature sensitivity of long-period gratings in B-Ge codoped fiber. IEEE Photonics Technol. Lett. **13**(8), 818–820 (2001)
3. Hochreiner, H., Cada, M., Wentzell, P.D.: Modeling the response of a long-period fiber grating to ambient refractive index change in chemical sensing applications. J. Lightwave Technol. **26**(13), 1986–1992 (2008)
4. Kher, S., Chaubey, S., Kishore, J., Oak, S.M.: Detection of fuel adulteration with high sensitivity using turnaround point long period fiber gratings in B/Ge doped fibers. IEEE Sens. J. **13**(11), 4482–4486 (2013)
5. Mishra, V., Jain, S.C., Singh, N., Poddar, G.C., Kapur, P.: Fuel adulteration detection using long period fiber grating sensor technology. J. Sci. Ind. Res. (JSIR) **46**(2), 106–110 (2008)
6. Libish, T.M., Linesh, J., Biswas, P., Bandyopadhyay, S., Dasgupta, K., Radhakrishnan, P.: Fiber optic long period grating based sensor for coconut oil adulteration detection. Sens. Transducers **114**(3), 102–104 (2010)
7. Kher, S., Chaubey, S., Kashyap, R., Oak, S.M.: Turnaround-point long-period fiber gratings (TAP-LPGs) as high-radiation-dose sensors. IEEE Photonics Technol. Lett. **24**(9), 742–744 (2012)
8. Gambhir, M., Gupta, S.: Review of turnaround point long period fiber gratings. J. Sens. Technol. **5**(04), 81–89 (2015)
9. Chiavaioli, F., et al.: Towards sensitive label-free immuno sensing by means of turn-around point long period fiber gratings. Biosens. Bioelectron. **60**, 305–310 (2014)
10. Tripathi, S.M., et al.: Long period grating based biosensor for the detection of Escherichia coli bacteria. Biosens. Bioelectron. **35**(1), 308–312 (2012)
11. Gambhir, M., Gupta, S.: Optimization of long period grating at phase matched turning points for bio-chemical sensing. In: 2016 International Conference on Fiber Optics and Photonics, Photonics, pp. W3A-39 (2016)
12. Ugale, S.P., Mishra, V.: Optimization of reversible LPFG for sensing application. Optik-Int. J. Light Electron. Opt. **125**(1), 111–114 (2014)
13. Oh, K., Paek, U.C.: Silica Optical Fiber Technology for Devices and Components: Design, Fabrication, and International Standards, vol. 240. Wiley, Hoboken (2012)
14. Rao, R.: Jaya: a simple and new optimization algorithm for solving constrained and unconstrained optimization problems. Int. J. Ind. Eng. Comput. **7**(1), 19–34 (2016)
15. Zhang, Y., Yang, X., Cattani, C., Rao, R.V., Wang, S., Phillips, P.: Tea category identification using a novel fractional Fourier entropy and Jaya algorithm. Entropy **18**(3), 77–86 (2016)
16. Rao, R.V., More, K.C., Taler, J., Ocłoń, P.: Dimensional optimization of a micro-channel heat sink using Jaya algorithm. Appl. Therm. Eng. **103**, 572–582 (2016)
17. Erdogan, T.: Cladding-mode resonances in short-and long-period fiber grating filters. JOSA A **14**(8), 1760–1773 (1997)

Strategy for Designing Single Electron Transistors

Raj Shah[1]([✉]) [iD], Rutu Parekh[2], and Rasika Dhavse[1]

[1] Sardar Vallabhbhai National Institute of Technology,
Surat 395007, Gujarat, India
shahraj9l@gmail.com, rsk@eced.svnit.ac.in
[2] Dhirubhai Ambani Institute of Information and Communication Technology,
Gandhinagar 382421, Gujarat, India
rutu_parekh@daiict.ac.in

Abstract. Silicon-processing, ultra-low-power dissipation, and scalability attract SET as the most emerging nanodevice. The SET, working on the principles of Coulomb blockade (CB) and Quantum mechanical tunneling (QMT), has many challenges at the design level. Its structure consists of two ultra-thin tunnel barriers and a conductive island which is always challenging to design. In this work, tunnel barrier optimization and island engineering are targeted to design SET with high current density and with appropriate CB. The Aluminum and N-type phosphorus-doped polysilicon materials are used as the island materials. The tunnel barrier thickness has been varied from 1 nm, 1.5 nm, 2 nm, 3 nm, and 4 nm. The simulations are carried out to plot I-V and Q-V plots in Sentaurus TCAD. The behavior of CB and QMT has been analyzed at 77 K, 150 K, 300 K, and 400 K. From the simulations of all structures the maximum drain current is found in range the 1 nA (T_J = 4 mm and at 77 K) to 3.5 µA (T_J = 1 mm and at 400 K) for Aluminum island and 2e-4 pA (T_J = 2 mm and at 77 K) to 0.35 nA (T_J = 1 mm and at 400 K) for Polysilicon island. Mathematical analysis for CB has been done for the above-mentioned temperatures and compared with simulations. The Effect of the gate on the controlling of QMT is analyzed on the 3 nm tunnel junction thick Aluminum island SET. The results of the maximum drain current have been compared to the other research works.

Keywords: Coulomb blockade · Emerging nanodevice · Island engineering · Quantum mechanical tunneling · Single electron transistor · Tunnel barriers

1 Introduction

SETs have been looking as under development before a decade as its dimensions control, room temperature operation and lack of current drive. But since the last decade, major development against its challenges shown its worthiness to succeed over matured CMOS technologies and contemporary FinFET technologies. It is an emerging device for both memory and logic circuit applications [1]. SETs unique behavior and characteristics have been very appealing for the ultra-low-power and high-speed circuits [2]. SETs are based on quantum mechanical effects at the sub-nanometer region with

© Springer Nature Singapore Pte Ltd. 2020
S. Gupta and J. N. Sarvaiya (Eds.): ET2ECN 2020, CCIS 1214, pp. 44–57, 2020.
https://doi.org/10.1007/978-981-15-7219-7_5

ultralow power and low operating bias conditions. But the afford to make SET based circuits and its large-scale processing is still not accomplished. The design methodology for circuit-level has been attained by many using spice netlist [3] and Verilog-A modeling [4] but the device-level design is still a challenge. A careful tunnel barrier optimization and island engineering are must for designing the best suitable dimension for SETs before fabrication [5, 6]. In this work, the attempt is to optimize the tunnel barrier thickness (1 nm, 1.5 nm, 3 nm, and 4 nm) for two different island materials viz. Aluminum and Phosphorous doped polysilicon. The devices have been simulated for temperatures 77 K, 150 K, 300 K, and 400 K. For device simulation, Doping Dependent Masetti, Phillips Unified Mobility model, Band to Band Schenk recombination model and Schenk Direct Tunneling model, have been used in Sentaurus TCAD [7]. In the initial set up, all devices are simulated with the grounded gate. After analyzing CB and QMT, the 3 nm Aluminum island SET, has been selected for its high current drive along with better CB. The effect of the gate on the device is also attempted. The controllability of the gate has been analyzed by plotting the number of electrons.

2 SET Device Planning and Mathematical Analysis

2.1 Mathematical Analysis

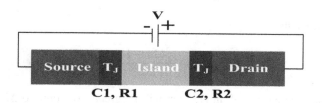

Fig. 1. SET cross section view for grounded gate

A bias supply of V volts has been applied between drain and source lead as shown in Fig. 1. Conductive island in the middle has been surrounded by the two tunnel barriers having capacitances $C1 = C2 = C_J$ and resistances $R1 = R2 = R_T$. These capacitances C1 and C2 can be calculated from their geometry by formula $C = A\varepsilon/d$, where $A = W \times t$. value of ε for SiO_2 is 34.51×10^{-3} aF/nm, W is the width, t is the depth and, d is the thickness. Total capacitance looking from the island can be calculated from the parallel plate model and given by $C = C1 + C2$. For zero temperature condition, the energy required to transfer an electron to or from the neutral island can be given by [8, 9].

$$E_C = \frac{(Q_0 - e)^2}{2C} \tag{1}$$

where, Q_0 is charge impurity or offset charge, e is an elementary charge of electron 1.6e-19 and C is the total capacitance [8, 9]. For room temperature or higher temperature, the thermal energy is also available. In this case

$$eV > \frac{e^2}{2C} - 2K_BT \tag{2}$$

and from Eq. 2, the condition of tunneling can be determined [8, 9]. Let, ΔE is the change in electrostatic energy required to transport an electron to or from island and n_0 is the minimum integer value of n that can be taken place when $\Delta E = 0$, which is closest to the $n = Q_0 \times e$. Change in electrostatic energy is given by [9],

$$\Delta E = \frac{(Q_0 - n_0e - e)^2}{2C} - \frac{(Q_0 - n_0e)^2}{2C} \tag{3}$$

Above Eq. 3. must be greater than zero ($\Delta E > 0$) when an electron has been added to the island. This condition gives,

$$\frac{(Q_0 - n_0e - e)^2}{2C} - \frac{(Q_0 - n_0e)^2}{2C} > 0 \tag{4}$$

$$\frac{e}{2C} \geq |Q_0 - n_0e| > 0 \tag{5}$$

For n electrons and $Q_0 = 0$,

$$\Delta E = \frac{e^2(2n + 1)}{2C} \tag{6}$$

Hence, when the energy of an electron will be greater or equal to ΔE, an electron can be added to the island [8, 9].

$$\frac{eC_2}{C_1 + C_2} V_{CB1} = \frac{e^2}{2C} \left[(2n + 1) - \frac{2Q_0}{e} \right] \tag{7}$$

$$V_{CB1} \geq \frac{2e}{C}(2n + 1) > 0 \tag{8}$$

So, the applied bias required to transfer an electron from source to drain will be $2V_{CB1}$ as $C_1 = C_2 = C_J$.

2.2 SET Design Strategy

The strategy of designing SET considers both for the mathematical analysis and the CMOS compatible fabrication processing. As the SET is having two ultra-thin tunnel barriers and a conductive island assembled between them, it is highly complex to fabricate it with proper dimensions. The fabrication of SET using nano-particles [10], nanowire [11], and graphene [12] can provide good characteristics but, large scale processing of SET using these is challenging and unfeasible in near future. Metal SETs provide good conductivity and also opens up the window for the 3D BEOL processing but Metal SETs are having more offset charges and defects than Silicon SETs [13]. So, in this work, CMOS compatibility and existing Silicon processing is adopted to design its critical dimensions [6, 14–16] for high current density and exploring the thermal behavior of SET.

As shown in Fig. 2, Sentaurus Structure Editor (SDE) is used for forming, meshing and processing structures. The source, drain, gate, and island are generated on the SOI substrate which can be patterned using EB lithography while the tunnel barriers can be grown using RTO [14–19] for fabrication.

Fig. 2. SET structure and top view

Here, as shown in Fig. 2, N-Type source and drain regions have created and are surrounded by the oxide. The conductive island at the center is bounded by two ultra-thin tunnel junctions. The gate is doped with N-Type polysilicon separated from the island with oxide. The design is strategized with island material and tunnel barrier optimization techniques. The Aluminum and N-type Polysilicon are preferred as the island material. The tunnel junction optimization of 1 nm to 4 nm for Aluminum island SET [6] and 1 nm to 3 nm for Polysilicon island SET have been carried out. Figure 3 shows the structures generated for tunnel barrier optimization with 1 nm, 1.5 nm, 3 nm and 4 nm of Aluminum island SET.

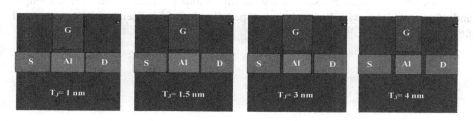

Fig. 3. Aluminum island SET tunnel barrier optimization

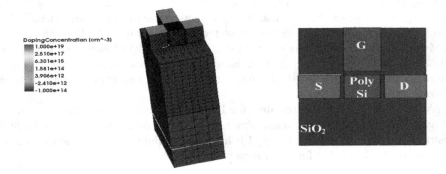

Fig. 4. Polysilicon island SET structure with meshing and its top view

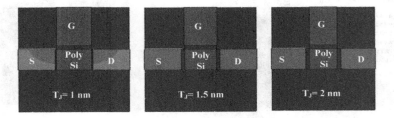

Fig. 5. Polysilicon island SET tunnel barrier optimization

Similar to aluminum island SET, polysilicon island SET structure is generated as shown in Fig. 4. The tunnel barrier optimization with T_J = 1 nm, 1.5 nm, and 2 nm has been done for the polysilicon island as shown in above Fig. 5.

2.3   SET Device Planning

The designed SET is shown in Fig. 6. The dimensions are designs from the process compatibility of 180 nm CMOS technology. However, the critical dimensions such as tunnel barrier thickness and island are designed to the get high current drive and at the same time adequate CB voltage. So, the dimensions of source, drain, and gate, as well as the length of island, can be scaled as per the processing equipment's availability. In this work, the SET having a substrate with dimensions (300 nm width, 450 nm length and 250 nm height) with P-type boron-doped (1e14 cm^{-3} concentration) is generated first.

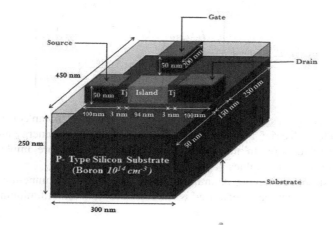

Fig. 6. SET device planning

On the substrate, a thick SiO_2 layer is deposited. N-type phosphorus-doped (1e19 cm^{-3} concentration) source and drain regions of silicon, and a gate of the polysilicon region are generated after etching SiO_2. Island material deposition (Aluminum/ Polysilicon) and tunnel barriers are then patterned. In Fig. 6. SET device planning of 3 nm tunnel barrier aluminum island SET is illustrated. Similarly, all remaining structures are planned.

For the designed structure, the capacitances can be calculated using a parallel plate capacitance [16–18]. Here, C_J, C_G, and C_Σ are junction capacitance, gate capacitance, and total capacitance respectively. Here, Total capacitance C_Σ can be evaluated as $C_\Sigma = (2C_J) + C_G$. Table 1 summarizes the calculated capacitances for all structures.

Table 1. SET capacitance calculations

T_J (nm)	C_J (aF)	C_G (eV)	C_Σ (aF)
1	263.50	3.51	530.32
1.5	175.67	3.51	354.85
2	131.75	3.51	267.02
3	87.83	3.51	179.18
4	65.87	3.51	135.26

3 Result and Analysis

3.1 SET Device Physics

For device simulation in TCAD for all above-generated structures, the doping dependent Masetti mobility model, Phillips Unified mobility model and the recombination model of SRH have been used as global physics. At Silicon/SiO_2, the direct tunneling model of Schenk is used to capture the electron tunneling at the interface. The current density of the direct tunneling model is given by,

$$J_n = \frac{qm_Ck}{2\pi^2}\hbar^3 \int_0^\infty \left\{ \begin{array}{l} T(0)\ln\left(e^{\left[\frac{E_{F,n}(0)-E_C(0)-E}{KT(0)}\right]}+1\right) \\[12pt] -T(d)\ln\left(e^{-\left[\frac{E_{F,n}(d)-E_C(0)-E}{KT(d)}\right]}+1\right) \end{array} \right\} \qquad (9)$$

Where m_C is the mass of carrier in semiconductor, K is Boltzmann constant, d is the thickness of the dielectric, T is the temperature in K, E_F is Fermi energy and E_C is the conduction band energy. In this work, these physics models are implemented for silicon and SiO_2 default values ($\varepsilon_{Si} = 11.7$, $\varepsilon_{OX} = 3.97$, and $m_{si,e-} = 1350$ V/cm^{-2}). For the SET structures having Aluminum island, band to band tunneling model and barrier lowering model have been used at the interface between Aluminum and oxide.

3.2   Simulation Results

All the structures are simulated using the device physics explained in the previous section. The observe the thermal behavior of all structures, simulations are carried out at 77 K, 150 K, 300 K, and 400 K. The temperature values are chosen by considering the characterization of the device at the liquid helium temperature (77 K), room temperature (300 K), below room temperature (150 K) and above room temperature (300 K).

Aluminum Island SET Simulations. Output characteristics of aluminum island SET structures have been plotted with the grounded gate.

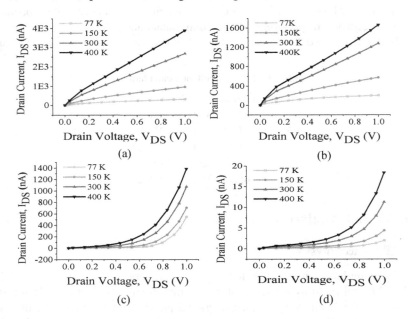

Fig. 7. Thermal behavior for Aluminum island SET for (a) $T_J = 1$ nm (b) $T_J = 1.5$ nm (c) $T_J = 3$ nm (d) $T_J = 4$ nm

The output characteristics have been plotted for tunnel barrier thicknesses of 1 nm in Fig. 7(a), 1.5 nm in Fig. 7(b), 3 nm in Fig. 7(c), and 4 nm in Fig. 7(d). Table 2 shows the extracted maximum drain current (I_{ON}) and CB voltage (V_{CB}) for all structure and theoretically calculated V_{CB} for all four structures.

Table 2. CB voltage and maximum drain current analysis for aluminum island SET (S: Simulated, T: Theoretical)

	400 K			300 K			150 K			77 K		
	S		T	S		T	S		T	S		T
T_J (nm)	I_{ON} (μA)	V_{CB} (mV)	V_{CB} (mV)	I_{ON} (μA)	V_{CB} (mV)	V_{CB} (mV)	I_{ON} (μA)	V_{CB} (mV)	V_{CB} (mV)	I_{ON} (μA)	V_{CB} (mV)	V_{CB} (mV)
1	3.5	0.16	0.233	2.5	0.22	0.25	0.9	0.38	0.26	0.25	0.59	0.28
1.5	1.52	0.25	0.38	1.3	0.28	0.39	0.51	0.40	0.425	0.15	0.63	0.43
3	0.33	6.3	0.84	0.52	9.8	0.85	0.12	20	0.867	1	98	0.88
4	0.018	1.2	1.11	0.012	1.4	1.13	0.004	2.1	1.16	0.001	19.22	1.17

The maximum current range is found to be 1 nA (T_J = 4 mm and at 77 K) to 3.5 μA (T_J = 1 mm and at 400 K). The range of CB voltage extracted is in the range of 0.16 mV (T_J = 1 mm and at 77 K) to 98 (T_J = 3 mm and at 400 K).

Polysilicon Island SET Simulations. Similar simulations have been done on Poly island SET to obtained the characteristics. The I-V characteristics are plotted as shown in Fig. 8 (Table 3).

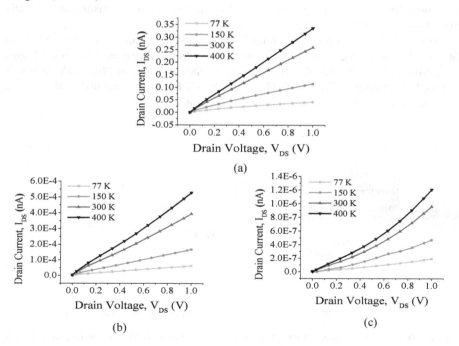

Fig. 8. Thermal behavior for polysilicon island SET for (a) T_J = 1 nm (b) T_J = 1.5 nm (c) T_J = 2 nm

Table 3. CB voltage and maximum drain current analysis for polysilicon island SET (S: Simulated, T: Theoretical)

| | $T_J = 1$ nm | | | $T_J = 1.5$ nm | | | $T_J = 2$ nm | | |
| | S | | T | S | | T | S | | T |
Temp (K)	I_{ON} (nA)	V_{CB} (mV)	V_{CB} (mV)	I_{ON} (nA)	V_{CB} (mV)	V_{CB} (mV)	I_{ON} (pA)	V_{CB} (mV)	V_{CB} (mV)
77	0.04	7.8	0.28	0.05	16.14	0.43	1.2	9.7	0.58
150	0.1	4.2	0.27	0.15	6.8	0.42	1	10.2	0.57
300	0.26	2.7	0.25	0.40	0.26	0.39	0.40	12.25	0.55
400	0.33	2.3	0.23	0.52	0.14	0.38	0.12	10.1	0.53

The maximum current range is found to be 2e-4 pA ($T_J = 2$ mm and at 77 K) to 0.35 nA ($T_J = 1$ mm and at 400 K). The range of CB voltage extracted is in the range of 0.16 mV ($T_J = 1$ mm and at 77 K) to 98 ($T_J = 2$ mm and at 400 K).

As the oxide thickness increases, the energy needed to transfer electron also increases. So, CB voltage increases and current decreases. But once CB overcomes, current increases rapidly as bias increases. Here, in all cases, temperature dependency has been observed on the CB and QMT. As temperature increases, the tunneling increases as well as CB voltage decreases. This can be justified as theoretically, an increase in temperature provides more thermal energy to electrons and that helps to overcome the CB region. The simulation point of view also can be justified as Schenk direct tunneling model which is responsible for tunneling current measurement, directly proportional to the temperature.

Out of all the structures, 3 nm tunnel barrier thickness aluminum island SET has shown the good amalgamation of CB and QMT. As the Aluminum is having higher conductivity and high current carrying capacity then polysilicon [20], high current is observed in aluminum island SET. The selected SET has been simulated to observe the effect of the gate and to plot the number of electrons.

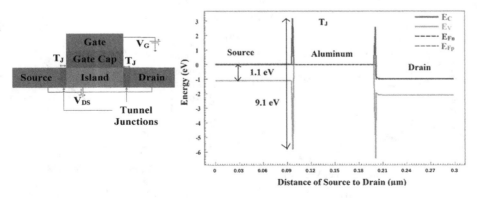

Fig. 9. SET device ($T_J = 3$ nm and Aluminum island) and its Energy Band Diagram (EBD)

The Fig. 9. illustrates the designed device and from the device simulation, its EBD is plotted. The EBD is observed by taking horizontal cut between source and drain.

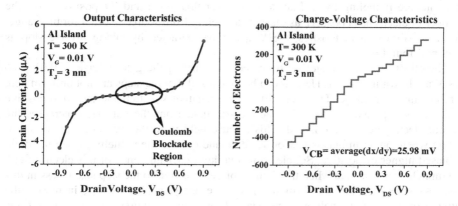

Fig. 10. Output I-V and charge-voltage characteristics for Aluminum island SET

Here, the output characteristics have been plotted to observe the CB region and to verify the symmetric behavior of the Al island SET with 3 nm tunnel barriers as shown in Fig. 10. From the above characteristics, the CB region at room temperature can be clearly observed at the center. The maximum current is in range of μA (max 5 μA) which justifies the high current capability of SET. Approximately 100 mV of V_{CB} can be extracted by observing the CB region but as the range of I_{DS} is in μA, it is not possible to calculate the exact V_{CB} from this. The gate voltage affects tunneling current in a very small margin. To visualize the effect, charge-voltage characteristics and the V_{CB} have been observed. The number of electrons from the charge has been calculated as n = Q = e where Q is the total charge and e is the elementary charge of an electron.

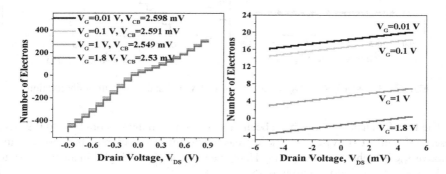

Fig. 11. Charge-voltage characteristics to observe the effect of gate voltage

The number of electrons has been plotted here for applied drain bias for fix gate voltage as shown in Fig. 11. The staircase pattern clearly shows the Coulomb staircase behavior of the device. For negative V_{DS}, the number of electrons is negative as the electrons are tunneling from drain to source for this range and for positive V_{DS}, the number of electrons is positive as they are tunneling from source to drain for this range. From the above characteristics, the V_{CB} can be extracted by taking inverse slop as 5.98 mV found here.

The effect of gate voltage has been seen by varying the gate voltage as 0.01 V to 1.8 V as shown in Fig. 11. Here, it can be visualized that the steps are not uniform here for the entire V_{DS} range. They are uniform for negative V_{DS} to 0 and then 0 to positive V_{DS}. As we applied the fix V_{GS}, the electric field from the gate side increases the overall electric field at the island. This electric field from the gate side supports tunneling when the drain bias is low or negative and oppose the tunneling when the drain is biased higher or positive. So, electrons that are under influence of this electric field, the tunnels at a slow rate when the drain is biased positive so the step size is less in this case. As shown in the above figure, it can be analyzed that as V_{GS} increases, the number of electrons tunneling to the island from source requires less energy. But, the potential difference between the island and drain increases. So, the number of electrons at the drain side decreases as they require higher energy.

The transfer characteristics has been plotted to observe the effect of the gate on CB and QMT at room temperature as shown in Fig. 12.

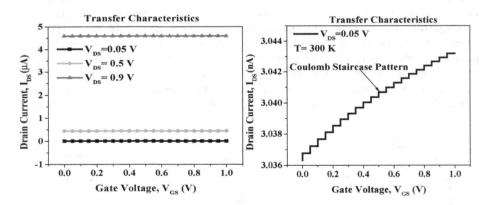

Fig. 12. Transfer I-V at V_{DS} = 0.05 V to 0.09 V and staircase pattern observation

The transfer characteristics have been plotted for V_{DS} ranging from 0.05 to 0.9 V to observe the effect of V_{DS}. As V_{DS} increases, the tunneling current increases so the range of I_{DS} is higher for higher V_{DS}. Here, we have observed ripples in all curves so to analyze it, we zoomed the curve as shown in Fig. 12.

The maximum drain current and the applied bias conditions of the different work have been compared in Table 4.

Table 4. Comparison of the maximum drain current and bias supply

Reference	Applied bias	Operating temperature	Maximum I_{DS}	SET material (Source-Island-Drain)
Dubuc 2008 [17]	1 V	296 K–430 K	10 nA–15 nA	Ti-Ti-Ti
Ray 2008 [10]	0.2 V	10 K–315 K	40 pA–315 K	Cr-Au-Cr
Lee 2011 [16]	0.1 V	4.4 K–77 K	40 nA–0.8 µA	Si-Al-Si
Puczkarski 2015 [12]	0.2 V	300 K	8 nA	Graphene
Durrani 2017 [21]	4 V	290 K	50 nA	Si-Si-Si
Majima 2017 [22]	0.2 V	9 K	12 nA	Au-Au-Au
Proposed Work, 2019	0.9 V	77 K–400 K	0.5 µA to 4.2 µA	Si-Al-Si

From the Table 4, the higher current density is obtained for the proposed research work compared to other research work. The proposed structure can be operated at higher applied bias and temperature with the advantages of CMOS compatibility and Silicon processing.

4   Conclusion

The proposed strategy is aimed to get high current drive along with adequate CB with CMOS process compatibility. The thermal behavior of SET devices also analyzed. Out of all devices generated using the strategy, 1 nm thick tunnel barrier SET of aluminum island exhibits maximum drain current of 4.1 µA. The range of drain current in aluminum island SETs has been observed in a few µA. CB voltage in the range of 0.23 mV to 1.17 mV has been calculated from mathematical analysis while 0.16 mV to 98 mV has been extracted from simulation results of aluminum island SET. The range of drain current in polysilicon island SETs has been observed in a few pA. CB voltage in the range of 0.14 mV to 16.14 mV has been extracted from simulation results of polysilicon island SET. From all structures, 3 nm aluminum island SET has provided the good drain current along with adequate CB. The gate voltage effect on CB for the final designed SET has been analyzed by plotting transient and output characteristics with gate voltage variation. The charge-voltage characteristics also plotted to analyze the effect of gate voltage on the number of electron as well as CB voltage. It is observed that at 0.05 V V_{DS}, the change in I_{DS} has been found in pA range which is very small compare to tunneling current in the range of nA. As V_{GS} increase, the number of electrons traveling to drain also decreasing in range of the 25-30 due to the high electric field near the gate. The results show the behavior of the gate voltage in controlling the number of electrons. The V_{CB} also decreases as V_{GS} increases. The proposed technique is compared with the other research work to show the excellency in the high current drive at suitable bias supply and temperature conditions. The designed SET can be suitable for ultra-low power logic and memory circuits in digital applications.

References

1. Chen, A.: Emerging research device roadmap and perspectives. In: 2014 IEEE International Conference IC Design & Technology (ICICDT), Austin, TX, pp. 1–4. IEEE (2014). https://doi.org/10.1109/icicdt.2014.6838616
2. Mahapatra, S., Ionescu, A.M.: Hybrid CMOS Single-Electron-Transistor Device and Circuit Design. Artech House, Norwood (2006)
3. Yu, Y.S., Jung, Y.L., Park, J.H.: Simulation of Single-Electron/CMOS hybrid circuits using SPICE macro-modeling. J. Korean Phys. Soc. **35**(4), 991–994 (1999)
4. Mahapatra, S., Vaish, V., Wasshuber, C., Banerjee, K., Ionescu, A.M.: Analytical modeling of single electron transistor for hybrid cmos-set analog ic design. IEEE Trans. Electron Devices **51**(11), 1772 (2004). https://doi.org/10.1109/TED.2004.837369
5. Hajjam, K.G.E., et al.: Tunnel junction engineering for optimized metallic single-electron transistor. IEEE Trans. Electron Devices, **62**(9), 2998–3003 (2015). https://doi.org/10.1109/ted.2015.2452575
6. Shah, R., Dhavse, R.: Tunnel barrier optimization for room temperature operation of single electron transistors. In: Proceedings of the Nanotech France 2018 International Conference (Nanotech France 2018), Sector, Paris, pp. 37–40 (2018)
7. SentaurusTM Device User Guide
8. Hanson, G.W.: Fundamentals of Nanoelectronics. Pearson/Prentice Hall, Upper Saddle River (2008)
9. Hamaguchi, C.: Basic Semiconductor Physics. GTP. Springer, Cham (2017). https://doi.org/10.1007/978-3-319-66860-4
10. Ray, V., Subramanian, R., Bhadrachalam, P., Ma, L.-C., Kim, C.-U., Koh, S.J.: CMOS-compatible fabrication of room-temperature single-electron devices. Nat. Nanotechnol. **3**(10), 603–608 (2008). https://doi.org/10.1038/nnano.2008.267
11. Sun, Y., Rusli, Singh, N.: Room-temperature operation of silicon single-electron transistor fabricated using optical lithography. IEEE Trans. Nanotechnol. **10**(1), 96–98 (2011). https://doi.org/10.1109/tnano.2010.2086475
12. Puczkarski, P., et al.: Three-terminal graphene single-electron transistor fabricated using feedback-controlled electroburning. Appl. Phys. Lett. **107**(13), 133105 (2015). https://doi.org/10.1063/1.4932133
13. Zimmerman, N.M., Huber, W.H., Fujiwara, A., Takahashi, Y.: Excellent charge offset stability in a Si-based single-electron tunneling transistor. Appl. Phys. Lett. **79**(19), 3188–3190 (2001). https://doi.org/10.1063/1.1415776
14. Joshi, V., Orlov, A.O., Snider, G.L.: Silicon single-electron transistor with oxide tunnel barriers fabricated using chemical mechanical polishing. J. Vac. Sci. Technol. B Microelectron. Nanometer Struct. **26**(6), 2587–2591 (2008). https://doi.org/10.1116/1.297887
15. Lee, Y.-C., Joshi, V., Orlov, A.O., Snider, G.L.: Si single electron transistor fabricated by chemical mechanical polishing. J. Vac. Sci. Technol. B Nanotechnol. Microelectron. Mater. Process. Measur. Phenom. **28**(6) C6L9-C6L13 (2010). http://dx.doi.org/10.1116/1.3498748
16. Lee, Y.-C., Orlov, A.O., Snider, G.L.: Fabrication of hybrid metal island/silicon single electron transistor. J. Vac. Sci. Technol. B Nanotechnol. Microelectron. Mater. Process. Measur. Phenom. **29**(6), 06FB02 (2011). http://dx.doi.org/10.1116/1.3644340

17. Dubuc, C., Beauvais, J., Drouin, D.: A nanodamascene process for advanced single-electron transistor fabrication. IEEE Trans. Nanotechnol. **7**(1), 68–73 (2008). https://doi.org/10.1109/TNANO.2007.913430
18. Parekh, R., Beaumont, A., Beauvais, J., Drouin, D.: Simulation and design methodology for hybrid SET-CMOS integrated logic at 22-nm room-temperature operation. IEEE Trans. Electron Devices **59**(4), 918–923 (2012). https://doi.org/10.1109/TED.2012.2183374
19. Kang, K.-C., et al.: Poly-silicon quantum dot single electron transistors. J. Korean Phys. Soc. **60**(1), 108–112 (2012). https://doi.org/10.3938/jkps.60.108
20. Gall, D.: Electron mean free path in elemental metals. J. Appl. Phys. **119**(8), 085101 (2016). https://doi.org/10.1063/1.4942216
21. Durrani, Z.A.K., Jones, M.E., Wang, C., Liu, D., Griffiths, J.: Excited states and quantum confinement in room temperature few nanometre scale silicon single electron transistors. Nanotechnology **28**, 125208 (2017). https://doi.org/10.1088/1361-6528/aa5ddd
22. Majima, Y., et al.: Three-input gate logic circuits on chemically assembled single-electron transistors with organic and inorganic hybrid passivation layers. Sci. Technol. Adv. Mater. **18**(1), 374–380 (2017). https://doi.org/10.1080/14686996.2017.1320190

Experimental Study on Etching of Fiber Bragg Grating for Sensing Application

Chhaya Suratwala[1,2(✉)] and Pranav Lapsiwala[1]

[1] Sarvajanik College of Engineering and Technology, Surat, India
{chhaya.suratwala,pranav.lapsiwala}@scet.ac.in
[2] Sardar Vallabhbhai National Institute of Technology, Surat, India

Abstract. Optical fiber sensors are popular due to its attractive feature. Chemically wet Etched Fiber Bragg Grating (EFBG) finds wide application in chemical and biochemical sensing domain. This paper demonstrate for the first time use of low cost high plastic polymer to hold FBG during wet chemical etching process. Experiment reveals etching rate of 4.7 µm/min for SM1500 (4/125) fiber using hydrofluoric (HF) 48% at room temperature. Original Bragg wavelength (λ_B) of 1547.528 nm shifts to 1548.322 nm and 1547.097 nm after etching for 15 min and 25 min. Shift in Bragg wavelength during etching process found not be linear. Initial red shift is noticed due to heating interaction and final blue shift is due to evanescent field interaction with HF. The use of EFBG for sensing surrounding refractive index (R.I.) for deionized water is experimentally demonstrated. It provides red shift of 0.067 nm. This low cost, fast, accurate, homogeneous, in house, indigenously adopted wet chemical etching process can be applied on photosensitive optical fibers for developing RI based biosensor and chemical application.

Keywords: Etching · Evanescent field · Etched FBG

1 Introduction

Optical fiber sensor are attractive due to its small size, light weight, chemical inertness, flexibility, absolute measurement capability, immunity to electromagnetic interference, low fabrication cost, wavelength multiplexing capability and distributed sensing possibilities [1–3]. FBG are very popular for strain and temperature sensing application. The partial or total removal of the FBG cladding enables the interaction of the external environment with evanescent field of propagating mode [4]. Evanescent field exist at the interface between core and cladding of fiber and it is attractive phenomenon for RI measurement for chemical and bio sensing related applications. Etched FBG is also key sensor in biomedical application via evanescent wave phenomenon based on the measurement of surface modification through a label-free configuration [5]. Nanostructure or thin film coating of few nm on core or on unclad surface improves interaction of evanescent field and external analyte [3].

J. Kumar et al. [6] analyses the adulteration using FBG for ethyl alcohol impure with methanol content and minimum RI change of 2×10^{-4} is found. J. Kumar et al. [7] determine petrol adulteration with kerosene using EFBG. S. Agarwala et al. [8]

© Springer Nature Singapore Pte Ltd. 2020
S. Gupta and J. N. Sarvaiya (Eds.): ET2ECN 2020, CCIS 1214, pp. 58–67, 2020.
https://doi.org/10.1007/978-981-15-7219-7_6

perform experiment using thinned FBG for study of adulteration of benzene, toluene and xylene: hydrocarbons. Razali N et al. [9] determine low nitrate concentration in source water using EFBG. Suneetha Sebastain et al. [10] demonstrate hydrostatic pressure sensor using nano layer Molybdenum (Mo) coated EFBG. Raquel da et al. [11] implements etched FBG written in multimode fibers in liquid fuel sector applications. Aliya Bekmurzayeva et al. [12] fabricate RI biosensors based on EFBG. NM Razai et al. [13] implement lead ion detection sensor using EFBG. Aliya bekmurzayeva et al. [5] detect thrombin using aptamer coated EFBG. Shridevi et al. [14] perform optical detection of glucose and glycated hemoglobin using EFBG coated with functionalized reduced graphene oxide. Shridevi et al. [15] demonstrate sensitive detection of C-reactive protein using optical FBG. Qiang Zhang et al. [16] demonstrate temperature-insensitive real-time inclinometer using EFBG. Many chemical and bio sensing application are based on EFBG. Several methods for reducing the cladding portion of the fiber to enable interaction of evanescent field have been reported. Wet chemical etching can be used for Single Mode fiber, D shape fiber or micro structure fiber [17]. Conventionally costly Teflon is used during etching process. This paper demonstrates use of low cost high plastic polymer during FBG etching process. Wet chemical etching using concentrated 48% HF is fast, best, low cost, in house, attractive alternative. This has been employed by various researcher to reduce FBG or any photo sensitive Fiber.

Section 2 briefs fundamentals about FBG and EFBG relation. Section 3 describes method and material needed of fabrication of FBG and process involved in EFBG. Section 4 discusses result of experiment on etching of FBG and Sect. 5 concludes the experimental work.

2 Fundamental

The Fiber Bragg Grating is a structure characterized by a periodic refractive index variation in core of a single-mode fiber. This period satisfies the phase matching condition between the fundamental forward propagating mode and back propagating core mode. FBG structure reflects wavelength of λ_B satisfying Bragg condition given by Eq. (1) where Λ is pitch and n^{eff} is the effective refractive index of core [18].

Strain and temperature bring change in physical parameter like period of FBG. Variation in refractive index of surrounding does not change any parameter like Λ or n^{eff}.

$$\lambda_B = 2\Lambda \, n^{eff} \tag{1}$$

$$\delta\lambda_B = 2\Lambda \, \eta_{po}(n_{cl} - n_{sur}) \tag{2}$$

External surrounding can be made sensitive by partial or total removal of cladding achieved through wet chemical etching process. This frames modified Bragg relation as given in Eq. (2) where $\delta\lambda_B$ is change in Bragg wavelength, η_{po} is the fraction of the total power of the unperturbed mode that flows in the etched region, n_{cl} is the refractive index of the cladding and n_{sur} is the RI of the surrounding medium [6].

3 Experimental Work

3.1 Fabrication of FBG

Figure 1 shows the experimental setup for writing Fiber Bragg grating using biprism. Second harmonic of Copper Laser Vapour (CVL) is used for UV beam generation. CVL beam of nearly 510 nm is focused on β-barium borate (BBO) crystal through cylindrical lenses. Crystal lenses are use to recollimate and separate fundamental and second harmonic (SH) beam. Mirrors are used for folding of UV beam. UV beam of 255 nm is allowed to write the FBG in photosensitive germanium doped SM-1500 fused silica fiber by passing it through biprism. Set up consists of a C band amplified spontaneous emission (ASE) source, optical spectrum analyzer (OSA) and computer to monitor online growth of the FBG [19, 20].

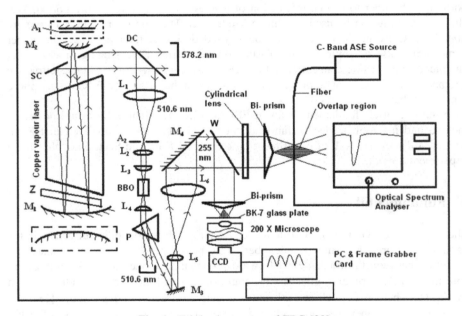

Fig. 1. Fabrication set up of FBG [20]

3.2 Etching of FBG

FBG containing fiber is spliced with Standard Connector (SC) pigtail using SUMOTO single fiber clever and SUMOTO electric micro core fusion splicer. Splicing loss is kept as low as 0.001 dB. In order to etch FBG, it is first cleaned by analytical grade acetone/isopropyl/ethanol for removing minute impurities. All images are taken with the help of microscope Labomed as shown in Fig. 2. All analysis and measurement for diameter measurement is carried out using lens 45 X and eyepiece 10 X. Container of analytical grade hydrofluoric acid (HF 48%) solution (RANKEM) is high plastic polymer material. Photo sensitive fiber of 15 mm length FBG is kept in same material vessel during etching. This removes the need of Teflon container. Precaution are taken that source end of the fiber does not get etch. During the experiment room temperature is maintained at 25 °C.

Fig. 2. Microscope labomade

The experimental setup for observing FBG response during etching process is shown in Fig. 3. It comprises of OSA (prolite 60), 3 dB coupler (1550 nm). OSA acts as a wide light source as well receiver. It is connected to 3 dB coupler to provide signal to sensor head and collect back reflected spectrum from it. FBG as sensor head is spliced to SC pigtail using fusion splicer. FBG as sensor head is immersed in 48% HF. Shift in Bragg wavelengths are noted timely from the beginning. Measuring etched diameter involves series of steps. Firstly EFBG is taken out from HF solution. Then after it is immerse in deionized (DI) water for a minute. Finally its surface is cleaned by ethanol and the diameter of etched FBG is measured at two different points with the help of microscope to know accurate value of reduced diameter.

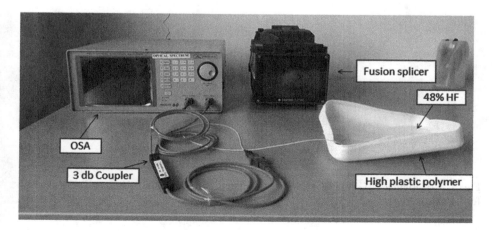

Fig. 3. Experimental set up for making etched FBG

Several times diameter of etched FBG is measured during the etching. Table 2 indicates the observation of reduced FBG diameter at instances measured from beginning of etching process. Non breaking of FBG due to over etching is taken care of. For the precaution, observations are taken between one minute intervals from 20 min of beginning. Fiber is allowed to be etched till 25 min. the diameters of the fiber are measured from relation of stage and ocular as shown in Fig. 4.

(a)   **(b)**

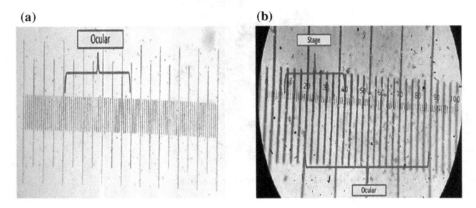

Fig. 4. Microscopic image of (a) ocular (b) relation in ocular and stage.

4   Results and Discussion

Microscope Labomed is used at the scale of 45 × and 10 × to measure object size approximately from 130 μm to 10 μm. It contain ocular of 1 mm divided in 100 division shown in Fig. 4(a).

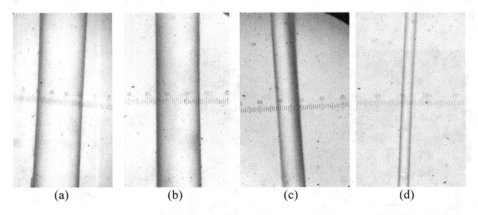

(a)   (b)   (c)   (d)

Fig. 5. (a) Original FBG (b) FBG etched for 12 min (c) FBG etched for 18 min (d) FBG etched for 24 min.

    Ocular and stages are kept overlapping to find relation between ocular and stage. Distance between successive stage is 0.0039 mm. It is calculated by two best overlapping between ocular and stage shown in Fig. 4(b). Optical fiber SM 1500(4.2/125) is observed under microscope during 48% HF etching process. Etched diameter of FBG is calculated at 0 min, 12 min, 18 min, and 24 min from the beginning of etching process. Figure 5 (a)–(d) shows microscopic image of segmented etched FBG after etching of 0 min, 12 min, 18 min, 24 min from the beginning of etching process.

Table 1. Etching time and FBG diameter using 48% HF for distingue samples

No of samples	Time (min)	FBG diameter (μm)
1	0 (Original)	125
2	12	66
3	18	39
4	24	15.6

    Table 1 indicates reduced FBG diameter at given time. Etching process is approximately linear with time. Etching rate of 4.75 μm/min is observed for FBG etching using 48% HF at room temperature. Figure 6 indicates relation between time require to etch FBG for reducing its diameter.

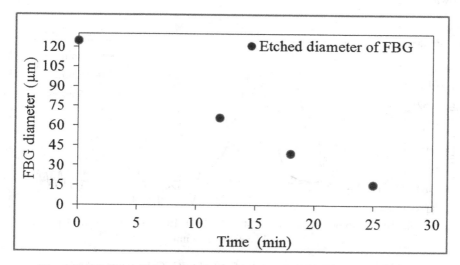

Fig. 6. (a) Response of time required etching verves etched diameter of FBG.

    Table 2 indicates various reported etching rate for different concentration of HF. These different etching rates are contributed due to different composition of pure Si clad and core Ge doping and photo sensitivity of fiber [5].

Table 2. Performance comparison of etching rate with different concentration of HF.

No. of samples	Etching rate	HF %	Reference
1	0.6	24	[21]
2	1.45	48 to 52	[22]
3	4.1	49	[23]
4	3.6	50	[18]
5	4.75	48	Performed

Spectral characteristics response of EFBG is conducted in reflection mode. Intermediate observation of the Bragg wavelength at t = 0 min, t = 15 min, t = 25 min are mentioned in paper, A continuous increment in λ_B from the start of the etching process t = 0 is apparent. During etching for initial 15 min Bragg wavelength increases because of liberation of heat due to interaction between silica and HF. Then after, HF starts interacting with evanescent wave. This reduces effective refractive index of propagating wave resulting in blue shift. Bragg wavelength of 1547.528 nm is measured at beginning of the process indicated by t = 0 min, Bragg wavelength till 15 min of etching is 1548.322 nm so maximum red shift of 0.794 nm noted at t = 15 min. Blue shift of 1.22 nm is noted at t = 25 min so Bragg wavelength till 25 min of etching is 1547.097 nm. During FBG etching experiment over all 0.430 nm of blue shift is observed at end of 25 min. Spectral shift for these FBG during etching is shown in Fig. 7.

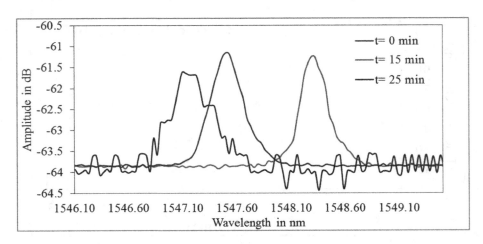

Fig. 7. Bragg wavelength shift of etched FBG (Color figure online)

After 25 min Bragg wavelength tends to more blue shift at the cost of sharp peak and spectral broadening as indicated in Fig. 7. Shifts in wavelength during etching are noted in Table 3. Positive sign indicate red shift in Bragg wavelength whereas negative sign indicate blue shift. The shits in wavelength are measured by keeping original Bragg wavelength as reference

Table 3. Bragg wavelength and consequent shift at different scenario of etching

Time (min)	Bragg wavelength (nm)	Shift (nm)
t = 0	1547.528	0
t = 15	1548.322	0.794
t = 25	1547.097	−0.430

The cladding portion of the FBG is partially etched using 48% HF now FBG can be used to sense change in surrounding refractive index. Figure 8 shows response for EFBG to sense change in refractive index demonstrated for deionized water. Set up for experiment is same as Fig. 2. EFBG is immersed in deionized water instead of HF. The red shift in wavelength is observed due to increase in surrounding n^{eff} as surrounding was replaced by deionized water.

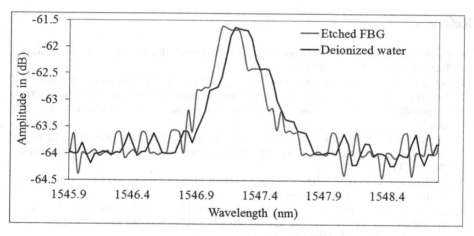

Fig. 8. Response for EFBG to sense change in refractive index

Table 4 indicates over all redshift of 0.067 nm λ_B for deionized water demonstrated with EFBG with the help of OSA.

Table 4. Bragg wavelength shift using EFBG

Time (min)	Bragg wavelength (nm)	Shift (nm)
Etched FBG	1547.097	0
Deionized water	1547.164	0.067

5 Conclusion

Wet etching is simple few steps process towards the fabrication of RI sensor using FBG. This is controlled and monitored technique for producing uniform etched FBG. It is quick process to generate RI sensor at room temperature with etching rate of 4.7 µm/min using HF 48%. This etching rate is fast as compared to reported etching rate. This etching rate is function of HF concentration and FBG fiber.

Shift in Bragg wavelength is not linear process. Bragg wavelength is 1547.527 nm at t = 0 and after etching for 15 min it shifts to 1548.322 nm and further etching till 25 min it shifts to 1547.097 nm. Over all blue shift in Bragg 0.430 nm is noted. EFBG to sense surrounding refractive index is demonstrated for deionized water showing red shift of 0.067 nm. This low cost, fast, accurate homogeneous etching process can be applied on photosensitive optical fibers for making RI sensor by interaction of evanescent wave and external surrounding. This EFBG find wide scope in chemical and bio sensing application.

Special thanks to RRCAT Indore for providing FBG and **Pollucon laboratory** Surat for providing technical support.

References

1. Shivananju, B.N., et al.: Detection limit of etched fiber Bragg grating sensors. J. Light. Technol. **31**(14), 2441–2447 (2013)
2. Iadicicco, A., et al.: Thinned fiber Bragg gratings for sensing applications. In: Proceedings of 2005 IEEE/LEOS Workshop on Fibres and Optical Passive Components, 2005. IEEE (2005)
3. Chiavaioli, F., et al.: Biosensing with optical fiber gratings. Nanophotonics **6**(4), 663–679 (2017)
4. Chryssis, A.N., Saini, S.S., Lee, S.M., Yi, H.: Detecting hybridization of DNA by highly sensitive evanescent field etched core fiber Bragg grating sensors. IEEE J. Sel. Top. Quantum Electron. **11**, 864–872 (2005)
5. Bekmurzayeva, A., et al.: Etched fiber Bragg grating biosensor functionalized with aptamers for detection of thrombin. Sensors **18**(12), 4298 (2018)
6. Kumar, J., et al.: HF-based clad etching of fibre Bragg grating and its utilization in concentration sensing of laser dye in dye–ethanol solution. Pramana **82**(2), 265–269 (2014). https://doi.org/10.1007/s12043-013-0674-5
7. Kumar, P., et al.: Graphene oxide coated fiber Bragg grating sensor for ethanol detection in petrol. Meas. Sci. Technol. **31**, 025109 (2019)
8. Agarwal, S., Prajapati, Y.K., Mishra, V.: Thinned fibre Bragg grating as a fuel adulteration sensor: simulation and experimental study. Opto-Electron. Rev. **23**(4), 231–238 (2015)
9. Razali, N., et al.: Etched fiber Bragg grating sensor for nitrate sensing application. In: 2018 IEEE 7th International Conference on Photonics (ICP). IEEE (2018)
10. Sebastian, S., et al.: Hydrostatic pressure response of Mo coated etched fiber Bragg grating sensor in side-hole packaging. In: CLEO: Applications and Technology. Optical Society of America (2019)
11. Corotti Jr., R., et al.: Etched FBG written in multimode fibers: sensing characteristics and applications in the liquid fuels sector. J. Microw. Optoelectron. Electromagn. Appl. **14**(1), 51–59 (2015)

12. Bekmurzayeva, A., Shaimerdenova, M., Tosi, D.: Fabrication and interrogation of refractive index biosensors based on etched fiber Bragg grating (EFBG). In: 2018 40th Annual International Conference of the IEEE Engineering in Medicine and Biology Society (EMBC) (2018)

13. Razali, N., Mohamed, H., et al.: Etched fiber Bragg grating sensor for lead ion detection, pp. 33–37 (2018)

14. Sridevi, S., et al.: Optical detection of glucose and glycated hemoglobin using etched fiber Bragg gratings coated with functionalized reduced graphene oxide. J. Biophotonics 9(7), 760–769 (2016)

15. Sridevi, S., et al.: Sensitive detection of C-reactive protein using optical fiber Bragg gratings. Biosens. Bioelectron. 65, 251–256 (2015)

16. Caucheteur, C., Guo, T., Albert, J.: Polarization-assisted fiber Bragg grating sensors: tutorial and review. J. Light. Technol. 35(16), 3311–3322 (2016)

17. Bal, H.K., et al.: Uniformly thinned optical fibers produced via HF etching with spectral and microscopic verification. Appl. Opt. 51(13), 2282–2287 (2012)

18. Shih, M.C., Yang, H.-H., Shih, C.H.: Measurement of the index of refraction of a liquid by a cladding depleted fiber Bragg grating. Opt. Quantum Electron. 48(2), 146 (2016)

19. Kumar, J., et al.: On the role of Ge-doping concentration in the refractive index rollover and thermal annealing characteristics of type IIa fiber Bragg gratings. Opt. Eng. 53(11), 117103 (2014)

20. Prakash, O., et al.: Study on the quality of interference fringes from a pulsed UV source for application in a biprism based fiber Bragg grating writing. Appl. Opt. 46(24), 6210–6217 (2007)

21. Iadicicco, A., Campopiano, S., Cutolo, A., Giordano, M., Cusano, A.: Thinned fiber Bragg gratings for sensing applications. In: Proceedings of the WFOPC 2005: 4th IEEE/LEOS Workshop on Fibres and Optical Passive Components, Palermo, pp. 216–221 (2005)

22. Liu, X.M., Zhang, X.M., Cong, J., Xu, J., Chen, K.S.: Demonstration of etched cladding fiber Bragg grating-based sensors with hydrogel coating. Sens. Actuators B Chem. 96, 468–472 (2003)

23. Ray, P., Srijith, K., Srinivasan, B.: Enhanced sensitivity etched fiber Bragg gratings for precise measurement of refractive index. In: International Conference on Optics and Photonics 2015. International Society for Optics and Photonics, vol. 9654 (2015)

Fabrication of Macro Porous Silicon Structures Using Pulsed Fiber Laser Technique for Capacitive Sensor Application

Shailesh M. Gheewala[✉]

Department of Electrical Engineering,
Government Polytechnic Valsad, Valsad, Gujarat, India
shaileshmgheewala@yahoo.co.in

Abstract. Porous silicon is a preferred material for making sensor devices due to its high surface to volume ratio. Porous silicon can be fabricated by advanced techniques like metal-assisted etching, layer-by-layer lithographic methods, Reactive Ion Etching (RIE), Inductive Coupled Plasma (ICP), and direct laser writing technique. These techniques have their advantages as well as disadvantages. Among them, Laser etching is a promising option for porous silicon devices due to the ease of fabrication, uniformity, and low cost. Laser etching has been reported for the fabrication of PCB, MEMS, aerospace, and medical industry. Here, we have reported the use of Pulse Fiber Laser of wavelength 1064 nm for the successful fabrication of porous silicon structure, which may be employed in sensor applications. Fabricated pore diameter, and pore depth are measured with Scanning Electron Microscope (SEM). Pores of diameter ranging from 42.44 μm to 83.30 μm, and pore depth of 49.00 μm to 98.90 μm have been synthesized. Pore size and depth modulation were observed with variation in the power of Pulsed Fiber Laser. The change in the output power of Pulsed Fiber Laser gives a linear relation with pore diameter and pore depth. The proposed porous silicon structure is useful for sensor devices application.

Keywords: Fabrication · Fiber Laser (FL) · Macro-fabrication pore · Porous silicon · Pore diameter · Pore depth · Pulsed Fiber Laser (PFL) · Scanning Electron Microscope (SEM)

1 Introduction

In the developed integrated sensor circuit technology, porous silicon is recognized in one of the most advanced materials in micro and nano-fabrication machining. In 1956, Arthur Uhlir Jr. and Ingeborg Uhlir discovered porous silicon at the Bell Labs in the U. S. Further, the detailed work was done by L. Canham with the help of electrochemical etchant who published the results [1, 2]. There are more than 20 methods available in different literature in order to fabricate the pore in silicon by etching technologies [3]. These methods are generally classified as either wet or dry etching process. Voids are generated in the crystalline silicon structure by removing a cluster of mono-crystalline in both the methods. The formation of lots of void in crystalline silicon is now known as porous silicon. According to the International Union of Pure and Applied Chemistry

© Springer Nature Singapore Pte Ltd. 2020
S. Gupta and J. N. Sarvaiya (Eds.): ET2ECN 2020, CCIS 1214, pp. 68–79, 2020.
https://doi.org/10.1007/978-981-15-7219-7_7

(IUPAC), the porous silicon can be classified as microporous for pore sizes below 2 nm, then as mesoporous for sizes below 50 nm, and as macroporous for pore diameters greater than 50 nm [4–7]. This porous silicon structure has a large surface to volume ratio as well as compatibility with microelectronics temperature. These micro, meso, and macro size sponge structures make the ideal host material for sensing different analytes in Porous silicon. The capacity of these sensing technologies, porous silicon, may be used in solar cells, health monitoring diagnosis, food industry technologies, graphene-based tunable Bragg superstructure, chemical sensing domestic and country safety purposes, etc. in sensor technologies [8–15].

Capacitive sensors are devices that transduce the measured physical parameter, which is in the form of mechanical displacement into variations of a capacitor's capacitance. Figure 1 shows the capacitance between two parallel plates separated by distance d:

$$C = \varepsilon_0 \varepsilon_r \left(\frac{A}{d} \right) \tag{1}$$

Where

A = Area of Plates (square meters),
d = Distance between the plates (Square meter),
ε_0 = Dielectric Constant of free space = 8.854×10^{-12} F/m,
ε_r = Relative dielectric Constant of the material between the plates,
C = Capacitance (Farads).

From above Eq. 1, capacitive sensors are realized by varying any of the three parameters of a capacitor: distance (d), area of capacitive plates (A), and dielectric constant (ε_r). Therefore, in Eq. 2,

$$C = f(d, A, \varepsilon_r) \tag{2}$$

These three factors are influencing capacitance values in the capacitive-sensor shown in Fig. 1:

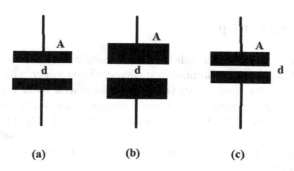

(a)   (b)   (c)

Fig. 1. Factors influencing capacitance value (a) Normal condition (b) Increase Surface area, increased capacitance, and (c) Decreased gap distance, increased capacitance [16].

The parameters of different capacitive sensors can be fabricated with the help of Eq. 2. The geometrical structure of porous silicon is used for sensing applications. Using geometry structure of porous silicon, a capacitive chemical sensor based on porous silicon for the detection of polar and non-polar organic solvents [4–6], a humidity sensor based on changing the capacitance based on humidity [17], a gas sensor based on capacitance changes due to dipole moment of gas [18], a pressure sensor based on changing the capacitance on pressure [19], in a oil-based Capacitive Micro-machined Ultrasonic Transducers based changing the impedance of frequency to measure peak shifting on oil-based environment [20], a Nitrogen (N_2) gas-based device, the current-voltage characteristic of sensor will change at the change of a Nitrogen (N_2) gas concentration [21].

First wet etching is done by electro-chemical [1, 2], while dry plasma etching is done by Reactive Ion Etching (RIE) [22, 23] as well as Inductively Coupled Plasma (ICP) [24]. The wet etching does not require any lithograph-masking pattern. So, its pore diameter size is not uniform. With the help of specific lithography technologies and materials in dry etching, pore diameter size is made uniform. The etching rates vary in these two processes. This etching rate depends upon the silicon-sample size, condition, time, and chemical contamination. Etching rates are very slow in the wet-chemical etching process, while the dry etching process required special tools, materials, and technologies. The use of a chemical in wet etching is harmful to humans and the environment, while the types of equipment used in dry etching are higher in cost. Both the processes are time-consuming, whether it is dry or wet.

Another way to fabricate micro-pore in silicon is by using Nd:Yag laser [25], and CO_2 laser [26]. The cost of Nd:Yag Laser cost is high compared to the CO_2 laser. In CO_2 laser, the primary disadvantage is that its wavelength is not absorbed by a silicon wafer. As a result, the CO_2 laser was not used to generate micropore in the silicon wafer. While comparing with these two, PFL requires less power, easy maintenance, high power efficiency, and less chiller power.

The objective of this work is the fabrication of macroporous silicon using a PFL for capacitive sensor device application. In Sect. 2, the experimental details of the macroporous silicon structure are presented. In Sect. 3, the geometrical structure of macroporous silicon is discussed. Section 4 concludes the paper.

2   Experimental Set-Up

In this experiment, we used a substrate as a single-side polished, Czochralski (CZ) produced 275-µm thick, Boron-doped p-type silicon wafer with <100> crystal orientation and resistivity of 0.01–0.02 Ω-cm. First, the silicon wafer was cleaned using standard piranha cleaning method. In piranha cleaning, the wafer was dipped in a mixture of Sulfuric Acid (H_2SO_4) and Hydrogen Peroxide (H_2O_2) (3:1 ratio by volume) for 20 min and washed with Deionized (DI) water and eventually blown with nitrogen gas. This method of cleaning was used to eliminate metals and organic contaminants from the wafer.

Different kinds of PFL machines are available in industries and research institutes. It is very convenient and easy to fabricate macropore in the silicon wafer. The used PFL machine was a Sparkle machine. The Sparkle machine PFL works at a maximum power output of 30 W. Its resolution frequencies range from 20 kHz–80 kHz, and its linear speed is 8000 mm/s. A 100 μm core diameter of an optical fiber is connected to the laser head, which transmits the PFL light on the silicon wafer. This PFL is operated by the embedded system, which allows the parameters to be modified like power, resolution frequency, loop count, and speed. We can improve our pore diameter and pore depth. The PFL parameters set for the porous silicon fabrication by us are shown in Table 1:

Table 1. PFL parameters fixed values for sample fabrication.

Sr. no.	Parameters	Value
1	Resolution frequency	20 kHz
2	Speed	50 (mm/s)
3	Loop count	1
4	PFL output power	30 W, 27 W, 25.50 W
5	PFL wavelength	1064 nm

A fundamental principle of FL is to convert low light energy into high output light energy. Figure 2 shows the schematic diagram of FL:

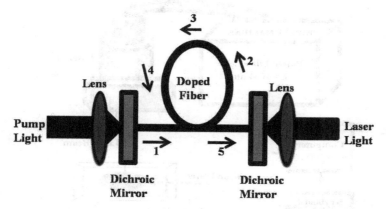

Number 1, 2, 3, 4, 5 Light Passing Direction in Doped fiber

Fig. 2. Schematic diagram of FL [26].

There are 3-main components in FL: 1) Diode laser as Pump, 2) Doped (Active) fiber medium, and 3) Dichroic mirror. Pump generates low energy light that gets transmitted into the doped fiber. This doped fiber is made up of rare earth material. Rare-earth materials-ions absorb light from the pump at a shorter wavelength than the light wavelength, except for up-conversion laser fiber. It allows the light amplification for stimulated emission. Doped fibers are referred to as active fibers and are a highly effective gain medium, mainly due to high light reprocessing. A Dichroic filter is a very accurate filter used to pass light of a small range selectively while reflecting on other light range. The working FL and PFL are explained by Macera Giuseppe and Tim Westphaling [27, 28]. In a PFL, this output light energy comes in the form of a pulse.

It is observed that pore diameter and depths increase with increasing PFL output power. Two process-reactions do this etching process at the same time in a sequence [26]. They are as follows:

1. As temperature increases, the band-gap energy in material silicon decreases because the crystal lattice expands, and the inter-atomic bonds are weaker. Consequently, more electrons are free, which encourages the pair of electron-photon to get high absorption of PFL output in order to make pore fabrication in the silicon wafer.
2. Due to the high-temperature, oxidation is created near the silicon wafer surface. This oxide surface on the silicon wafer also takes part with PFL to make pore fabrication in the silicon wafer.

Figure 3 shows the simplified set-up diagram, including the PFL source, with the laser beam, laser head, and p-type silicon wafer:

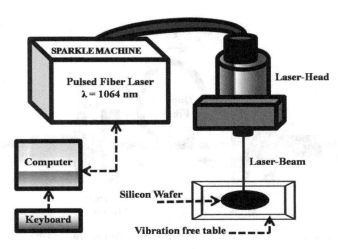

Fig. 3. Experiment of the PFL for Si etching.

The fabrication of macropore silicon depends on apply PFL power. Here the maximum output power of the machine is 30 W (100%). The geometry of pore diameter and pore depth will change according to the output power of Pulsed Fiber

Laser. Here the output power, which is 100%, 90%, and 85%, is respectively used to change the geometrical structure of the proposed structure.

Figure 4 shows SEM micrograph top view of the sample. The sample has the following steps:

1) The silicon wafer was cut in 1.5 cm × 1.5 cm.
2) 7922 pores are fabricated in an inner 1 cm diameter at 27 W.

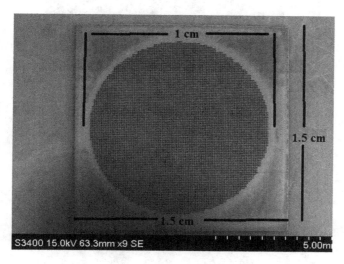

Fig. 4. The SEM top view micrograph of 1.5 cm × 1.5 cm single side polished, 275 μm thick wafer <100> with macropore formed in inner 1 cm diameter at 27 W power (90%).

3 Results and Discussion

SEM was used to study the morphological structure properties of the samples. Top-view and cross-sectional micrographs of the samples were taken and studied. A wide field-of-view micrograph was taken and analyzed to research the effect and PFL output power on the porous structures.

The top view of a micrograph with pore diameter and depths for PFL output power less than 80% does not show any pore formation. Hence, it is not shown here. Further, PFL output power varied like 85%, 90%, and 100% of the PFL specification, and its effect on pore diameter and pore depth is discussed as follows in the Figs. 5a, b, and c:

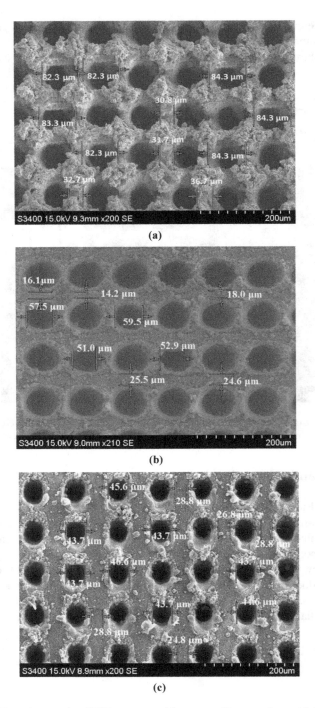

Fig. 5. The SEM micrograph of PFL output etching on a silicon wafer at (a) Power at 100% (30 W), (b) Power at 90% (27 W), and (c) Power at 85 (25.50 W)%.

The change in pore diameter with respect to output power is shown in Table 2. The effect of PFL output power on the average pore diameter is shown in Fig. 6.

Figures 7a and b show the cross-section micrograph of the pore depth at different output powers, namely, 90% and 50%, respectively. Pore depth at PFL output power 90%, is 98.90 μm, and at PFL output power 50%, it is 49.00 μm.

Table 2. Pulse fiber laser power v/s average pore diameter.

Sr. no.	Power (%)	Average pore diameter (μm)
1	100 (30 W)	83.30 μm
2	90 (27 W)	55.22 μm
3	85 (25.50 W)	42.44 μm

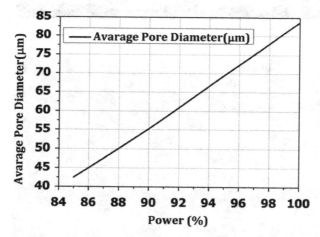

Fig. 6. The relationship between average pore diameter and power.

The change in pore depth to PFL output power is shown in Table 3. The relationship between PFL output power and pore depth is shown in Fig. 8.

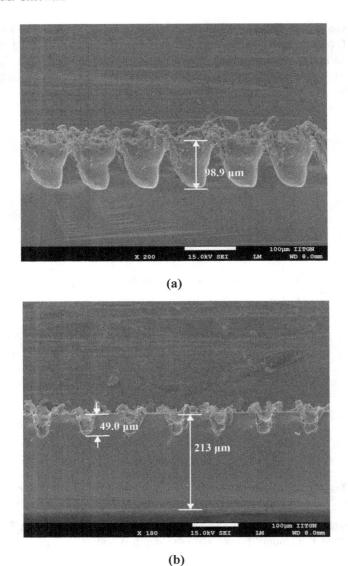

(a)

(b)

Fig. 7. The cross-sectional SEM micrograph etched in silicon depth at (a) Depth at 90% (27 W) output power and (b) Depth at 50% (15 W) output power.

Table 3. Pulse fiber laser power v/s pore depth.

Sr. no.	Power (%)	Pore depth (μm)
1	90 (27 W)	98.90 μm
2	50 (15 W)	49.00 μm

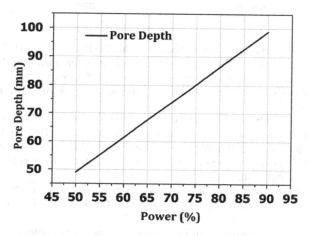

Fig. 8. The relationship between pore depth and power.

4 Conclusions

The low-cost unique etching process experiment in silicon wafer has been exposed to PFL. The pore diameter varies from 42.44 μm to 83.30 μm, and pore depth varies from 49.00 μm to 98.90 μm using changed in output power of Pulsed Fiber Laser. This experiment shows that pore diameter and depth increase by increasing the PFL output power. This macroporous structure fabricating in a silicon wafer is economical and easily manufactured without using environmentally harmful chemicals and expensive manufacturing process. These fabricated porous silicon structures should be used for capacitive sensor devices such as chemical sensing, biochemical sensing, bacterial detection in water, and food.

Acknowledgments. The authors thank the Technical Education Quality Improvement Program Phase-III (TEQIP-III), Sardar Vallabhbhai National Institute of Technology, Surat for supporting this research work. They would also like to acknowledge the Sensor Research Laboratory, Sardar Vallabhbhai National Institute of Technology, Surat, for providing the research facility. This paper is a result of the R&D work attempted under the Visvesvaraya Ph.D. Scheme of Ministry of Electronics and Information Technology, Government of India, being executed by Digital India Corporation (Formerly Media Lab, Asia). The authors are also thankful to the Central Instrumentation Facility (CIF) at IIT, Gandhinagar for the structural characterization of samples. The authors are also thankful to Shri Sagar Jagtap from Sophisticated Instrumentation Centre, Mechanical Engineering Department at Sardar Vallabhbhai National Institute of Technology, Surat for the structural characterization of samples.

References

1. Canham, L.T.: Properties of Porous Silicon, 1st edn. INSPEC, London (1997)
2. Canham, L.T.: Silicon quantum wire array fabrication by electrochemical and chemical dissolution of wafers. Appl. Phys. Lett. **57**(10), 1046–1048 (1990)
3. Karbassian, F.: Porous Silicon - Porosity - Process, Technologies, and Applications – Chapter (2018)
4. Harraz, F.A.: A highly sensitive and durable electrical sensor for liquid ethanol using thermally-oxidized mesoporous silicon. Superlattices Microstruct. **100**, 1064–1072 (2016)
5. Harraz, F.A., Ismail, A.A., Bouzid, H., Al-Sayari, S.A., Al-Hajry, A., Al- Assiri, M.S.: A capacitive chemical sensor based on porous silicon for detection of polar and non-polar organic solvents. Appl. Surf. Sci. **307**, 704–711 (2014)
6. Harraz, F.A., Ismail, A.A., Bouzid, H., Al-Sayari, S.A., Al-Hajry, A., Al-Assiri, M.S.: A capacitive chemical sensor based on porous silicon for detection of polar and non-polar organic solvents. Appl. Surf. Sci. **307**, 704–711 (2016)
7. Harraz, F.A.: Organic analytes sensitivity in meso-porous silicon electrical sensor with front side and backside contacts. Arab. J. Chem. (2017)
8. Pancheri, L., Oton, C.J., Gaburro, Z., Soncini, G., Pavesi, L.: Very sensitive porous silicon NO_2 sensor. Sens. Actuators B Chem. **89**(3), 237–239 (2003)
9. Lammel, G., Schweizer, S., Renaud, P.: Microspectrometer based on a tunable optical filter of porous silicon. Sens. Actuators Phys. **92**(3), 52–59 (2001)
10. Massad-Ivanir, N., Shtenberg, G., Raz, N.: Porous silicon-based biosensors: towards real-time optical detection of target bacteria in the food industry. Sci. Rep. **6**, 1–12 (2016)
11. Jalkanen, T., Määttänen, A., Mäkilä, E., Tuura, J., Kaasalainen, M.: Fabrication of porous silicon-based humidity sensing elements on paper. J. Sens., 1–10 (2015)
12. Balucani, M.: Porous silicon solar cells. In: IEEE 15th International Conference on Nanotechnology (IEEE-NANO-2015), Rome, pp. 724–727 (2015)
13. Salman, K.A., Hassan, Z., Omar, K.: Effect of silicon porosity on solar cell efficiency. Int. J. Electrochem. Sci. **7**, 376–386 (2012)
14. Levitsky, I.A.: Porous silicon structures as optical gas sensors. Sensors **15**(8), 19968–19991 (2015)
15. Patel, S.K., Ladumor, M., Sorathiya, V., Guo, T.: Graphene based tunable grating structure. Mater. Res. Express **6**(2), 1–11 (2018)
16. Robbins, A., Miller, W.: Circuit Analysis: Theory and Practice. Delmar, Albany (2000)
17. Kim1, S.-J., Park, J.-Y., Lee, S.-H., Yi, S.-H.: Humidity sensors using porous silicon layer with mesa structure. J. Phys. D Appl. Phys. **33**, 1781–1784 (2000)
18. Kim, S.-J., Jeon, B.-H., Choi, K.-S., Min, N.-K.: Capacitive porous silicon sensors for measurement of low alcohol gas concentration at room temperature. J. Solid State Electrochem. **4**(6), 363–366 (2000)
19. Knese, K., et al.: Novel technology for capacitive pressure sensors with monocrystalline silicon membranes. In: IEEE 22nd International Conference on Micro Electro Mechanical Systems (2009)
20. Lascaud, J.: Porous silicon as backing material for capacitive micromachined ultrasonic transducers. In: IEEE International Ultrasonics Symposium (IUS), Tours, 2016, pp. 1–4 (2016)
21. Bahar, M., Eskandari, H., Shaban, N.: Electrical properties of porous silicon for N_2 gas sensor. J. Theor. Comput. Sci. **4**(1), 1–6 (2017)
22. Chou, T.K.A., Najafi, K.: Fabrication of out-of-plane curved surface in Si by utilizing RIE lag. In: Proceedings of SPIE Journal of MEMS2002, pp. 145–148 (2002)

23. Chung, C.K.: Geometrical pattern effect on silicon deep etching by an inductively coupled plasma system. J. Micromech. Microeng. **14**, 656–662 (2004)
24. Pratiwi, N.D., Handayani, M., Suryana, R., Nakatsuka, O.: Fabrication of porous silicon using photolithography and reactive ion etching (RIE). Mater. Today Proc. **13**(1), 92–96 (2019)
25. Xia, Y., et al.: Laser ablation of Si, Ge, ZrO, and Cu in air. J. Phys. D Appl. Phys. **24**, 1933–1941 (1991)
26. Chung, C.K., Wu, M.Y., HIsiao, E.J., Sung, Y.C.: Etching behaviour of silicon using CO_2 laser. In: Proceedings of 2nd IEEE International Conference of Nano/Micro Engineered and Molecular Systems, Bangkok, pp. 59–62 (2006)
27. Westphäling, T.: Pulsed fiber lasers from ns to ms range and their applications. Phys. Procedia Part A **5**, 125–136 (2010)
28. Nufern, B.S.: Fiber laser-chapter. In: Handbook of Solid State Lasers Materials, Systems and Applications, pp. 403–462 (2013)

Communication

Target Tracking Using a Hybrid KF-PSO Tracking Model in WSN

Dhiren P. Bhagat[1]([envelope]) and Himanshukumar Soni[2]

[1] Electronics and Communication Department,
Sarvajanik College of Engineering and Technology, Surat, India
dhiren.bhagat@scet.ac.in
[2] Electronics and Communication Department,
G. H. Patel College of Engineering and Technology, Vallabh Vidyanagar, India
principal@gcet.ac.in

Abstract. Wireless Sensor Networks (WSNs) have smart commercial application in tracking, healthcare, surveillance, smart homes, habitat monitoring, and intrusion detection. Target tracking is well examined and demanding application of WSNs. Such application needs accurate estimate of a target's changing spot which composes position and velocity or/and defined measure of distance of target from each sensing nodes. These measures are treated as prerequisites and are necessary to be delivered to the sink node for the further processing. Commonly used techniques to do so involve use of algorithms based on prediction like Kalman Filter (KF). Precise tracking of target is reticent due to restricted properties in WSN like battery capacity, computing and communicating capacity, ageing, sensors breakdown, noises etc. These constraints disturb the tracking process and affects tracking efficiency too. In order to achieve high tracking efficacy, detection and tracking of moving target requires coordination among sensor nodes. Proposed is the Hybrid model of KF and Particle Swarm Optimization (PSO) for tracking the target trajectory and to estimating target position. Different target moving trajectory paths are considered to examine efficiency of Hybrid KF-PSO tracking approach. It is to be noted from the obtained results that Hybrid KF-PSO works well compared to standard KF by notably reducing Root Mean Square Error (RMSE), hence increases 5 to 15% of tracking efficiency for various unlike paths of target moving in.

Keywords: WSN · Hybrid KF-PSO

1 Introduction

In target tracking WSN, intention is to notice the target existence and to track its moving trajectory. Looking at the application and are to be monitored, sensor nodes are to be placed in a planned or arbitrary mode. Applications consist of examining pressure, temperature, wind, humidity etc. including security and surveillance in indoor and outdoor environments. In outdoor application like habitat monitoring, tracking mechanism is used to track animals roaming where and in which area of the forest or park. To monitor and track assets in asset monitoring, WSN is deployed to sense location of assets and report to the centralized entity to get required information of assets when needed. WSN

© Springer Nature Singapore Pte Ltd. 2020
S. Gupta and J. N. Sarvaiya (Eds.): ET2ECN 2020, CCIS 1214, pp. 83–98, 2020.
https://doi.org/10.1007/978-981-15-7219-7_8

with small in size sensor nodes with less sensing and communication capacity is a resource limited network consist of processing unit, sensing unit, trans-receiver and small battery to power up and make all the units functional. To do so, moderate energy is used which may influence the operation of sensing and break up tracking process. For an unbroken process of tracking, sensing should be done constantly and should be brought quickly to a sink node in order to process subsequently [1].

Kalman Filter (KF), Extended Kalman Filter (EKF), Particle Filter (PF) and Information Filter (IF) are few among well-known prediction filters used to predict moving target trajectory in various applications. These predicted information of moving target is passed to the sink node for subsequent process. Tracking process can be seen as single sensor or collaborative sensors sensing [2–5]. Collaborative sensing is quite effective as sensing through single sensor may result in heavy drain out of node's battery energy and this cause reduced lifetime of the network due massive computational burden on that sensor. Synchronization and sensing from numerous sensors offer superior estimation about moving target state. These estimations are less precise but nearby to actual location of target henceforth, estimations from numerous detecting sensor nodes assist to obtain superior tracking performance of a target being tracked [6]. Various mechanism which offers tracking process are considered and evaluated according to tracking accuracy, energy consumption, and security, modality of sensing, motion, and fault tolerance.

To track the target effectively is a complex procedure as sensed readings from various nodes are influenced by delay, consumed energy, battery exhaust, communication and connectivity capability, collection of data etc. Tracking mechanism used must be executed fast enough so that target miss will not happen and should preserve tracking accuracy [7]. This paper proposes Hybrid KF-PSO model in which, both KF and PSO backs the tracking of target. Tracking results from both the individual technique is combined to propose Hybrid KF-PSO. Hybrid KF-PSO uses initial tracking estimations resulted from KF operation and then later tracking estimations given by PSO. Obtained results through Hybrid KF-PSO technique is compared with standard KF to show the improved target tracking efficiency.

Paper is planned as; Sect. 2 calls trends in target tracking in WSN, Sect. 3 labels proposed Hybrid KF-PSO mechanism of target tracking and outline of system, Sect. 4 refer to system behavior, in Sect. 5 simulation and results are shown followed by conclusion.

2 Target Tracking in WSN

Localizing target is significant and essential to track the target. To do so, use of GPS is one of the widely used solutions. As use of GPS makes mechanism difficult and highly energy consumed, it is not always feasible to mount GPS on devices contributing to localization. Use of such thing results in poor delivery of tracking accuracy in sensor network along with less lifetime of network. RADAR could be used which offers good tracking accuracy and trustworthy too. But observed to be quite expensive hence, mounting GPS and RADAR on devices contributing to localization price a lot. This asks for development of target tracking WSN using cheaper sensor nodes as monitored area could be heavily deployed with amply of nodes which gives good collaborative sensing to get closest target estimation with respect to actual target trajectory. This essentially helps to achieve good tracking efficiency.

In [8], authors define target tracking as central or scattered network. Central body is accountable for intricate calculations to be done on sensed data from sensing field. This gives pretty good performance but not that scalable. Calculations are blowout over the entire network in scattered mechanism which is distributed in nature and permits individual sensor node to function individually and offers collective sensing. This gives pretty good scalability and sturdiness but planning a scattered and collective algorithm is quite difficult.

Distance is one of the network metrics widely used in major prediction based algorithm for state estimate of the target, few of them being Kalman Filter (KF), Extended Kalman Filter (EKF), and Information Filter (IF) etc. Such techniques are noticeable and acknowledged way out for tracking but having limitations to function fine for non-linear trajectories. All the prediction based filters have two functional stages, prediction and update stage to accurate estimate [9].

In [10], authors have used PSO to choose appropriate cluster leader in clusters formed. These leaders are responsible to pass on data to sink node. Selection of proper cluster leader does the job of passing data to sink node effectively which helps to minimize over all network's energy expense and maximize the overall network coverage. In [11], PSO is utilized to remove out sample impoverishment problem that occurs in PF. FIR filter sense the causes of sample impoverishment problem. PF gets reset by the outcome of an auxiliary FIR filter and retrieves the failed PF [12, 13].

Proposed method uses novel hybrid model of KF and PSO where, fine approximation of target state is obtained from output of KF and PSO. PSO will converge well for nonlinear target trajectory and KF gives good estimation in liner region of moving target. To exert fine approximation of target state, combined results from KF and PSO is used. Initially, there won't be any fitness function established for PSO hence it will not converge well to estimate target trajectories. Proposed model uses target state estimates of KF initially and later PSO estimates are used to give over all fine approximation of target state. Such estimates are compared with standard KF results and shows improvements in tracking accuracy. Proposed work includes PSO to contribute to the target tracking in addition to KF that is the new work presented.

3 Proposed Hybrid KF-PSO Tracking Model

Sensing vicinity in Fig. 1 is considered for Hybrid KF-PSO model, having moving target assumed to be cooperative in nature [14, 15]. Nodes deployed systematically in sensing area to be monitored. PSO setup is done by assigning four particles to four corner nodes of the network. Proposed Hybrid KF-PSO tracking model includes, KF and PSO in tracking of a target to exert fine tracking outcome to get good tracking accuracy. KF being a decent target state predictor in linear path where's PSO converge very well in nonlinear path. Exclusive assets of each method issued in proposed hybrid tracking model results into worthy tracking mechanism. KF being recursive predictor operates in first tier and second tier consist of approximation of KF is appended in a position of personal best value of PSO to appraise position of target. This allows PSO to track target and gives fine approximation, move its particles in the direction and closer to moving target. Proposed Hybrid KF-PSO gives twofold advantages; KF tracks the target fine in linear section and in nonlinear trajectory of target, PSO gives best position estimation. Objectives achieved here through proposed Hybrid KF-PSO tracking are; expectation about target state of unknown target is maximized, square error per tracking step and root mean square error (RMSE) is reduced. Different target paths have been utilized on which Hybrid KF-PSO tracking is applied to verify performance of proposed method and noticing its target tracking efficiency.

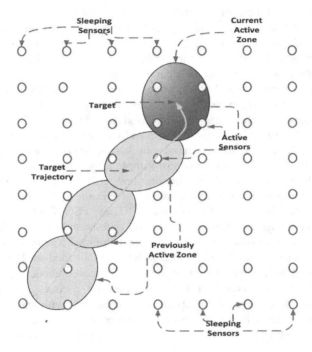

Fig. 1. Sensor network model for proposed Hybrid KF-PSO tracking

PSO works with fitness function which is initiated in the PSO by first move of particles. Particles' coordination builds up and PSO gets converged as global and personal best values builds up per tracking step as per the fitness function. Convergence of PSO depends on fitness function, coordination amongst particles and swarm strength.

Proposed Hybrid KF-PSO could be used and mapped with indoor LIFI application where moving user with LIFI device treated as target and should be connected to nearby LIFI spot for data access. Hybrid KF-PSO locate the LIFI spot near to moving target and let user get connected to it for data access.

4   System Model

4.1   Kalman Filter

In KF prediction; time sequence, inaccuracies and statistical noise are measured over a time and generates state estimates of unknown target. Prediction of unknown target is done in two phase by KF; prediction and update step. Timed measurements are done in prediction step and in update step corrections given to timed measurements to diminish uncertainties, inaccuracies and errors caused.

Weighted average estimate is generated at the end of KF prediction which falls between measured and predicted state. Equations (1) to (5) are standard KF filter equations used in literature.

State of Prediction
Prediction-State:

$$\overline{x_{n+1}} = \emptyset x_n \tag{1}$$

Prediction-Error covariance:

$$\overline{P_{n+1}} = \emptyset P_n \emptyset^T + \Gamma Q \Gamma^T \tag{2}$$

Where, $\emptyset$ is matrix-state transition, x_n is state vector-current, $\overline{x_{n+1}}$ is state of the target-predicted next, P_n is error covariance, $\overline{P_{n+1}}$ is error covariance-predicted, T is time interval-sampling, Γ is matrix-process noise, Q is covariance matrix.

State of Update
Update-Kalman gain:

$$K_{n+1} = \overline{P_{n+1}} H^T \left(H \overline{P_{n+1}} H^T + R \right)^{-1} \tag{3}$$

Update-Estimation:

$$\widehat{x_{n+1}} = \overline{x_{n+1}} + K_{n+1}(Y_{n+1} * H \overline{x_{n+1}}) \tag{4}$$

Update-Error covariance:

$$P_{n+1} = (1 - K_{n+1}H)\overline{P_{n+1}} \tag{5}$$

Where, K_{n+1} is kalman gain, H is matrix-observation, Y_n is state vector-observation, R is noise-measurement.

4.2   Particle Swarm Optimization

PSO is inspired by shared actions of biological populations similar to fish schools and birds flocking. PSO mostly applicable to deterministic, non-linear space problems to obtain superior results with a superior efficiency [16–18]. Such PSO properties make it quite appropriate for tracking of unknown target mainly for nonlinear regions. Control parameters like swarm and personal confidence factor gives fine sense of balance between global and local search all over the significant course of run of moving trajectory of target. Proposed Hybrid KF-PSO model performs well in linear path of target through KF and in nonlinear path through PSO. PSO works with updates in velocity and position, whose equations are given in Eqs. (6) and (7), respectively [18].

Velocity update:

$$
\begin{aligned}
v_i[n+1] = w[n] * v_i[n] + cp[n] * rp_i[n] * (p_i[n] - x_i[n]) \\
+ cg[n] * rg_i[n] * (g[n] - x_i[n])
\end{aligned} \tag{6}
$$

Position update:

$$
x_i[n+1] = x_i[n] + v_i[n+1] \tag{7}
$$

For each i particle, $v_i[n]$ is velocity-current, $v_i[n+1]$ is velocity-new, $x_i[n]$ is position-current, $x_i[n+1]$ is position-next, $p_i[n]$ is personal best (*pbest*) particle position, $g[n]$ is value of global best (*gbest*) amongst the entire particles, $w[n]$ is inertia weight, $cp[n]$ is confidence factor-personal, $cg[n]$ is confidence factor-swarm, $rp_i[n]$ is random variable-personal confidence factor, $rg_i[n]$ is random variable-swarm confidence factor.

4.3   Proposed Network Modeling

Network Dimensions
Network (n/w) area is given as dimensions by height and width as follows,

$$
n/w\, dimensions = \begin{cases} h, height \\ w, width \end{cases} \tag{8}
$$

$$
n/w\, area = \prod(h, w) \tag{9}
$$

Node Count
Node count in sensor n/w to be used and placed by the following Eq. (10),

$$
node\, count\, n = \prod_h^w \tag{10}
$$

Node Placement
Nodes systematically placed to create systematic grid using the formula as (11).
For each node, $i = 1: node\, count$

$$
Population_{nodes(i,X,Y)} = \begin{cases} mod(i-1,w), & X \\ floor\left(\frac{i-1}{w}\right), & Y \end{cases} \tag{11}
$$

Structure and Placement of Particles

To avoid any bias related to any path or shape, 4 particles are populated at each corner grid position. Particle's population is given as $(1, 1)$, $(1, w)$, $(h, 1)$ and (h, w).

Target Moving Trajectory

Different target moving trajectories includes sudden transition, curve, nonlinear and liner path are used and shown in simulation and results section.

RSSI Measurement

Measurement of RSSI gives the fitness measure for best value of the target moving. We use measured distance between the particle and target as RSSI measurement is not possible directly. RSSI is then derived using target's distance from every particle by following equations:

$$pdist_{particle\ to\ target} = \sqrt{(pX - x)^2 + (pY - y)^2} \tag{12}$$

$$max_{particle}\ RSSI\ \alpha\ \frac{1}{min\ pdist_{particle\ to\ target}} \tag{13}$$

Where, $pdist$ is distance to target-particle, pX is x position-particle, pY is y position-particle, x is x position-target and y is y position-target.

Fitness Function

Fitness function is a merit representing nearness of the resulting outcome to moving target set. Hybrid KF-PSO uses fitness values to get new particle position near the target to shift onto.

$$Fitness = m - \frac{1}{max_{particle}RSSI} \tag{14}$$

Global Best Particle

A particle with maximum fitness among every particle is global best particle.

$$gBestParticle = max_{particle}Fitness \tag{15}$$

Particle's Next Position

Particles next position decides by fitness and particle jump onto node with good fitness. Particles' change their position by comparing current fitness with new fitness based on which is higher as indicated in Eq. (16).

For i = 1: particle count

$$if$$
$$fitness(x_i) > fitness(pbest)$$
$$pbest = x_i$$
$$if$$
$$fitness(pbest) > fitness(gbest) \tag{16}$$
$$gbest = pbest$$
$$endif$$
$$endif$$

Velocity and position are updated using values of pbest and gbest.

Flow of Proposed Hybrid KF-PSO Based Tracking Model

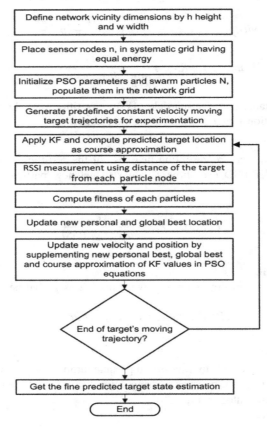

5 Simulation Results

Simulation results through Hybrid KF-PSO tracking is discussed in this section. To demonstrate the efficiency of the proposed tracking model, various simulations carried out in MATLAB by implementing KF and Hybrid KF-PSO tracking model on various target moving tracks shown in Fig. 2(a–c). Network matrices used to measure and compare performance of proposed Hybrid tracking are; RMSE and square error per tracking step. Simulation is performed with various personal confidence ($cp[n]$) and swarm confidence factor ($cg[n]$) values as mentioned in parameter Table 1.

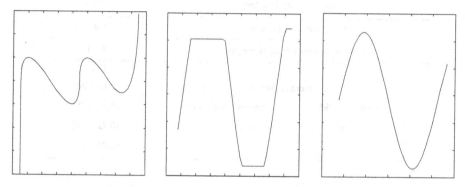

Fig. 2. (a) Sample path 1 (b) Sample path 2 (c) Sample path 3

Assumptions
Following assumptions are considered during the simulation;

1. Single, moving and cooperative target
2. Sensor nodes placed systematically are static and not moving
3. Location information is known to all the sensor nodes
4. Sensor nodes equipped with same initial energy
5. Sensor node's residual energy can be measured
6. Time synchronization among nodes

5.1 Simulation Parameters

Simulation parameters are as shown in Table 1.

5.2 Results

This section shows recital of KF and Hybrid KF-PSO for (a) Tracking efficiency (b) Square error per tracking step (c) RMSE and its percentage improvement and (d) Average square error per tracking steps throughout the course of run of simulation

Table 1. Simulation parameters

Parameters		Values
Environment		Indoor
Network vicinity, (h by w)		100 m by 100 m
Node count, ($h * w$)		100
Initial energy of all nodes		1 J
Particle count, N		4
Velocity of moving target		1 m/s
Large value m, ($h * w$)		100
Random variables ($rp_i[n], rg_i[n]$)		[1, 1]
		[1 0]
Confidence factors		[0.80 0.20]
Personal confidence	Swarm confidence	[0.75 0.25]
$cp[n]$	$cg[n]$	[0.72 0.28]
		[0.71 0.29]

for different cases. Simulation is done for various personal and swarm confidence factors presented in Table 1, but graphical results for three different confidence factors [0.71 0.29] [0.70 0.30] [0.69 0.31] are presented here.

It is to be noted that Hybrid KF-PSO tracking with combination [1 0] behaves same as KF because whole model is driven and balanced by personal confidence factor of PSO which is responsible to supplement KF's predicted values in place of personal best position in PSO. As shown, target is moving in predefined trajectory, KF and Hybrid KF-PSO tracking model's predictions are plotted.

Proposed Hybrid KF-PSO tracking performs superior by giving close enough prediction of target state then KF filter. Plots of square error per tracking step are also shown as estimated error comparison. RMSE and average square error per tracking step of proposed Hybrid KF-PSO tracking model are shortened and compared with KF filter in Table 2 and Table 3 respectively.

Figure 3, 4 and 5 show the simulation results for KF and proposed Hybrid KF-PSO applied on moving target in trajectory path 1. Graphs displayed for personal and swarm confidence factor combinations [0.71 0.29] [0.70 0.30] [0.69 0.31]. Figure 3(a), 4(a) and 5(a) shows tracking graphs and square error per tracking step are presented in Fig. 3(b), 4(b) and 5(b), respectively. It could be observed from graph that tracking accuracy for Hybrid KF-PSO tracking is superior to standard KF filter.

It is to be noted that, initially PSO won't converge well hence predicted points are far away then KF predicted points. Later, once PSO starts converging well giving close predicted points then KF though tracking graph does not look smooth. But importantly good tracking efficiency is achieved with reduced RMSE.

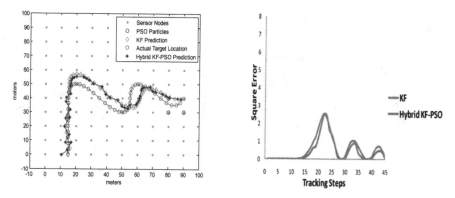

Fig. 3. (a) Tracking graph Path 1-cp(n) = 0.71 & cg(n) = 0.29 (b) Square error vs. Tracking steps Path 1-cp(n) = 0.71 & cg(n) = 0.29

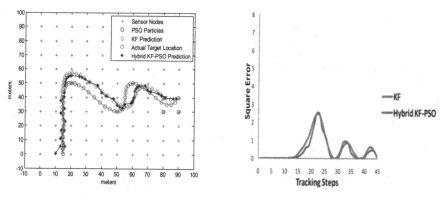

Fig. 4. (a) Tracking graph Path 1-cp(n) = 0.70 & cg(n) = 0.30 (b) Square error vs. Tracking steps Path 1-cp(n) = 0.70 & cg(n) = 0.30

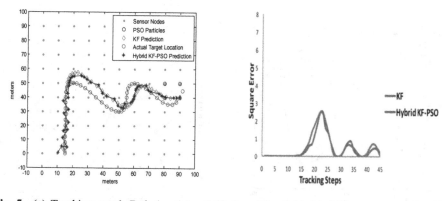

Fig. 5. (a) Tracking graph Path 1-cp(n) = 0.69 & cg(n) = 0.31 (b) Square error vs. Tracking steps Path 1-cp(n) = 0.69 & cg(n) = 0.31

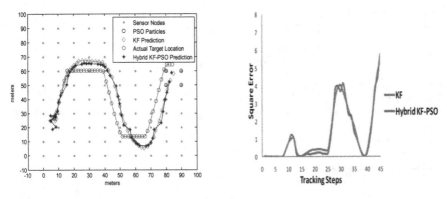

Fig. 6. (a) Tracking graph Path 2-cp(n) = 0.71 & cg(n) = 0.29 (b) Square error vs. Tracking steps Path 2-cp(n) = 0.71 & cg(n) = 0.29

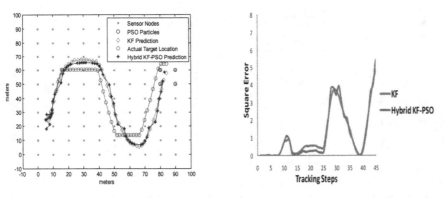

Fig. 7. (a) Tracking graph Path 2-cp(n) = 0.70 & cg(n) = 0.30 (b) Square error vs. Tracking steps Path 2-cp(n) = 0.70 & cg(n) = 0.30

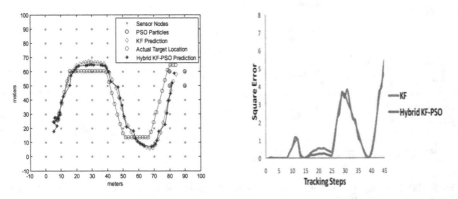

Fig. 8. (a) Tracking graph Path 2-cp(n) = 0.69 & cg(n) = 0.31 (b) Square error vs. Tracking steps Path 2-cp(n) = 0.69 & cg(n) = 0.31

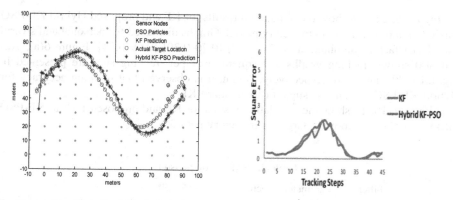

Fig. 9. (a) Tracking graph Path 3-cp(n) = 0.71 & cg(n) = 0.29 (b) Square error vs. Tracking steps Path 3-cp(n) = 0.71 & cg(n) = 0.29

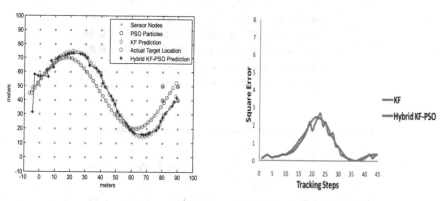

Fig. 10. (a) Tracking graph Path 3-cp(n) = 0.70 & cg(n) = 0.30 (b) Square error vs. Tracking steps Path 3-cp(n) = 0.70 & cg(n) = 0.30

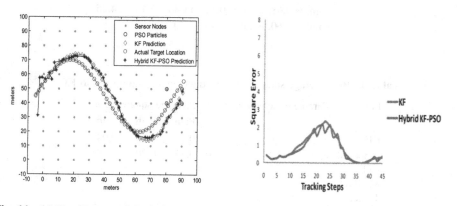

Fig. 11. (a) Tracking graph Path 3-cp(n) = 0.69 & cg(n) = 0.31 (b) Square error vs. Tracking steps Path 3-cp(n) = 0.69 & cg(n) = 0.31

Figure 6, 7 and 8 show the simulation results for KF and proposed Hybrid KF-PSO applied on moving target in trajectory path 2. Graphs displayed for personal and swarm confidence factor combinations [0.71 0.29] [0.70 0.30] [0.69 0.31]. Figure 6(a), 7(a) and 8(a) shows tracking graphs and square error per tracking step are presented in Fig. 6(b), 7(b) and 8(b), respectively. Again, it is observed that tracking accuracy for Hybrid KF-PSO tracking is superior to standard KF.

Figure 9, 10, 11 show the simulation results for KF and proposed Hybrid KF-PSO tracking applied on moving target in trajectory path 3.

Table 2. RMSE comparison

Filter	Parameter selection	RMSE		
		Path 1	Path 2	Path 3
Kalman	—	0.74	0.95	0.94
Proposed Hybrid KF-PSO Target Tracking	$Cp[n] = 1, Cg[n] = 0$	0.74	0.95	0.94
	$Cp[n] = 0.80, Cg[n] = 0.20$	0.73	0.945	0.927
	$Cp[n] = 0.71, Cg[n] = 0.29$	0.669	0.94	0.91
	$Cp[n] = 0.70, Cg[n] = 0.30$	0.66	0.93	0.90
	$Cp[n] = 0.69, Cg[n] = 0.31$	**0.65**	**0.90**	**0.89**
	$Cp[n] = 0.68, Cg[n] = 0.32$	0.655	0.92	0.90
	$Cp[n] = 0.60, Cg[n] = 0.40$	0.70	0.94	0.925

Table 3. Percentage improvement of RMSE compared to KF

Filter	Parameter selection	RMSE in %		
		Path 1	Path 2	Path 3
Proposed Hybrid KF-PSO Target Tracking	$cp[n] = 1, cg[n] = 0$	0	0	0
	$cp[n] = 0.80, cg[n] = 0.20$	1.35	0.52	1.38
	$cp[n] = 0.71, cg[n] = 0.29$	9.45	1.05	3.19
	$cp[n] = 0.70, cg[n] = 0.30$	10.81	2.10	4.25
	$cp[n] = 0.69, cg[n] = 0.31$	**12.16**	**5.26**	**5.31**
	$cp[n] = 0.68, cg[n] = 0.32$	11.48	3.15	4.25
	$cp[n] = 0.60, cg[n] = 0.40$	5.40	1.05	1.59

Table 4. Best average square error vs. tracking step compared to KF

Filter	Parameter selection	Average square error		
		Path 1	Path 2	Path 3
KF	–	0.57	0.93	0.94
Proposed Hybrid KF-PSO Target Tracking	$cp[n] = 0.69, cg[n] = 0.31$	0.35	0.90	0.89

6 Conclusion

Results obtained evidently recommend benefit of using Hybrid KF-PSO model compared to KF for application of target tracking in WSN, in particular when target path is nonlinear. Calculation of RMSE and average square error per tracking step displayed in Table 2 and Table 3 respectively also provides edge of using proposed Hybrid KF-PSO tracking model. Around 5% to 15% of more tracking accuracy is achieved through proposed Hybrid KF-PSO compared to KF for various target moving path. Proposed Hybrid KF-PSO provides good tracking results in terms of reduced square error per tracking step and improved RMSE for set of personal and swarm confidence factors cp(n) = 0.69, cg(n) = 0.31. This is the set of value at which PSO converges well and sensor network becomes more stable and balanced. Table 4 shows decreased average square error as a result of proposed Hybrid KF-PSO tracking compared to tracking through KF filter only.

References

1. Demigha, O., Hidouci, W.-K., Ahmed, T.: On energy efficiency in collaborative target tracking in wireless sensor network: a review. IEEE Commun. Surv. Tutor. **15**(3), 1210–1222 (2013)
2. Hu, X., Xu, B., Hu, Y.-H.: Generalised Kalman filter tracking with multiplicative measurement noise in a wireless sensor network. IET Signal Process. **8**(5), 467–474 (2014)
3. Wang, X., Fu, M., Zhang, H.: Target tracking in wireless sensor networks based on the combination of KF and MLE using distance measurements. IEEE Trans. Mob. Comput. **11**(4), 567 (2012)
4. Bhuiyan, M.Z.A., Wang, G., Vasilakos, A.V.: Local area prediction-based mobile target tracking in wireless sensor networks. IEEE Trans. Comput. **64**(7), 1968–1982 (2015)
5. Fu, P., Tang, H., Cheng, Y., Li, B., Qian, H., Yuan, X.: An energy-balanced multi-sensor scheduling scheme for collaborative target tracking in wireless sensor networks. Int. J. Distrib. Sens. Netw. **13**(3) (2018)
6. Demigha, O., Slimane, H.O., Bouziani, A., Hidouci, W.-K.: Energy efficient target tracking in wireless sensor networks with limited sensing range. In: The Sixth International Conference on Systems and Networks Communications, pp. 181–187 (2011)
7. Chen, C.P., Mukhopadhyay, S.C., Chuang, C.L., Liu, M.Y., Jiang, J.A.: Efficient coverage and connectivity preservation with load balance for wireless sensor networks. IEEE Sens. J. **15**(1), 48–62 (2015)
8. Ez-Zaidi, A., Rakrak, S.: A comparative study of target tracking approaches in wireless sensor networks. J. Sens. Article ID 3270659, 11 pages (2016)
9. Huo, Y., Cai, Z., Gong, W., Liu, Q.: A new adaptive Kalman filter by combining evolutionary algorithm and fuzzy inference system. In: IEEE Congress on Evolutionary Computation (CEC), Beijing, pp. 2893–2900 (2014)
10. Yu, Y.: Distributed target tracking in wireless sensor networks with data association uncertainty. IEEE Commun. Lett. **21**(6), 1281–1284 (2017)
11. Xia, G., Ludwig, S.A.: Object-tracking based on particle filter using particle swarm optimization with density estimation. In: IEEE Congress on Evolutionary Computation (CEC), Vancouver, BC, pp. 4151–4158 (2016)

12. Pak, J.M., Ahn, C.K., Shmaliy, Y.S., Shi, P., Lim, M.T.: Accurate and reliable human localization using composite particle/FIR filtering. IEEE Trans. Hum. Mach. Syst. **47**(3), 332–342 (2017)
13. Pak, J.M., Ahn, C.K., Shmaliy, Y.S., Lim, M.T.: Improving reliability of particle filter-based localization in wireless sensor networks via hybrid particle/FIR filtering. IEEE Trans. Ind. Inform. **11**(5), 1089–1098 (2015)
14. Bai, H., et al.: Improving cooperative tracking of an urban target with target motion model learning. In: 4th IEEE Conference on Decision and Control (CDC), Osaka, pp. 2347–2352, December 2015
15. Ramos, H.S., et al.: Cooperative target tracking in vehicular sensor networks. IEEE Wirel. Commun. **19**(5), 66–73 (2012)
16. Trojanowski, K., Kulpa, T.: Particle convergence time in the PSO model with inertia weight. In: 7th International Joint Conference on Computational Intelligence (IJCCI), Lisbon, Portugal, pp. 122–130 (2015)
17. Juneja, M., Nagar, S.K.: Particle swarm optimization algorithm and its parameters: a review. In: International Conference on Control, Computing, Communication and Materials (ICCCCM), Allahabad, pp. 1–5 (2016)
18. Taherkhani, M., Safabakhsh, R.: A novel stability-based adaptive inertia weight for particle swarm optimization. Appl. Soft Comput. **38**, 281–295 (2016)

New Modelisation of Silicon DWDM Demux, AND Gate for Wavelengths in C and L Bands

Mira Ganesh[✉], Venkatachalam Rajarajan Balaji, R. Sri Nivedha, and D. Kavya

Department of Electronics and Communication Engineering,
St. Joseph's Institute of Technology, Chennai 600119, Tamil Nadu, India
mira.ganesh@gmail.com

Abstract. Realization of fast speed information processing device for communication and its application. In this paper, optical device with the 2D Photonic Crystals is proposed. The photonic DWDM (Dense Wavelength Division Multiplexing) demultiplexer uses the concept of splitting the incoming signals to the defined network. The work proposes a integrated 4 channel Photonic crystal DWDM demultiplexer. One side of the demultiplexer is designed to support 100 GHz and another side of demultiplexer is supported to drop 200 GHz. The proposed demultiplexer is also designed to support drop desired wavelength in C and L band. The Photonic optical AND gate is designed using constructive interfernce. The proposed device support with high bit rate and contrast ratio of 11.76 Tbps and 11 dB. The size of the proposed device is 230.64 μm^2 and results of the proposed device is best suitable for Photonic Integrated Circuits (PIC)

Keywords: Demultiplexer · AND gate · Linewidth · Fabrication · Waveguide · Integrated · Photonic crystal

1 Introduction

Photonic Crystals are manmade artificial crystals with a new way of light confinement in ultra compact size along with low energy losses. The unique feature in PhC is Photonic Band Gap (PBG), due to the arrangement of the periodicity of dielectric material [1]. The PBG completely blocks the propagation of light inside the devices like a reflector [2]. The light can be guided with an idea of breaking the periodcity. This principle allows the researchers to find many useful devices like photonic demultiplexer [3], logic gates [4], encoders [5], switches [6], sensors [7] and many more. A photonic demultiplexer splits the incoming signals to the designated network [3]. The DWDM network provides high utilization of bandwidth due to narrow channels spacing of 0.1 nm/12.5 GHz, 0.2 nm/25 GHz, 0.4 nm/50 GHz, 0.8 nm/100 GHz and 1.6 nm/200 GHz [8].

In literature survey it is found that many researches carried out in PC demultiplexer. The demultiplexer designed with point & line defect resonant cavity [9–11] ring resonant cavity (Square, Rectangular, circular, hexagonal) [3, 12–14]. However, there is no

© Springer Nature Singapore Pte Ltd. 2020
S. Gupta and J. N. Sarvaiya (Eds.): ET2ECN 2020, CCIS 1214, pp. 99–108, 2020.
https://doi.org/10.1007/978-981-15-7219-7_9

attempt made in combining both to support 100 GHz and 200 GHz bandwidth in C & L communication band. To the best of our knowledge, It is the first time to propose.

So far in many works, research work has been realized in PC AND gate using Y shaped [15], Multimode interference [16]. The work failed to show the high contrast ratio and bit rate to support high speed processing circuits. In the proposed design constructive interference based edge rod is utilized to get high contrast ratio and bit rate of 11 dB and 11.7 Tbps.

The paper is presented as follows, The proposed PC geometry analysis is studied in Sect. 2. In Sect. 3 design of integrated band (C & L) and bandwidth (100 GHz & 200 GHz) in single chip is described. The design of PC AND gate is explained in Sect. 4. In Sect. 5 process flow to fabricate PC device with air rod is explained, the conclusion is provided in Sect. 6.

2 Photonic Band Gap

The structure consists of high refractive index of Si rods (n = 3.45), dielectric constant = 11.4. The 20 × 35 array of Si rods have been utilized with following parameters a = 550 nm (Lattice Constant), r = 170 nm (non defect rod size), n = 1 (background index) as shown in Fig. 1.

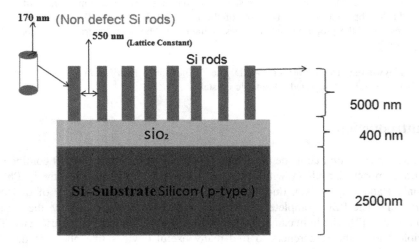

Fig. 1. Square lattice rods in air with dimensions

The PC with high index Si rods supports TE polarization, which is observed in Fig. 1, unlike TM polarization in Triangular lattice air holes [17]. The extensive PBG is observed 0.31 (2193 nm) < a/λ < 0.44 (1539 nm) for r/a = 0.1774. The three TE PBG and two TM PBG for the proposed structural parameter is shown in Fig. 2. The First TE PBG is used for designing demultiplexer.

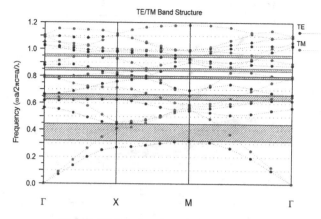

Fig. 2. PBG before introducing the defects

From Fig. 3(a) The optimum value of non defect rod radius is selected at 170 nm, lattice constant 550 nm, refractive index 2,45 is optimized from the gap map analysis and its highlighted in yellow line proposed device. The PBG is depend on structural parameter of optmized nano optical device.

3   Proposed Design

3.1   DWDM Demultiplexer

Figure 4(a) shows the proposed integrated dual band-bandwidth four channel demultiplexer. The proposed device supports to split 0.8 nm and 1.6 nm channels separately. The top of the DRC is used to drop 0.8 nm channels whereas 1.6 nm channels are selected by the bottom DRC. Both 0.8 nm channels & 1.6 nm are combined to output port through coupling rods between the bus waveguide to the DRC. DRC is used to suppress the side bands, by adjusting the radius of diamond edge.

The desired wavelength has been optimized with the optimizing the rods and studying the PBG show in Table 1.

PhC square resonant cavity is create with removing $(4 + 4)2$ rods to couple the resonat wavelength to drop waveguide.

$$\frac{da}{dt} = \left(j\omega_1 - \frac{\omega_1}{Q_1} - \frac{\omega_1}{2Q_2} - \frac{\omega_1}{2Q_3} \right) a + e^{j\theta_b} \sqrt{\frac{\omega_1}{2Q_2}} S_{+1} + e^{j\theta_b} \sqrt{\frac{\omega_1}{2Q_2}} S_{+2} + e^{j\theta_c} \sqrt{\frac{\omega_1}{Q_3}} S_{+3} \tag{1}$$

Equation (1) of the first channel denoted as, S_{+1}, S_{+2}, S_{+3} are the incoming waves of channel [18]. Similarly, S_{-1}, S_{-2}, and S_{-3} are the amplitude of the outgoing waves. Proposed model shown with the arrangement of 2 D taper (Si) between SMF to 2D PhC, this arrangement reduce the insertion loss in real time systems. The coupling theory proposed model is shown in Fig. 4(b)

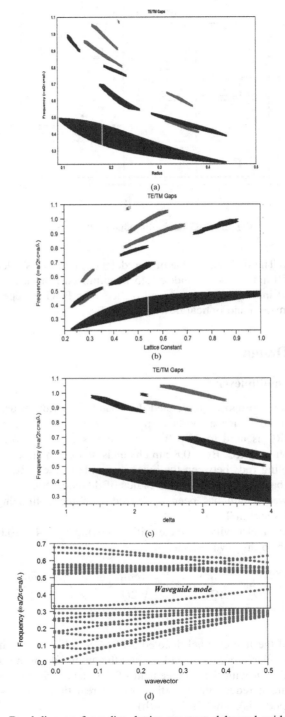

Fig. 3. Band diagram for radius, lattice constant, delta and guided mode

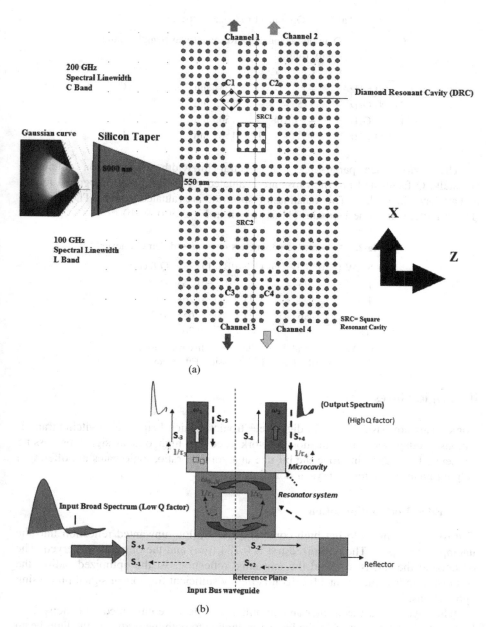

Fig. 4. (a) Proposed Integrated dual band demultiplexer with taper and 3D view (b) Sketch of proposed model based on coupling theory

Table 1. Optimized rod size of the cavity

Channel	Diamond resonant cavity (nm)				Resonant wavelength	Band
	C1	C2	C3	C4		
1–200 GHz	112	–	–	–	1551 nm	C
2–200 GHz	–	115	–	–	1555 nm	C
1–100 GHz	–	–	108	–	1565 nm	L
2–100 GHz	–	–	–	105	1569 nm	L

The performance parameters like spectral linewidth, transmission efficiency, crosstalk, Q factor and insertion loss are evaluated for the proposed integrated model and are listed in Table 2. The transmission spectrum is evaluated from FDTD algorithm (Finite Difference Time Domain) [1] as shown in Figs. 5(a) & (b)

Table 2. Performance parameters of proposed demultiplexer

S.LW (nm)	T.E (%)	C.T (dB)	I.L	Q factor
1.6	93	−23	−0.264	970
1.6	94	−23	−0.268	972
0.8	86	−27	−0.655	1956
0.8	94	−27	−0.26	1958

S.L.W = Spectral linewidth, I.L = Insertion loss. C.
T = Cross talk, T.E = Transmission Efficiency

4   Logic Gates

Logic gates are basic blocks in digital electronics, which help in all switching applications. Today telecommunication network need the high optical signal processing elements. In order to improve the bit rate and contrast ratio, logic gates are offering a helping hand in photonics crystal domain.

4.1   Edge Rod Optimization

The rod is optimized to get high contrast ratio and low unwanted reflection into the unemployed inputs. The optimized rod is 0.184 (μm) and the output is observed. The optimizing the rod is to avoid the unwanted reflection. At the optimized radius, the contrast ratio is achieved at 11.7 dB it is highly sufficient for optical signal processing applications.

The edge rods act as a filter and amplifier it neglect the unwanted reflections from both ends. For the input of 11 the logic 1 is applied to both the ports i.e., the light beam is applied to both the ports and due to constructive interference it gives a high power compared to 01 and 10. The 10% in the time curve observed at 18.265 μm similarly, for 90% it gives a result of 27.397 μm. The pulse width is calculated by $2t_2$, which gives the ON, and OFF logic levels. To our knowledge it is high-proposed logic gate operate in the bait rate of 11.76 Tbps

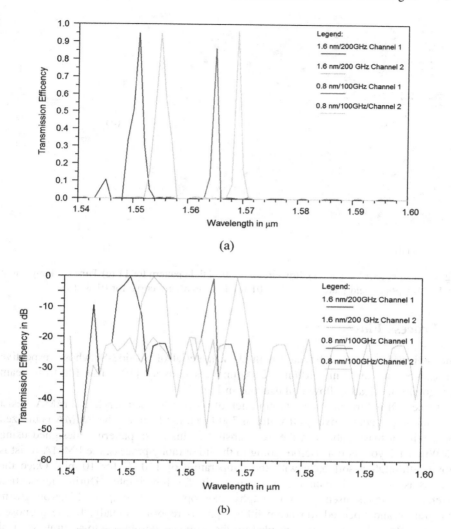

Fig. 5. Transmission Spectrum in a) Linear scale and b) dB

Like wise, due to the logic 01 and 10 given in the ports there is a destructive interference caused which has a phase difference of 180 the low power is generated due to the logic 0 resulting in output. This makes the logic 11 more compelling for high contrast ratio compared to other two logic inputs which is shown in Fig. 6.

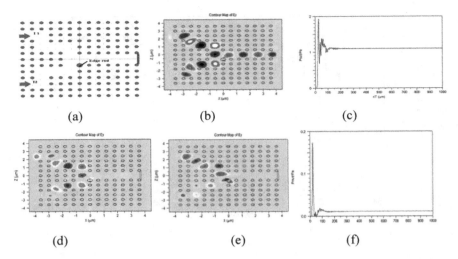

Fig. 6. Stair case AND gate (a) Structure (b) Optical field pattern for 11 (c) Time evolving curve for 11 (d) Optical field pattern for 01 & 01 (e) Time evolving curve for 01 & 10

5 Process Flow

The SOI wafer can be fabricated with stack material of Si-Sio2-Si whose respective thicknesses are 5000 nm–400 nm–2500 nm, respectively [19]. The Electron beam lithography fabrication flow is illustrated in Fig. 7.

Once SOI is formed, then 100 nm thick of polymethylmethacrylate (PMMA) resist material is spin coated over SOI wafer at 7000 rpm for 15 min. The PMMA is utilized for making a mask pattern in the SOI substrate. This mask pattern is designed using CleWin 4.1-layout editor. Before going to the lithography process, the PMMA resist is moving through a soft bake with the temperature of 110 °C for 10 min. Once the process is completed, then the wafer is ready for lithography. During fabrication several techniques used for lithography like optical lithography, Electron Beam lithography and Focused Ion beam lithography is reported already. In the proposed design, E-Beam Lithography is needed for the proposed design due to accurate vertical etching for few tens of nanometers [20]. The other techniques do not have capability to control the feature size in sub nm size Particularly, Raith E line direct electron beam lithography is needed as it provides ultra-high resolution, maximum acceleration voltage of up to 30 kV and nano manipulators to get the pattern of the air hole structure. Then, the developed substrate is hot baked with 180° C for dehydration process.

The Deep Reactive Ion Etching (DRIE) is the deep vertical dry etching which is used to form the array of rods based on the masking pattern. Next wet etching process is used to remove the Sio2 oxide layer rinse with BHF acid for 16 min. The SiO_2 oxide layer is acting as sacrificial layer for suspending the PC in air. By having the afore-mentioned fabrication steps, the proposed demultiplexer will be realized.

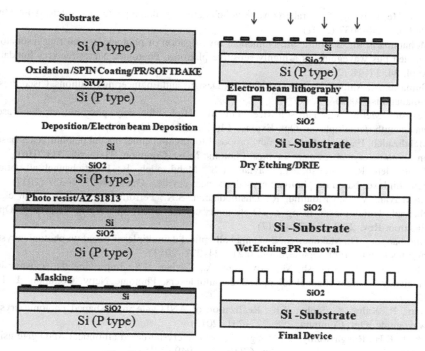

Fig. 7. Process in electron beam lithography

6 Conclusion

In this paper, the realization of ultra compact dual band (0.8 nm/1.6 nm) demultiplexer in single 2D PhC and optical AND gate is discussed. The DRC effectively suppresses side bands in turn offers better transmission efficiency. The AND gate provides a bit rate of 11.6 Tbps with minimum contrast ratio of 11 dB. The size of proposed device is small as it can be needed device in optical signal processing.

References

1. Joannopoulos, J.D.: Photonic crystals, Molding the flow of light, 2nd edn. Princeton University Press, Princeton (2008)
2. Soukoulis, C.M.: Photonic Band Gap Materials, vol. 315. Springer, New York (2012)
3. Mohammadi, M., Seifouri, M.: A new proposal for a high-performance 4-channel demultiplexer based on 2D photonic crystal using three cascaded ring resonators for applications in advanced optical systems. Opt. Quantum Electron. **51**(11), 350 (2019)
4. D'souza, N.M, Mathew, V.: Interference based square lattice photonic crystal logic gates working with different wavelengths. Opt. Laser Technol. **80**, 214–219 (2016)
5. Mehdizadeh, F., Soroosh, M., Alipour-Banaei, H.: Proposal for 4-to-2 optical encoder based on photonic crystals. IET Optoelectron. **11**(1), 29–35 (2016)

6. Li, J., He, J., Hong, Z.: Terahertz wave switch based on silicon photonic crystals. Appl. Opt. **46**(22), 5034–5037 (2007)

7. Mohammadi, M., Seifouri, M.: Numerical investigation of photonic crystal ring resonators coupled bus waveguide as a highly sensitive platform. Photonics Nanostructures Fundam. Appl. **34**, 11–18 (2019)

8. Gumaste, A., Antony, T.: DWDM Network Designs and Engineering Solutions. Cisco Press, Indianapolis (2003)

9. Tekeste, Meron Y., Yarrison-Rice, Jan M.: High efficiency photonic crystal based wavelength demultiplexer. Opt. Express **14**(17), 7931–7942 (2006)

10. Mehdizadeh, F., Soroosh, M.: A new proposal for eight-channel optical demultiplexer based on photonic crystal resonant cavities. Photonic Netw. Commun. **31**(1), 65–70 (2016)

11. Talebzadeh, R., Soroosh, M., Kavian, Y.S., Mehdizadeh, F.: Eight-channel all-optical demultiplexer based on photonic crystal resonant cavities. Optik **140**, 331–337 (2017)

12. Kannaiyan, V., Savarimuthu, R., Dhamodharan, S.K.: Performance analysis of an eight channel demultiplexer using a 2D-photonic crystal quasi square ring resonator. Opto Electron. Rev. **25**(2), 74–79 (2017)

13. Ghorbanpour, H., Makouei, S.: 2-channel all optical demultiplexer based on photonic crystal ring resonator. Front. Optoelectron. **6**(2), 224–227 (2013)

14. Mohammadi, B., Soroosh, M., Kovsarian, A., Kavian, Y.S.: Improving the transmission efficiency in eight-channel all optical demultiplexers. Photonic Netw. Commun. **1**, 1–6 (2019)

15. Rani, P., Kalra, Y., Sinha, R.K.: Realization of AND gate in Y shaped photonic crystal waveguide. Opt. Commun. **298**, 227–231 (2013)

16. Shaik, E.H., Rangaswamy, N.: Design of photonic crystal-based all-optical AND gate using T-shaped waveguide. J. Mod. Opt. **63**(10), 941–949 (2016)

17. Wen, F., David, S., Checoury, X., El Kurdi, M., Boucaud, P.: Two-dimensional photonic crystals with large complete photonic band gaps in both TE and TM polarizations. Opt. Express **16**(16), 12278–12289 (2008)

18. Olivier, S., Benisty, H., Weisbuch, C., Smith, C.J., Krauss, T.F., Houdré, R.: Coupled-mode theory and propagation losses in photonic crystal waveguides. Opt. Express **11**(13), 1490–1496 (2003)

19. Bogaerts, W., et al.: Fabrication of photonic crystals in silicon-on-insulator using 248-nm deep UV lithography. IEEE J. Sel. Top. Quantum Electron. **8**(4), 928–934 (2002)

20. Subramania, G., Lin, S.Y.: Fabrication of three-dimensional photonic crystal with alignment based on electron beam lithography. Appl. Phys. Lett. **85**(21), 5037–5039 (2004)

Outage and SNR Performance of Tropical Optical Wireless Links Using Receiver Diversity

Gireesh G. Soni[✉]

Shri G S Institute of Technology and Science, Indore, India
gireeshsoni@gmail.com

Abstract. This work investigates the performance of various receiver diversity combining techniques in mitigating the rain induced impairments experienced by optical wireless communication (OWC) links under tropical rainfall. An on-off keying (OOK) modulated 10 Mb/s optical signal is used to study rain specific attenuation (RSA) using laboratory testbed with controlled rainfall intensity up to 250 mm/hr. Various combining techniques at the receiver i.e. selection combining (SelC), equal gain combining (EGC) and maximum ratio combining (MRC) are employed to observe diversity improvement. Significant compensation of rain induced impairments in a 1×2 single input multiple output (SIMO) link is observed when compared to conventional single input single output (SISO) link. The outage probability and signal to noise ratio (SNR) based comparative is evaluated at varying rain conditions which show MRC to be superior diversity technique followed by EGC and SelC.

Keywords: Optical wireless communication · Rainfall · Diversity techniques

1 Introduction

Optical wireless communication (OWC) or Free Space Optics (FSO) is currently seen as a promising alternative technology for large bandwidth applications particularly for last mile access networks where fiber is not available due to deployment issues, cost constraints and time. Feasibility of such links is limited by the localized atmospheric conditions such as fog, rain, haze and scintillation [1]. In tropical regions, rainy events are a major factor of attenuation and distortion in terrestrial OWC. The rain specific attenuation in such regions could be up to 100 dB [2]. Also scattering and absorption due to raindrops results in performance degradation inducing deep fades, pointing errors and beam sway. There are a number of techniques to address these channel induced effects such as adaptive optics, coding, spatial diversity, modulation format and aperture averaging etc., which have conventionally been used in FSO channels [3–5].

In this work, we analyze the performance of rain interrupted OWC signals using a 1×2 SIMO link. Receiver diversity with various combining techniques i.e. equal gain combining (EGC), selection combining (SelC) and maximum ratio (MRC) is employed. A comparative analysis of SISO and the SIMO link on the basis of outage

S. Gupta and J. N. Sarvaiya (Eds.): ET2ECN 2020, CCIS 1214, pp. 109–121, 2020.
https://doi.org/10.1007/978-981-15-7219-7_10

probability and SNR is shown to demonstrate the potential of diversity to compensate rain induced degradations.

1.1 Rain Specific Attenuation

There are two different mechanisms that produce energetic deficits of the spread of electromagnetic wave when encountered to raindrops. At first, water droplets absorbs energy and later disperse on different directions [6, 7]. An underlying entity in the calculation for attenuation statistics is the RSA, which is basically the attenuation per unit distance as mathematically defined in Eq. 1 [8]:

$$\gamma_{rain} = k \cdot R^{\alpha} \tag{1}$$

where k and α are the power-law parameters and depends upon the frequency, temperature and micro structure of rain, R is the rain rate in mm/hr. Table 1 shows the 'k' and 'α' values for different models [9–11].

Table 1. Empirical values of 'k' and 'α' for several rain attenuation models.

Model name	Carbonneau	Japan	Marshall & Palmer	Prague	Suriza's	Samir's
K	1.076	1.58	0.365	0.231	0.4195	2.03
α	0.67	0.63	0.63	0.7	0.8486	0.74
Country/ Region	France/ Temperate	Japan/ Temperate	Prague/ Temperate	Prague/ Temperate	Malaysia/ Tropical	Malaysia/ Tropical

2   Receiver Diversity and Combining Methods

Mostly, the loss of SNR performance can be palliated through increased input power, but the power requisite in many situations may not be practical. A substitute to increasing transmitter power at the input may be enhanced receiver aperture area (size). Although the use of large aperture sizes in direct detection links can reduce the negative effects induced by scintillation through aperture averaging, this may not correspond to the optimal solution for a list of practical reasons. However, it is possible to accomplish spatial diversity advantage of a large-aperture area collecting lens by using multiple smaller apertures separated sufficiently far apart that each received output acts independent of the others [12]. As schematic shown in Fig. 1, the summated output from such an array of receivers shall display aperture averaging effects similar to that of a single large aperture.

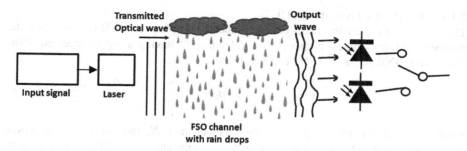

Fig. 1. Schematic of OWC link with receiver diversity (SelC)

Assuming that net output of M statistically uncorrelated detectors be given by Eq. (2):

$$i = \sum_{i \to 1}^{M} (i_{S,j} + i_{N,j}) \tag{2}$$

where, i_S and i_N are random signal and nonzero noise component respectively. In Eq. 2, identical mean/variance of i_S and i_N is assumed. It therefore follows the mean and variance of the total current, which is expressed by:

$$\langle I \rangle = M \langle I_{s1} \rangle$$

$$\sigma_{SN}^2 = M[\langle i_{S,1}^2 \rangle - \langle i_{s,1} \rangle^2 + \langle i_{N,1} \rangle^2] = M\sigma_{SN,1}^2 \tag{3}$$

Hence, we conclude that the mean rms of the SNR magnitude can be written as:

$$\langle SNR_M \rangle = \frac{M \langle i_{S,1} \rangle}{\sqrt{M} \sigma_{SN,1}} = \sqrt{M} \langle SNR_1 \rangle \tag{4}$$

Here, $\langle SNR_1 \rangle = \langle i_{S,1} \rangle / \sigma_{SN,1}$ is the mean SNR of a single PD. This analysis points that the output SNR from an M detectors array can enhance the output SNR of a single PD by the factor of M [1].

2.1 Combining Techniques

There are various methods for combining the received signal in a near optimum or optimum way in order to have substantial diversity improvement. Commonly used combining methods are discussed below [1, 13]:

2.1.1 Selection Combining (SC)

This method of combining picks out the branch having highest SNR output. More the number of diverse routes, higher is the probability of having a higher received SNR. The instant SNR in the ith route is given by:

$$\gamma_i = \frac{E}{N_0}|h_i|^2 \tag{5}$$

where E is the symbol energy, h_i is the channel gain, N_0 the noise spectral power density presumed to be similar in all branches. The instantaneous SNR at the output of selection combiner is as follows:

$$\gamma_{SC} = max\{\gamma_1, \gamma_2, \ldots \ldots \gamma_M\}$$

The pdf of instantaneous SNR of all diverse routes follows exponential distribution as given below:

$$f(\gamma_i) = \frac{1}{\gamma_{av}}\exp\left(-\frac{\gamma_i}{\gamma_{av}}\right), \quad for \ \gamma_i > 0,$$

where, $\gamma_{av} = \overline{\gamma_i} = \frac{E}{N_0}|\overline{h_i}|^2$ is the average SNR. The associated cumulative distribution function (CDF) can be expressed by following equation.

$$P(\gamma_i \leq \gamma) = \int_{-\infty}^{\gamma} f(\gamma_i)d\gamma_i = 1 - \exp\left(-\frac{\gamma_i}{\gamma_{av}}\right), \tag{6}$$

The CDF for instantaneous SNR after selection combining can be expressed as:

$$F(\gamma_{SC}) = P(\gamma_i \leq \gamma_{SC}, i = 1, 2 \ldots \ldots M) = \prod_{i=1}^{M} P(\gamma_i \leq \gamma_{SC})$$

$$= \prod_{i=1}^{M} 1 - \exp\left(-\frac{\gamma}{\gamma_{av}}\right) = 1 - \exp\left(-\frac{\gamma}{\gamma_{av}}\right)^M, \ \gamma_{SC} \geq 0 \tag{7}$$

The above expression is the outage probability (P_{out}) of ith branch which is another performance parameter of diversity system under the effect of fading paths. Outage probability is specified as the instantaneous error probability that the received SNR falls below a certain pre-specified threshold γ_{th} i.e. CDF of γ, obtained at $\gamma = \gamma_{th}$.

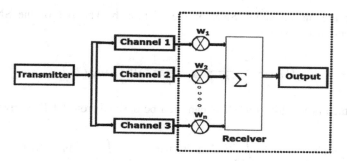

Fig. 2. Maximum ratio combining scheme.

2.1.2   Maximum Ratio Combining (MRC)

This method, allocates different weights to diversity paths for SNR optimization as depicted in Fig. 2. The information signal of different diversity paths can be expressed as:

$$r_i(t) = h_i s(t) + z_i(t),$$

Where h_i is the channel (complex) gain, $s(t)$ is the transmitted signal, and $z_i(t)$ is additive white Gaussian noise. The received signal is given to the linear combiner; therefore output can be given as:

$$y(t) = \sum_{i=1}^{M} w_i r_i = \sum_{i=1}^{M} w_i(h_i s(t) + z_i(t)) = s(t) \cdot \sum_{i=1}^{M} w_i h_i + \sum_{i=1}^{M} w_i z_i(t).$$

The instantaneous signal and noise power at the combined output is given as:

$$\sigma_y^2 = E\left[|s(t)|^2\right] \cdot \left|\sum_{i=1}^{M} w_i h_i\right|^2; \ \sigma_{nc}^2 = \sigma_n^2 \cdot \sum_{i=1}^{M} |w_i|^2 \tag{8}$$

Now, in accordance with the Schwarz inequality used for complex parameters,

$$\left|\sum_{i=1}^{M} w_i h_i\right|^2 \leq \sum_{i=1}^{M} |w_i|^2 \cdot \sum_{i=1}^{M} |h_i|^2 \tag{9}$$

which holds true when $w_i = a h_i^*$, where a is an arbitrary constant. If $a = 1$, the instantaneous SNR is maximized when chosen weights are conjugate of channel gain, i.e., $w_i = h_i^*$; and it becomes

$$\gamma_{MRC} = \gamma_{av} \sum_{i=1}^{M} |h_i|^2 = \sum_{i=1}^{M} \gamma_i \tag{10}$$

where γ_i is the instantaneous SNR of the ith branch. The pdf of the SNR at the combined output is given as

$$f(\gamma_{MRC}) = \frac{1}{(M-1)!} \cdot \frac{\gamma_{MRC}^{M-1}}{\gamma_{av}^M} \exp(-\gamma_{MRC}/\gamma_{av}).$$

The outage probability for MRC can then be derived from CDF as given by:

$$P(\gamma_{MRC} \leq \gamma) = \int_{-\infty}^{\gamma} f(\gamma_{MRC}) d\gamma_{MRC} = 1 - \int_{-\infty}^{\gamma} f(\gamma_{MRC}) d\gamma_{MRC}$$

$$= 1 - \exp(-\gamma_{MRC}/\gamma_{av}) \sum_{i=1}^{M} \frac{(\gamma_{MRC}/\gamma_{av})^{i-1}}{(i-1)!}. \tag{11}$$

2.1.3   Equal Gain Combining (EGC)

In this technique, instead of different weights, equal weights are assigned to every branch which in turn lowers down the receiver complexity.

2.2   The SNR in Presence of Absorption and Scattering

In presence of atmospheric hurdles like fog, rain, aerosols, haze etc. between the link of transmitter and receiver, the received signal manifests random fluctuation of irradiance. If we let $I(0, L)$ denoting the instantaneous irradiance at the receiver collecting lens, the instantaneous input signal power is related by:

$$P_S = \frac{1}{8} \pi D^2 I(0, L)$$

The output signal current (i_S) over long measurement intervals must be treated like a random variable due to these random irradiance fluctuations. Consequently, the mean signal current is:

$$\langle i_S \rangle = \frac{\eta e \langle P_S \rangle}{h\nu} \tag{12}$$

Where, allowing also for attenuation caused by absorption and scattering, the mean signal power can be approximated by:

$$\langle P_S \rangle = \frac{1}{8} \pi D^2 \langle I(0, L) \rangle \exp(-\alpha L) \cong \frac{1}{8} \pi D^2 I^0(0, L) \left[\frac{\exp(-\alpha L)}{1 + 1.63\sigma_1^{12/5} \Lambda_1} \right] \tag{13}$$

The parameter $\alpha(\lambda)$ is the extinction coefficient $\Lambda_1 = 2L/kW_1^2$, W_1 is the spot radius of the beam incident on the collecting lens, and $\sigma_1^2 = 1.23 C_n^2 k^{7/6} L^{11/6}$ is the Rytov variance. The output photocurrent from the detector $i = i_S + i_N$ in this case has mean $\langle i_S \rangle$ and variance:

$$\sigma_{SN}^2 = \langle i_S^2 \rangle - \langle i_S \rangle^2 + \langle i_N^2 \rangle = \left(\frac{\eta e}{hv}\right)^2 \langle \Delta P_S^2 \rangle + \frac{2\eta e^2 B P_S}{hv}, \tag{14}$$

Where $\langle \Delta P_S^2 \rangle = \langle P_S^2 \rangle - \langle P_S \rangle^2$ represent power perturbations in the signal that become major component of the detector noise. Based on (12) and (14), the mean SNR, $\langle SNR \rangle$, at the output of the photo-detector takes the form:

$$\langle SNR \rangle = \frac{\langle i_S \rangle}{\sigma_{SN}} = \frac{\langle P_S \rangle}{\sqrt{\langle \Delta P_S^2 \rangle + \frac{2hvB\langle P_S \rangle}{\eta}}},$$

But, $\langle \Delta P_S^2 \rangle = A \langle P_S \rangle^2$ where A ≤ 1 is the coefficient of aperture averaging. Therefore (8) can be rewritten as:

$$SNR = \frac{SNR_0}{\sqrt{\frac{P_{S0}}{\langle P_S \rangle} + A SNR_0^2}}, \tag{15}$$

Where $SNR_0 = \frac{i_S}{\sigma_N} = \sqrt{\frac{\eta P_S}{2hvB}}$ and P_{S0} is the signal power in absence of atmospheric effects. Therefore, the power ratio $P_{S0}/\langle P_S \rangle \cong \left(1 + 1.63\sigma_1^{\frac{12}{5}}\Lambda_1\right)e^{\alpha L}$ gives a measure of SNR degradation caused by rain induced beam scattering and attenuation as the entry inside the brackets will approximately equals 1. The Rytov variance σ_1 is of the order of 10^{-4} for clear atmosphere. Thus rain induced absorption and scattering effects will dominate and turbulence will be negligible. Therefore it is neglected here in all further calculations.

3 Experimental Set-up

The laboratory prototype to implement receiver diversity is shown in Fig. 3. Atmospheric conditions of rainfall (intensity varies from 0 to 250 mm/hr) have been artificially generated in the chamber. A 5 mW, 650 nm laser source with 0.8 miliradian divergence is mounted on XYZ positioning stage for handling three dimensional motions while conserving line of vision. A 10 Mbps OOK-NRZ (80 mV$_{PP}$) modulates the optical radiation which is collimated prior to travelling 15 m free space channel. The transmitter and receiver apertures are 5 mm and 25 mm respectively. Two PIN-Si photodiode (PD) (Thor lab: DET 10A) having responsivity of 0.45 A/W (central wavelength 700 nm with rise time, $t_r \approx 1$ ns) are accompanied with optical power meters (Newport-1815 C). Transparent sheets made up of acrylic are used to configure a closed atmospheric unit having $5 \times 0.6 \times 0.6$ m^3 dimension. The effective length of free propagation is increased by placing two front coated mirrors at the end of chamber, each one has reflection loss $\approx 4\%$.

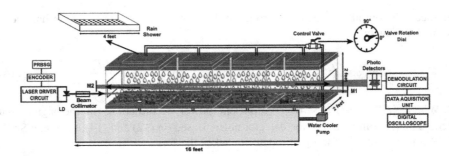

Fig. 3. Schematic of experimental setup.

To affirm the validity of the laboratory testbed, RSA is calculated employing the calibrated unit as shown in Fig. 3 and equated with RSA observed using conventional empirical relations. For every precipitation rate, experiments are carried out to calculate the RSA employing standard Beer's-Lamberts law. A comparative of the RSA obtained using various empirical relations have been discussed in [14].

3.1   Implementation of Receiver Diversity Combining

The system with receiver diversity consists of one transmitter and N number of receivers, usually kept apart by a radial distance larger than spatial coherence for uncorrelated outputs. In our case, two identical PDs are taken (Fig. 5a) and its receiver diversity is schematically illustrated in Fig. 4 and real setup in Fig. 5(b). Multiple receivers reduce the scintillation index by a factor of M and improve the SNR by a factor of $\sqrt{M}$. Thus the average SNR always increases with an increase in M. These various distinct paths are statistically self-reliant and hence produce averaged-out irradiance fluctuation. On the contrary, diversity improvement is abated with an increase in number of routes. The peak gain in diversity is obtained, when number of branches equals two. However, one needs to compromise with the outage probability. Thus there is a tradeoff between the probability of outage and diversity improvement.

The SelC combining method is less complex among all as it processes the aperture with the highest received irradiance (or electrical SNR). Apparently, the choice is made according to $I_{SelC} = \max\{ I_1, I_2 \cdots, I_N \}$. If I_n are self-reliant and evenly distributed random variables, then for SelC receivers, the probability of outage is readily achieved from Eq. (16) [1]

$$P_{out} = f\left(\sqrt{\frac{SNR_{th}}{SNR}} \right) \tag{16}$$

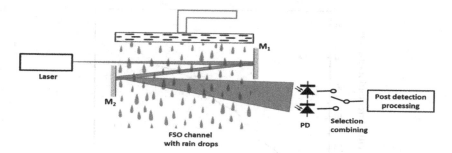

Fig. 4. 1×2 SIMO OWC link with SelC.

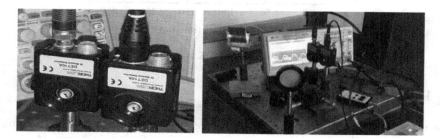

Fig. 5. Photographs of (a) two identical Si- PIN-PDs (b) lab testbed for receiver diversity.

According to the receivers employed within the observed irradiance plane, we conclude that there exist M self-reliant diversity branches carrying the same information bearing signal. The received signal envelope on all branches is evenly Rayleigh distributed. The noise on each branch is independent, additive and evenly distributed. It is also independent of the signal [15, 16].

The output from the PD1 may be approximated as $\alpha_1 E_b^{1/2} b + n_1$, similarly output from the PD2 as $\alpha_2 E_b^{1/2} b + n_2$ where, b = Transmitted bit i.e. 1 or 0; E_b = Bit energy; n_i = AWGN of ith branch, α_i = Fading complex envelope on the ith branch.

The received signal from the two PDs is captured using a DSO and is fed to the MATLAB environment for processing. The diversity combining i.e. MRC, EGC and SelC on the received outputs is implemented in the MATLAB domain.

3.2   Channel Response of 10 Mbps-OOK Under Tropical Rain Intensities

Here the response of an OOK test signal of 10 Mbps is analyzed which is required for all further observations of combining i.e. receiver diversity. The RSA is calculated for increasing precipitation rates using Beer's- Lamberts law. The Fig. 6 shows the channel response or the rain induced attenuation of the modulated optical signal under consideration.

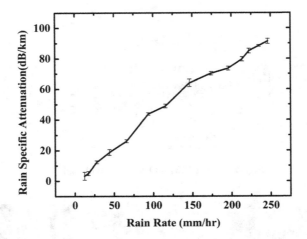

Fig. 6. Channel response to 10 Mbps-OOK signal under heavy precipitation.

4 Results and Discussions

One of the key advantages of using multiple receivers for diverse routes is to minimize the probability of pointing errors due to scattering from rain drops. A 1×2 SIMO OWC link is employed to observe the effect of receiver diversity in compensating rain induced losses. The PDs are kept in proximity of the irradiance received and are placed apart by spatial coherence radius. The performance improvement is observed in terms of SNR and the Outage probability.

4.1 SNR

The uncorrelated outputs from the two PDs are fed to the digital storage oscilloscope (DSO) from where they are processed using MATLAB. Bit-by-bit comparison is made by comparing the instantaneous bit energy for each bit is and the one having higher energy is taken for evaluating SNR. Since here we intend to enhance the SNR i.e. in terms of diversity improvement, we have used two PDs as diversity gain is maximized for two diversity routes. The potential of combining can be visualized from Fig. 7 as the observed SNR (MRC) at zero precipitation point is 3.7 dB higher than that of SISO.

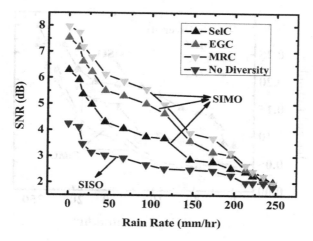

Fig. 7. SNR for SISO and 1 × 2 SIMO OWC link under heavy precipitation.

With reference to SISO, the average diversity improvement factor in terms of average SNR obtained using MRC, EGC and SelC is 1.76, 1.62 and 1.35 dB respectively. In other words:

$$SNR_{avg.}(MRC) = 1.76\ SNR_{avg.}(SISO)$$
$$SNR_{avg.}(EGC) = 1.62\ SNR_{avg.}(SISO)$$
$$SNR_{avg.}(SelC) = 1.35\ SNR_{avg.}(SISO)$$

Also even at higher rainfall rates, this SNR enhancement is quite significant. Though in SelC, the much simpler technique to implement, the SNR improvement obtained is lesser than that of MRC and/or EGC, it is still much better than that of SISO link.

4.2 Outage Probability

The outage dictates the probability that the mean SNR of the link may lie below a specific threshold SNR. The threshold SNR to calculate this probability in case of 1 × 2 SIMO link is kept at 1.5 dB. The graph in Fig. 8 clearly indicate that the outage performance with diversity is improved, however this is expected to reduce further if more than two diversity routes will be used.

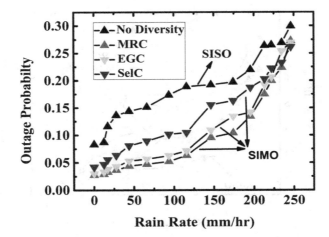

Fig. 8. Probability of outage for SISO and SIMO OWC link under heavy precipitation.

As for PDs array (M = 4, 8, 16 ...) the diversity improvement reduces but the probability of outage becomes better. Moreover, much better outage performance can be achieved at relatively higher received power. The average outage probability of SISO link is 19% while with SIMO, it reduces to 10%, 11% and 13% for MRC, EGC and SelC resp. For RR > 170 mm/hr, both SNR and outage performance degrades sharply.

5   Conclusion

To account for rain influenced degradations, receiver diversity is investigated using two identical receivers employing SelC, EGC and MRC techniques. A 10 Mbps OOK-SISO and a 1 × 2 SIMO link is investigated and the performance is evaluated on the basis of outage probability and SNR. With reference to SISO, the average diversity improvement factor using MRC, EGC and SelC is 1.76, 1.62 and 1.35 respectively. The average outage probability of SISO link is 19% while with SIMO; it reduces to 10%, 11% and 13% for MRC, EGC and SelC respectively. For rain intensities >170 mm/hr, both SNR and outage performance degrades sharply.

References

1. Ghassemlooy, Z., Popoola, W., Rajbhandari, S.: Optical Wireless Communications: System and Channel Modelling with MATLAB®. CRC Press, Boca Raton (2017)
2. da Silva Mello, L.R., Pontes, M.S., de Souza, R.M., Pérez García, N.A.: Prediction of rain attenuation in terrestrial links using full rainfall rate distribution. Electron. Lett. **43**(25), 1442 (2007)
3. Popoola, W.O., Ghassemlooy, Z.: BPSK subcarrier intensity modulated free-space optical communications in atmospheric turbulence. J. Light. Technol. **27**(8), 967–973 (2009)

4. Viswanath, A., Jain, V.K., Kar, S.: Aperture averaging and receiver diversity for FSO downlink in presence of atmospheric turbulence and weather conditions for OOK, M-PPM and M-DPPM schemes. Opt. Quantum Electron. **48**(9), 435 (2016)
5. Kaur, P., Jain, V.K., Kar, S.: Comparison of aperture averaging and receiver diversity techniques for free space optical links in presence of turbulence and various weather conditions. J. Opt. Commun. **35**(4), 319–326 (2014)
6. Grabner, M., Kvicera, V.: Multiple scattering in rain and fog on free-space optical links. J. Light. Technol. **32**(3), 513–520 (2014)
7. Olsen, R.L., Rogers, D.V., Hodge, D.B.: The $_aR^b$ relation in the calculation of rain attenuation. IEEE Trans. Antennas Propag. **26**(2), 318–329 (1978)
8. Crane, R.K.: Prediction of Attenuation By Rain. IEEE Trans. Commun. **28**(9), 1717–1733 (1980)
9. Suriza, A.Z., Rafiqul, I.M., Wajdi, A.K., Naji, A.W.: Effects of rain intensity variation on rain attenuation prediction for Free Space Optics (FSO) links. In: International Conference on Computer and Communication Engineering (ICCCE), pp. 680–685 (2012)
10. Gombak, J., Suriza, A.Z., Islam, R., Wajdi, A.-K., Naji, A.W., Rafiqul, Md.: Analysis of rain effects on terrestrial free space optics based on data measured in tropical climate. IIUM Eng. J. **12**(5), 45–51 (2011)
11. Marshall, J.S., Palmer, W.M.K.: The distribution of raindrops with size. J. Meteorol. **5**(4), 165–166 (1948)
12. Kaur, P., Jain, V.K., Kar, S.: Performance analysis of FSO array receivers in presence of atmospheric turbulence. IEEE Photonics Technol. Lett. **26**(12), 116–1168 (2014)
13. Peppas, K., Nistazakis, H.E., Assimakopoulos, V.D., Tombras, G.S.: Performance analysis of SISO and MIMO FSO communication systems over turbulent channels. In: Optical Communication. InTech (2012)
14. Soni, G.G., Tripathi, A., Mandloi, A., Gupta, S.: Compensating rain induced impairments in terrestrial FSO links using aperture averaging and receiver diversity. Opt. Quantum Electron. **51**, 244:1–13 (2019)
15. Hulea, M., Ghassemlooy, Z., Rajbhandari, S., Tang, X.: Compensating for optical beam scattering and wandering in FSO communications. J. Light. Technol. **32**(7), 1323–1328 (2014)
16. Tsiftsis, T.A., Sandalidis, H.G., Karagiannidis, G.K., Uysal, M.: Optical wireless links with spatial diversity over strong atmospheric turbulence channels. IEEE Trans. Wirel. Commun. **8**(2), 951–958 (2009)

A Comparative Evaluation of Low-Complexity LAS Detection Algorithm for Massive MIMO Systems

Mitesh S. Solanki[✉]

Prachitirth Laundry Equipments, Rajkot, India
smittesh89@gmail.com

Abstract. For multiple-input multiple-output (MIMO) to work, both network and mobile devices need to be tightly integrated. Now the requirements for the design of the 5G network, the MIMO becomes "massive" and exceedingly necessary for the deployment point of view. The main intention of our work is to generate as many potential solutions or outputs as we can select among the best one. We introduce low complexity detection algorithms into large scale MIMO systems where they can perform better than heuristic algorithms known in the literature, such as MIMO detection algorithms likelihood ascent search (LAS) detector. This contribution explains the potential for simple local search such as LAS for near-optimal performance in a large-scale antenna MIMO system. In this article, we analyze the behaviour of common indices used in the linear approach such as ZF and MMSE, to measure rates of convergence of error performance of a LAS algorithm and most importantly, observed execution time costs of all schemes. Simulation outcomes are presented to corroborate the study.

Keywords: Multiple-input multiple-output (MIMO) · Likelihood ascent search (LAS) · Zero-forcing (ZF) · Minimum mean square error (MMSE)

1 Introduction

4G incentives and new achievements in the current decade bring the consent of the next generation of mobile systems (5G). 5G interruptions will bring huge waves in potential telecom surfing. Expected 5G to be able to access applications and services with various capabilities. By eliminating later concerns, it will increase resilience, consistency, and greater resource efficiency [1, 2]. With all these significant reductions in energy consumption. The large multiple-input multiple-output MIMO is an important technological ingredient in the evolution of 5G. It has the potential to significantly increase network capacity and end-user experience. Large scale MIMO signal detection is a vital view of 5G, and it is essential to know how to efficiently and accurately detect the broadcasted signal from the large MIMO system at the receiver. Because of a large number of antenna array elements as well as the radio frequency chain operating, the complexity of the symbol detector in the large MIMO downlink receiver progressed rapidly [2].

© Springer Nature Singapore Pte Ltd. 2020
S. Gupta and J. N. Sarvaiya (Eds.): ET2ECN 2020, CCIS 1214, pp. 122–135, 2020.
https://doi.org/10.1007/978-981-15-7219-7_11

Consequently, investigations to obtain the best large MIMO detection algorithm with less complexity have triggered much concentration during the past decade [3, 4]. Suggestion have been made in the literature [3, 5], including the detection algorithm of a purely evolutionary neighborhood. Although the research community recognizes the theoretical advantages of this, many algorithms are being investigated to perform signal detection [3, 6]. In prevailing, these algorithms can be split into linearly detection algorithms and nonlinearly detection algorithms, as stated by several computations schemes. Although the nonlinear detection of the linear detection algorithm is less harsh than the algorithm, even so, it is yet a potent signal detection schemes of a large scale MIMO system in some cases owing to its low complexity. Under the linear detection algorithm, it is important to calculate the inverse of large matrices, especially when operating a large antenna array; this increase poses challenges for the design and implementation of systems [6].

Therefore, in this article, we present a low complexity detection algorithm for large scale MIMO signal detection. Working on this algorithm, we can use this approach and use it to avoid direct inverse of vectors or matrices under a large-scale system in each iteration and to reduce the computation of the algorithms. We have addressed the likelihood ascent search (LAS) detection algorithm in large-scale MIMO system where they can achieve near-optimal performance in the large-scale MIMO literature [7–9]. This contribution explains the possibility of simple spatial detection such as 1-LAS for the near optimal performance in large scale antenna MIMO system. It is interesting to achieve near optimal performance among the more antenna regimes using LAS for Sphere Decoder SD's at this stage is prohibited. When it needs to allow for some additional complexity compared to 1-LAS complexity, efforts can be made to achieve 2-LAS or 3-LAS and Tabu search algorithm [7, 9].

The LAS detection algorithm begins with the initial vector and finds the optimal solution vector in the neighboring vector until ML improves the cost satisfaction. Therefore, we identify by a linear scheme such that the matched filter, zero-forcing, and minimum mean square error is sufficient to use the initial vector in the algorithm; the ZF-LAS detector uses the zero-forcing output as the initial vector and the MMSE-LAS detector acts as the initial vector to the MMSE output. The algorithm starts with quadratic amplitude modulation (QAM) symbol mapping. A LAS algorithm is addressed even under the consideration of perfect known CSI has been widely investigated in [7]. In particular, we observe a low complexity detection algorithm for large MIMO system and evaluate its performance under the consideration of fully known CSI. Recognizing the low computations and performance superiority of LAS detectors in large systems, we, in this article, generously accept LAS detectors in large MIMO systems to describe spatial multiplexing and impressive results.

1.1 Outline

The memories of this article is formed as follows: In Sect. 2, the system model explains and expresses the most prominent LAS detection algorithm. Section 3 discusses about analytical evaluation of likelihood ascent search (LAS) algorithm and derives the asymptotic analysis of the LAS detector. In Sect. 4, we analyze the relevant computational efficiency and Sect. 5 provides simulation results to promote the importance of LAS approach which as outlined in Sect. 4 and finally, Sect. 6 concludes this article.

1.2 Notations

A vector and a matrix are represented with lowercase and uppercase boldface letters, respectively. $(.)^T, (.)^H, (.)^{-1}, \|.\|^2, Tr\{.\}, \mathbb{E}\{.\}\mathbb{R}\{.\}, |.|, \mathcal{Q}\{.\}, sign(.)$ denote the transpose, complex conjugate transpose, inverse, l_2 norm, trace of matrix, mathematical expectation, real domains, absolute value, quantization operation, sign to the nearest integer, sequentially. $\mathcal{CN}(x, R)$ is used to represent circularly symmetric complex Gaussian random vectors where x is the mean and R the covariance matrix. The notation $\triangleq$ is used for definitions.

2 System Model

In this part, we present the LAS detector signal model for Vertical Bell Laboratories Layered Space-Time (V-BLAST). Consider of a V-BLAST system with n_t transmit antenna and get n_r antenna $n_t \leq n_r$, where the n_t signals are simultaneously transmitted from the n_t transmit antenna. On the transmitter side, the information is generated in the source and mapped to the symbol of M-QAM. Let $s(0) \in \{-1, 1\}$ be a symbol transmitted by transmitter antenna. The received signal and the broadcasted signal are the following relations

$$\tilde{y} = \tilde{H}\tilde{s} + \tilde{n} \tag{1}$$

where $\tilde{s} = \{\tilde{s}_1, \tilde{s}_2 \cdots, \tilde{s}_{n_t}\}^T$ is denotes the transmitted signal vector where $\tilde{s}_i \in \Omega$, $\tilde{y} = \{\tilde{y}_1, \tilde{y}_2 \cdots, \tilde{y}_{n_r}\}^T$ represents the received signal vectors. $\tilde{n} = \{\tilde{n}_1, \tilde{n}_2 \cdots, \tilde{n}_{n_r}\}^T$ represents additive noise vector with each $\tilde{n}_i \sim \mathcal{CN}(0, \sigma_n^2)$. $\tilde{H}$ indicates channel gain matrix of dimension $n_r \times n_t$ with each coefficient $h_{ij} \sim \mathcal{CN}(0, 1)$. The complex signal model in (1) can be estimated as the equivalent real signal model written as follows

$$y = Hs + n, \tag{2}$$

where $s \in \mathbb{R}^{2n_t \times 1}$ represents a real equivalent transmitter vector, $y \in \mathbb{R}^{2n_r \times 1}$ denotes a real equivalent received vector and $n \in \mathbb{R}^{2n_r \times 1}$ represents equivalent noise vector. Herein, transmit vector is mapped with discrete values from $\{\Omega_m, m = 1, \cdots, M\}$ where $\Omega_m = \{\pm 1, \pm 3, \cdots, \pm(\sqrt{M} - 1)\}$. $H \in \mathbb{R}^{2n_r \times 2n_t}$ indicates equivalent real channel matrix defined as follow

$$H = \begin{vmatrix} Re(\tilde{H}) & -Im(\tilde{H}) \\ Im(\tilde{H}) & Re(\tilde{H}) \end{vmatrix} \tag{3}$$

We will use the real signal model (2) of this system in this article. At the receiver, our main objective is to detect the vector s in all possible $\sqrt{M}^{2n_t}$ [7, 9] broadcast vector sets adjacent to the received vector y given a H. H is supposed to be known on the receiver, but not on the transmitter side. Consider defining a bit vector as d. Mathematically, this is defined as

$$\hat{s}_{ML} = \arg \min_{s \in \Omega^{2n_t}} \|y - Hd\|^2, \tag{4}$$

and the Maximum Likelihood ML is associated with this solution. $\|.\|$ indicates L_2 norm. We determine the ML cost function as follows

$$\phi(d) = \|y - Hd\|^2 = \sum_{i=1}^{2n_r} \left| y_i - \sum_{j=1}^{2n_t} h_{ij} d_j \right|^2, \tag{5}$$

and the rest of the paper calls it the ML cost or simply cost.

2.1 LAS Detection Algorithm

The essential idea of the local search algorithm is to start with the initial solution vector and then to obtain the optimal solution vector from the neighboring vectors set. The process is replicated until ML costs (5) are reduced. The LAS algorithm essentially finds the sequence of the required solution vectors that are given a certain point; this sequence is determined by the update rule [7, 10]. LAS with the initial solution vector $d^{(0)}$. The algorithm is given by the starts $d^{(0)} = \mathcal{Q}(\mathcal{G}y)$, where $\mathcal{G}$ denotes the initial vector as a linear scheme such as MF, ZF, or MMSE and where $\mathcal{Q}(.)$ represents quantization process. The index value m denotes in $d^{(m)}$ represents number of iteration in search levels. The cost function specified by the addressed kth iteration followed by the provided search level

$$C^{(k)} = d^{(k)^T} H^T H d^{(k)} - 2y^T H d^{(k)} \tag{6}$$

In the $(k+1)th$ recurrence, it tries to update a symbolic effort to increase the possibilities by updating the existing data vector $d^{(k)}$ current entry [10, 11]. If we update pth symbol in $(k+1)th$ iteration; in system p can take value from $1, \cdots, 2n_t$ form M-QAM mapper. Depending on the update rule, it may be revised as follows

$$d^{(k+1)} = d^{(k)} + \lambda_p^{(k)} e_p, \tag{7}$$

where e_p expresses a unit vector with its only pth entry, and places zero in the residual entries. Also, for any iteration, $d^{(k)}$ must be refer to space $\mathbb{A}$, and so $\lambda_p^{(k)}$ can only take specific integer values. There are several types available to select a fraction of the neighbours' vectors [10]. A low complexity neighbourhood can be a "k-coordinate away" neighbourhood, where neighbours differ only from the solution given in k coordinates, thereby increasing the neighbourhood size

$$|\mathcal{N}_k(s)| = \binom{2n_t}{k}.$$ (8)

For example, for $n_t = 2$ and $s = [-1, 1, 1, -1]$, the size of the 1-symbol update away from the set of the neighborhood is $|\mathcal{N}_1(s)| = 4$, where

$$\mathcal{N}_1(s) = \{[1, 1, 1, -1], [-1, -1, 1, -1], [-1, 1, -1, -1], [-1, 1, 1, 1]\}.$$

Using (6) and (7), and defined as matrix F

$$F \triangleq H^T H$$ (9)

The cost difference, we can write this

$$\Delta C_p^{k+1} \triangleq C^{(k+1)} - C^{(k)} = \lambda_p^{(k)^2} (F)_{p,p} - 2\lambda_p^{(k)} z_p^{(k)},$$ (10)

when h_p is the pth column of H, $z^{(k)} = H^T (y - Hd^{(k)})$, $z_p^{(k)}$ is the pth entry of the $z^{(k)}$ vector, and $(F)_{p,p}$ is the (p,p)th entry of the F matrix [10, 11]. Also, let's obtain a_p and $l_p^{(k)}$

$$a_p = (F)_{p,p} \qquad l_p^{(k)} = \left| \lambda_p^{(k)} \right|.$$ (11)

With the above defined variables (10), we can rewrite

$$\Delta C_p^{k+1} = l_p^{(k)^2} a_p - 2l_p^{(k)} \left| z_p^{(k)} \right| sgn \left(\lambda_p^{(k)} \right) sgn \left(z_p^{(k)} \right),$$ (12)

where the $sgn(.)$ the signum function indicates. In order to reduce the ML cost function from the kth to the $(k+1)$th iteration, the cost differentiation should be negative [10]. Based on the approach that a_p and $l_p^{(k)}$ is non-negative variables, we can compile from (12) that the sign of $\lambda_p^{(k)}$ should be satisfied

$$sgn \left(\lambda_p^{(k)} \right) = sgn \left(z_p^{(k)} \right).$$ (13)

Using (13) in (12), ML can override the cost difference as

$$\mathcal{F} \left(l_p^{(k)} \right) \triangleq \Delta C_p^{k+1} = l_p^{(k)^2} a_p - 2l_p^{(k)} \left| z_p^{(k)} \right|.$$ (14)

Set as negative for $\mathcal{F} \left(l_p^{(k)} \right)$, the needed and satisfactory condition of (14) is as follows

$$l_p^{(k)} < \frac{2 \left| z_p^{(k)} \right|}{a_p}.$$ (15)

However, we can find the value of $l_p^{(k)}$ which is a solution of Eq. (15) as well as the largest descendant and at the same time, gives the largest slope of the function for the ML cost function while repeating the kth to the $(k+1)$th iteration (when symbol p is improved) [10]. In addition, $l_p^{(k)}$ is intended to take only certain integer values, and so it is possible to evaluate the brute-force $\mathcal{F}\left(l_p^{(k)}\right)$ for optimum $l_p^{(k)}$ values of $l_p^{(k)}$. This will be computationally expensive because the M size of the constellation is greater [7, 10]. However, in the case of a one-symbol improvement, we can find the nearest form, the optimization of the expression is reduced by $l_p^{(k)}$ which decrease by $\mathcal{F}\left(l_p^{(k)}\right)$, which is given by

$$l_{p,opt}^{(k)} = 2\left\lceil \frac{\left|z_p^{(k)}\right|}{2a_p} \right\rceil, \tag{16}$$

where $[.]$ indicates the rounding process, where for a real number d, $\lceil d \rceil$ is an integer closer to d. If the pth symbol in $d^{(k)}$, i.e., $d_p^{(k)}$, is actually modified, then the new value of the vector will be updated

$$\tilde{d}_p^{(k+1)} = d_p^{(k)} + l_p^{(k)} sgn\left(z_p^{(k)}\right). \tag{17}$$

However, $\tilde{d}_p^{(k+1)}$ can only take the values of the $\mathbb{A}_p$ set, and consequently, we should examine for the occurrence of more than $\tilde{d}_p^{(k+1)}$ being greater than $(M-1)$ or less than $-(M-1)$. If $\tilde{d}_p^{(k+1)} > (M-1)$, then $l_p^{(k)}$ is arranged so that the updated value of $\tilde{d}_p^{(k+1)}$ with the arranged value of $l_p^{(k)}$ using (17) is $(M-1)$. Similarly, if $\tilde{d}_p^{(k+1)} > -(M-1)$, then $l_p^{(k)}$ is adjusts so a new value of $\tilde{d}_p^{(k+1)}$ is $-(M-1)$. After these adjustment, let us $l_{p,opt}^{(k)}$. It is shown that if $\mathcal{F}\left(l_{p,opt}^{(k)}\right)$ is non-positive, then $\mathcal{F}\left(\tilde{l}_{p,opt}^{(k)}\right)$ is also non-positive. We calculate $\mathcal{F}\left(\tilde{l}_{p,opt}^{(k)}\right), \forall p = 1, \cdots, 2n_t$. Now, let

$$s = \arg\min_p \mathcal{F}\left(\tilde{l}_{p,opt}^{(k)}\right) \tag{18}$$

If $\mathcal{F}\left(\tilde{l}_{s,opt}^{(k)}\right) < 0$, $(k+1)$th is updated for iteration

$$d^{(k+1)} = d^{(k)} + \tilde{l}_{s,opt}^{(k)} sgn\left(z_s^{(k)}\right)e_s, \tag{19}$$

$$z^{(k+1)} = z^{(k)} - \tilde{l}_{s,opt}^{(k)} sgn\left(z_s^{(k)}\right)f_s, \tag{20}$$

where f_s indicates sth column of F. The modified in (20) follows the description of $z^{(k)}$ in (10). If $\mathcal{F}\left(\tilde{l}_{s,opt}^{(k)}\right) \geq 0$, at that stage, an 1-symbol update search ends. At this position, the 1-symbol update in the data vector is recognised as the local minima [10]. At this stage a 1-symbol update reaches at the local minima point, we can look a further reduction in cost value by updating with multiple symbols vectors updates [10].

3   Analytical Evaluation of LAS Algorithm

In this part, we have concerned an asymptotic convergence of the error performance of the LAS detection algorithm, similar to the ML detector for the $n_t, n_r \to \infty$ with $n_t = n_r$ in the MIMO system [11]. Data vector $d \in \Omega$ on an n-symbol update such as $(d - \Delta d_n) \in \Omega$ are transform d to $(d - \Delta d_n)$. Further, $(d - \Delta d_n)$ is collected by replacing n-symbols the emblems in d on different index values by the $n-$ tuple $u_n \triangleq (i_1, i_2, \cdots, i_n), 1 \leq i_j \leq 2n_t, \forall_j = 1, \cdots, m$. Therefore, we can write Δd_n as

$$\Delta d_n = \sum_{k=1}^{n} 2d_{i_k} e_{i_k}, \tag{21}$$

where d_{i_k} is the $i_k th$ element of d. Let $\mathbb{L}_n \subseteq \Omega$ indicate a set of data vectors for anyone $d \in \mathbb{L}_n$, if the n symbol on d is updated as result of the vector $(d - \Delta d_n)$, then $\|y - H(d - \Delta d_n)\| \geq \|y - Hd\|$. The objective is to derive the error probability of LAS detector in this section with the help of Theorem 2. To derive Theorem 2, we need the following Lemmas 1 to 5, Slutsky's theorem, and Theorem 1 from [11].

Lemma 1: Grant $d \in \Omega$. when, $d \in \mathbb{L}_n$ if and only if, for given any n-update on $d, n \in [1, 2, \cdots, 2n_t]$ [11],

$$\|y - H(d - \Delta d_n)\|^2 \geq \|y - Hd\|^2,$$
$$\left(y - Hd + \frac{1}{2} H\Delta d_n\right)^T (H\Delta d_n) \geq 0. \tag{22}$$

If we adopt $d \in \mathbb{L}_1$, then applying Lemma 1 and (2), we can address

$$\left(n + H(x - d) + h_p d_p\right)^T \left(h_p d_p\right) \geq 0, \forall_p = 1, \cdots, 2n_t. \tag{23}$$

Lemma 2: Regarding the specificity of the optimal vector, the symbol vector $d \in \Omega$ is the optimal vector supporting the noise vector n performs the following set of equation

$$\left(n + H(x - d) + \left(\sum_{j=1}^{n} h_{i_j} d_{i_j}\right)\right)^T \left(\sum_{j=1}^{n} h_{i_j} d_{i_j}\right) \geq 0, \tag{24}$$

$\forall n = 1, \cdots, 2n_t$ and for all possible n-tuples $\{i_1, \cdots, i_n\}$ for each n [11].

Definition: For each $d \in \Omega$ and for each integer $m, 1 \leq m \leq 2n_t$, we connect a domain $\mathbb{R}_{d^m} \in \mathbb{R}^{2n_t}$, such as a noise vector $n \in \mathbb{R}_{d^m}$ if only if n serves the set of Eq. (24) $\forall n = 1, \cdots, m$ and for all possible n-tuples $\{i_1, \cdots, i_n\}$ for each n [11]. Then determine $\mathbb{R}_d \triangleq \mathbb{R}_{d^{2n_t}}$.

Lemma 3: If $n \in \mathbb{R}_d$, then d is the optimal vector. Let $d_i, d_j \in \Omega$ and $d_i \neq d_j$. Then $\mathbb{R}_{d_i}$ and $\mathbb{R}_{d_j}$ are disjoint [11].

Lemma 4: Make $h \in \mathbb{R}^m$ with a random vector along with (i.i.d) elements distributed as $\mathcal{N}(0, 1/2)$. Make $\{h_i\}, i = 1, 2, \cdots, m$ is a set of all vectors, with each $h_i \in \mathbb{R}^m$ and becoming i.i.d elements distributed as $\mathcal{N}(0, 1/2), \mathbb{E}\left[h_i h_j^T\right] = 0$ for $i \neq j$, and $\mathbb{E}\left[h h_j^T\right] = 0$ for $j = 1, \cdots, m$. Then

$$\lim_{n_t \to \infty} \frac{\sum_{k=1}^m h^T h_k}{m n_t} = 0. \tag{25}$$

Lemma 5: Let $i_j \in u_n, j = 1, \cdots, n$. Define a random variable z_{u_n} as

$$z_{u_n} \triangleq \frac{\sum_{k=1}^n \sum_{j=k+1}^n h_{i_j}^T h_{i_k} d_{i_j} d_{i_k}}{\sum_{j=1}^n \left\| h_{i_j} \right\|^2}. \tag{26}$$

For any $d \in \Omega, z_{u_n}$ the conversion reaches zero [11] in probability defines as $n_t \to \infty$, i.e., $z_{u_n} \xrightarrow{p} 0$ as $n_t \to \infty \forall n = 2, 3, \cdots, 2n_t$.

Theorem 1: Let $d \in \epsilon \Omega$ and $n \in \mathbb{R}_{d^1}$. Then $n \in \mathbb{R}_d$ in probability as $n_t \to \infty$, i.e., for any $\delta, 0 \leq \delta \leq 1$, it is indicate as an integer $n(\delta)$ such as for $n_t > n(\delta), p(n \in \mathbb{R}_d) > 1 - \delta$.

Theorem 2: The error probability of data vector of the LAS detector converts the near-optimal detector [11] as $n_t, n_r \to \infty$ keeping $n_t = n_r$.

Proof: The d_{LAS} is detected symbol vector of the LAS detector provided data s, H and n. The algorithm ends if and only if 1-symbol update outcomes in no more reduction of cost. This terms that for the addressed s, H and $n, d_{LAS} \in \mathbb{L}_1$, and so it must be true that n contents (23) with d replace by d_{LAS}. This is similar to the set of equations that define this region $\mathbb{R}_{d^1}$. Hence, by changing d by d_{LAS}, we can further claim that asymptotically as $n_t \to \infty, n \in \mathbb{R}_{d_{LAS}}$ in the probability [11]. From Lemma 3, we know if $n \in \mathbb{R}_{d_{LAS}}$, then d_{LAS} is actually the optimal vector in the probability. That is, for any $\delta, 0 \leq \delta \leq 1$, there is an integer $n(\delta)$ such that for $n_t > n(\delta)$

$$P(d_{LAS}) > (1 - \delta). \tag{27}$$

Therefore, we can write that for $n_t \geq n(\delta)$

$$P_{LAS_e} = P(d_{LAS} \neq s)$$
$$= P(d_{LAS} \neq s | d_{LAS} = d_{ML}) P(d_{LAS} = d_{ML}) \tag{28}$$
$$+ P(d_{LAS} \neq s | d_{LAS} \neq d_{ML}) P(d_{LAS} \neq d_{ML}).$$

From (27), we have $(d_{LAS} \neq d_{ML}) \leq \delta$. Also, $P(d_{LAS} \neq s | d_{LAS} = d_{ML})$ is a probability of error for the optimal detector, which we express by P_{ML_e}. Utilizing this, we can fix the probability of error for the LAS algorithm as

$$P_{LAS_e} \leq P_{ML_e} + \delta P(d_{LAS} \neq s | d_{LAS} \neq d_{ML}) \leq P_{ML_e} + \delta. \tag{29}$$

Since δ can be arbitrarily small, so we can draw conclusions from (29) that fact $n_t \rightarrow \infty$, the symbol vector of the LAS detector converges the error probability to an optimal detector. This can be adapted to show that the evidence that the LAS, except for the symbol vector error probability [11], the slightest error performance of the detection algorithm also convergence with that of the best solution detection [7]. The indication for the BER converges is with the same Eqs. (28) and (29), rather defining an error event as $d_{LAS} \neq s$, we determine an error events for each bit; for example, for the pth bit, the occurrence of the error is determined as $d_{p,LAS} \neq s_p$.

4   Computational Complexity

The analysis of the complexity of the LAS detector is as follows. Given the initial vector, the LAS algorithm alone has on average a little complexity in the fraction of $\mathcal{O}(n_t n_r)$ [7]. These can be described as follows. The complexity of the LAS algorithm is defined in the three parts: (i) initial calculation of $\mathcal{C}^{(k)}$ in (6), (ii) an update of $z^{(k)}$ in each step (20), and (iii) the average number of steps needed to reach a certain point. Calculating of $\mathcal{C}(0)$ requires the calculation of $H^H H$ for each MIMO channel realization, which requires a per bit complexity of the order $\mathcal{O}(n_t n_r)$ [3, 7]. In addition to the aforementioned complexity, the initial vector generation also contributes to the overall complexity. The average per-bit complexity of generating initial vectors using MF, ZF, and MMSE is $\mathcal{O}(n_r), \mathcal{O}(n_t n_r)$, and $\mathcal{O}(n_t n_r)$, respectively [7]. The high complexity of ZF and MMSE compared to MF is due to the need to perform matrix inversion operation in ZF/MMSE. Again, considering the complexity of the LAS part and the initial vector generation part together, we find that the overall average per-bit complexity of the MF/ ZF/ MMSE-LAS detector for V-BLAST is $\mathcal{O}(n_t n_r)$ [3, 7].

5   Simulation Results and Discussion

Our approach is to find the optimal solution that is limited to the given Euclidean distance around the initial solution. It finds all the neighbors of the initial solutions that fall under the dynamically assessed square Euclidean distance based on the cost function. We have adopted that the LAS detector is initiated by the ZF and MMSE filter respectively. We define, the number of data frame lengths are set to 1024 and the number of antennas, respectively. Simulation curves corresponding to the 4-QAM symbol mapper are generated. During the simulation, we assume that the channel matrix elements are constant during the transmission symbols. In this section, we define the BER performance of the LAS detection algorithm for V-BLAST obtained by elaborate simulations. This section will also describe the convergence rate of BER performance of LAS detectors.

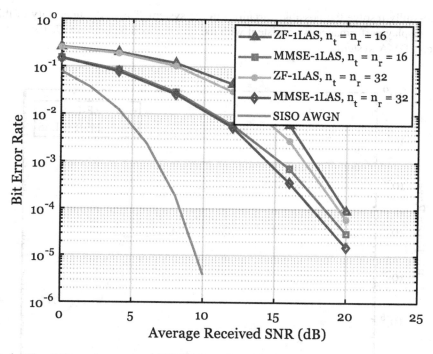

Fig. 1. The BER performance of ZF-1LAS vs. MMSE-1LAS as a function of the average received SNR for 16×16 and 32×32 MIMO system with a 4-QAM constellation.

The BER performance of the LAS algorithm in a MIMO system with $n_t = n_r = 16, 32$ and 4-QAM modulation is presented in Fig. 1. The MMSE and ZF filters output is adopted as the initial solution vector. Therefore, the detection algorithm is referred to as ZF-1LAS and MMSE-1LAS in the figure, respectively. From Fig. 1, it is observed that MMSE-1LAS performs better than ZF-1LAS for $n_t = n_r = 16, 32$. Which is an attribute of the ML detector. It can be observed that the MMSE-1LAS influence comes very close to the unfaded SISO AWGN for $n_t = n_r$. This explains the ability of simple local search such as LAS to achieve near-optimal performance in the MIMO system with the number of antennas [7, 10].

MMSE-1LAS gives better performance than ZF-LAS for enhancing $n_t = n_r$: Fig. 2, we visualize the BER performance of ZF-1LAS and MMSE-1LAS detectors for MIMO as a function $n_t = n_r$ at an average received SNR of 16 dB with 4-QAM.

A plot has been plotted to compare the performance of ZF-1LAS and MMSE-1LAS detectors. From Fig. 2, observations can be made: the behavior of ZF-1LAS and MMSE-1LAS is interesting to increase $n_t = n_r$. More interestingly, this improved performance of MMSE-1LAS increases significantly with increasing $n_t = n_r$ compared to ZF-1LAS. For example, for $n_t = n_r = 24$, performance is improved by the order of the BER (i.e., 4.5×10^{-3} BER for MMSE-1LAS versus 8.2×10^{-3} BER for ZF-LAS). The LAS detection is due to a large system effect in the algorithm which can successfully resolve the possible variations in the system. The LAS superiority of this large display performance is consistent with the observations reported in [7, 10] for the larger CDMA system.

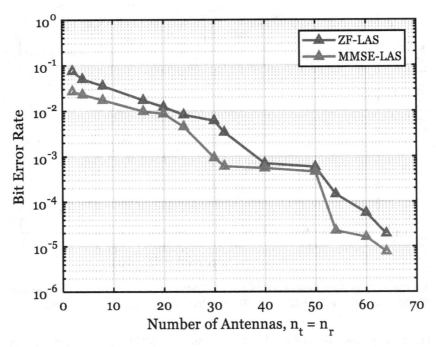

Fig. 2. The BER performance of ZF/MMSE-1LAS detectors as a function of number of transmitting/receiving antennas ($n_t = n_r$) for the MIMO system, average SNR = 16 dB with 4-QAM constellation.

The simulation results for BER convergence, ZF-1LAS, and MMSE-1LAS up to $n_t = n_r = 16, 32$, which are illustrated in Fig. 3, are the main observations in this figure, the average SNR range from 0 to 30 dB to achieve a specific BER for ZF-1LAS and MMSE-1LAS detectors. The convergence speed of both ZF-1LAS and MMSE-1LAS detectors can be compared in terms of the number of BER generated during algorithm execution. It is observed that the faster convergence rate of MMSE-1LAS compared to ZF-1LAS to all BER sample points. This property makes it attractive for the practical implementation of the LAS algorithm.

Finally and most importantly, Table I summarizes time costs. The detection cycle represents the average clock cycle used to perform the detection process for each slot in the process. Table I shows the execution time costs of all detectors on a regular 2.5 GHz desktop computer. Due to the more computational of the LAS algorithm, the execution time costs of the MMSE-1LAS is 6.67% higher than that of the ZF-1LAS detectors at $n_t = n_r = 32$.

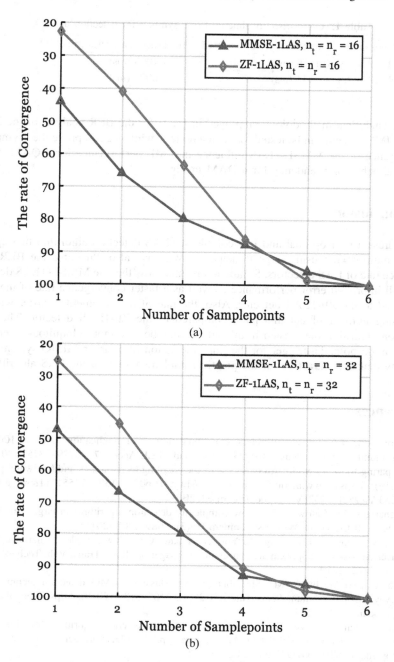

Fig. 3. The convergence curve of BER performance of ZF/MMSE-1LAS detectors as a function of number of BER sample points (a) For $n_t = n_r = 16$, (b) For $n_t = n_r = 32$ MIMO system with a 4-QAM constellation.

Table 1. Comparison of time cost (per symbol) for detection process.

Algorithms	Detection cycles (time) 16×16	Detection cycles (time) 32×32
ZF-LAS	0.1216 (ms)	1.4000 (ms)
MMSE-LAS	0.7134 (ms)	1.6000 (ms)

The analytical methodology employed in [3, 7] for the BER analysis of the large-scale MIMO system can be tested for such a review, while we can prove the asymptotic convergence of the MMSE-1LAS influence into ML performance for 4-QAM. Show the same behavioral tendency for 4-QAM in Fig. 2.

6 Conclusion

We address a near-optimal and low complexity LAS detection algorithm that applies spatial multiplexing using large dimensions. We have also illustrated the BER convergence rate of LAS detectors. Simulation results show that the MMSE-1LAS detector has well-improved error performance as well as a faster convergence rate of the BER compared to the ZF-1LAS detector. Also, the rate of improvement is faster with the increasing number of antenna pairs compared to the ZF-1LAS detector. The LAS detection algorithm manifested in this article may be of a more ubiquitous interest in theory and a potential trigger for the implementation of a larger MIMO system. This property makes it attractive for the practical implementation of the LAS algorithm.

References

1. Rappaport, T.S., et al.: Wireless communications and applications Above 100 GHz: opportunities and challenges for 6G and beyond. IEEE Access **7**, 78729–78757 (2019)
2. Preparing for a 5G world: An overview of the enabling technologies and hardware, pp. 1–9 (2019). https://www.ti.com/lit/wp/slwy003/slwy003.pdf?ts=1594372551911&ref_url=https%253A%252F%252Fwww.google.com%252F
3. Elghariani, A., Zoltowski, M.: Low complexity detection algorithms in large-scale MIMO systems. IEEE Trans. Wireless Commun. **15**(3), 1689–1702 (2016)
4. Tan, X., Ueng, Y.-L., Zhang, Z., You, X., Zhang, C.: A low-complexity massive MIMO detection based on approximate expectation propagation. IEEE Trans. Veh. Technol. **68**(8), 7260–7272 (2019)
5. Albreem, M.A., Juntti, M., Shahabuddin, S.: Massive MIMO detection techniques: A survey. IEEE Commun. Surv. Tutorials **21**(4), 3109–3132 (2019). https://ieeexplore.ieee.org/document/8804165
6. Liu, L., Peng, G., Wei, S.: Linear massive MIMO detection algorithm. Massive MIMO Detection Algorithm and VLSI Architecture, pp. 71–123. Springer, Singapore (2019). https://doi.org/10.1007/978-981-13-6362-7_2
7. Vardhan, K.V., Mohammed, S.K., Chockalingam, A., Rajan, B.S.: A low-complexity detector for large MIMO systems and multicarrier CDMA systems. IEEE J. Select. Areas Commun. **26**(3), 473–485 (2008)

8. Sah, A.K., Chaturvedi, A.K.: Beyond fixed neighborhood search in the likelihood ascent algorithm for MIMO systems. In: 2016 IEEE International Conference on Communications (ICC), Kuala Lumpur, Malaysia, pp. 1–6 (2016)
9. Sah, A.K., Chaturvedi, A.K.: An unconstrained likelihood ascent based detection algorithm for large MIMO systems. IEEE Trans. Wireless Commun. **16**(4), 2262–2273 (2017)
10. Chockalingam, A., Rajan, B.S.: Large MIMO Systems. Cambridge University Press, New York (2014)
11. Mohammed, S.K., Chockalingam, A., Rajan, B.S.: Asymptotic analysis of the performance of LAS algorithm for large-MIMO detection. arXiv:0806.2533 [cs, math], October 2009

Evaluation of Gain and Noise Figure Spectrum of EDFA by Optimizing its Parameters with Different Pumping Schemes in the Scenario of WDM System

Gandhi Divyangna[(✉)]

Institute of Technology and Engineering, Indus University, Ahmedabad, India
divyangnagandhi.ec@indusuni.ac.in

Abstract. Wavelength Division Multiplexing is employed in an optical communication network for upgrading the system capacity. The advent of erbium-doped fiber amplifier with WDM system is considered as one of the advanced technology in recent years. The performance of EDFA depends on several parameters such as Er^{+3} doping, pump power, input signal power, fiber length and different pumping schemes. In this paper, performance analysis of 16×10 Gbps WDM system is evaluated for gain and noise figure under co, count, and bi directional pumping schemes. Results elucidates that the maximum 44 dB gain is obtained by bidirectional pumping with -30 dBm input signal power and 500 mW pump power. Lowest 3.73 dB noise figure is achieved by co directional pumping with -30 dBm input signal power and 100 mW pump power. However, counter pumping has higher noise figure compare to co and bi-directional pumping.

Keywords: WDM · DWDM · Gain · Noise figure

1 Introduction

The optical signal passing through the fiber is affected by attenuation [1]. If the data rate is higher than 10 Gb/s, then it experiences dispersion. Therefore, to reimburse these losses optical amplifiers are used [2]. In optical fiber communication systems, amplifiers are vital for regenerating, amplifying and retransmitting the optical signals which improve the performance of long-haul communication systems [3].

Number of optical amplifiers are available but the significant component in the WDM system is EDFA [4, 5]. Nowadays EDFAs is considered an essential part of every WDM and DWDM systems [6] due to many advantages [7–9]. It permits amplification of signal irrespective of their modulation type or data rate. EDFA can operate in a board range within a 1550 nm window, where silica attenuation is minimum [10, 11].

O. Mahran et al. [12] reported a gain flatness in the wavelength range of 1545–1565 nm with 31 dB maximum gain and 3.8 dB noise figure. Shinji Yamashita et al. [13] presented improvement in the gain flatness of EDFA by using co pumping with

© Springer Nature Singapore Pte Ltd. 2020
S. Gupta and J. N. Sarvaiya (Eds.): ET2ECN 2020, CCIS 1214, pp. 136–146, 2020.
https://doi.org/10.1007/978-981-15-7219-7_12

high pump power. It also proves the flatness with experiment as well as numerical calculation. Mishal Singla et al. [14] presents the impact of 32 channels EDFA based WDM system by using bidirectional pumping. In his work, the system is observed with received power, Q-factor, bit error rate at different pumping power. Channel spacing of 0.8 nm in the wavelength range of 1530 nm to 1555 nm, with input signal power of −26 dBm. Honde et al. [15] presented EDFA performance with forward and bidirectional pumping which provides 27 dB flatten gain with less than 14 dB noise figure. Sivanantha et al. [16] revealed that hybrid amplifier (EYDFA) with Raman amplifier provides better performance with forward pumping scheme compared to another pumping scheme.

The performance of the WDM and DWDM systems utilizing EDFA largely depends on how the later performs in terms of gain and noise [17, 18]. The aim of this paper is to present the performance analysis of EDFA characteristics with co, counter, and bidirectional pumping. Analysis has been carried out by varying the parameters such as input signal power, input signal wavelength, pump power, pump wavelength and fiber length.

This paper is divided in to four sections. The system model is explained in Sect. 2. Section 3 contains simulation results and conclusion is discussed in Sect. 4.

2 System Model

Tremendous improvement in network bandwidth capacity is offered by wavelength division multiplexing technology with erbium-doped fiber. WDM will perform foremost role in the high-speed networks of the next generation.

The structure of EDFA with WDM system comprises of a 16 input signals from tunable laser source of C band, multiplexer, isolators, 980 nm pump laser with different pump power, pump couplers, erbium-doped fiber, demultiplexer, photo detector and optical spectrum analyzer as shown in the Fig. 1. In this system three different pumping techniques are used such as co, counter and bi-directional.

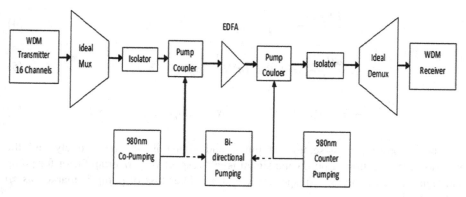

Fig. 1. Simulation setup of EDFA with different pumping configuration

In co directional pumping configuration, the input signal as well as pump signal propagates in the same forward direction. In the counter direction pumping configuration, input signal and pump power signal propagates in the opposite direction. In Bi-direction pumping configuration, input signal propagates in the forward direction and two pump power signals propagates in both the direction, forward and backward.

2.1   Amplification of EDFA Signal

Both the cross-sections, absorption and emission can be calculated for EDFA using following question [19].

$$\sigma_a(v) = \frac{\lambda^2}{8\pi n^2 \tau \Delta v} g_a(v) \tag{1}$$

The absorption cross-section $\sigma_a(v)$ and the emission-cross section $\sigma_e(v)$ are related by following equation and it states by McCumbers relation [20].

$$\sigma_e(v) = \sigma_a(v) \exp\left(\varepsilon - \frac{hv}{kT}\right) \tag{2}$$

Where boltzmann constant is k, absolute temperature is marked as T and, the optical frequency is labeled with v. The parameter ε is defined as following [20].

$$\exp\left(\frac{\varepsilon}{kT}\right) = \frac{\sum_{j=1}^{8} exp\left(-\frac{E_{1j}}{kT}\right)}{\sum_{j=1}^{7} exp\left(-\frac{E_{2j}}{kT}\right)} \exp\left(\frac{E_0}{kT}\right) = R \exp\left(\frac{E_0}{kT}\right) \tag{3}$$

where the energy difference is E_0 [20].

For simplicity two level EDFA is considered instead of three levels, the propagation equations of the pump, signal, and amplified spontaneous emission (ASE) power can be written as following [21].

$$\frac{dP_{p(z,t)}}{dz} = -P_p \Gamma_p (\sigma_a^p N_1 - \sigma_e^p N_2) - \alpha_p P_p \tag{4}$$

$$\frac{dP_{s(z,t)}}{dz} = +P_s \Gamma_s (\sigma_e^s N_2 - \sigma_a^s N_1) - \alpha_s P_s \tag{5}$$

$$\frac{dP_{ASE(z,t)}}{dz} = +P_{ASE} \Gamma_s (\sigma_e^s N_2 - \sigma_a^s N_1) + 2\sigma_e^s N_2 \Gamma_s P_{ASE} - \alpha_s P_{ASE} \tag{6}$$

The absorption cross-section of pump and signal is $\sigma_a^{p,s}$ respectively and the emission-cross section of pump and signal is $\sigma_e^{p,s}$ respectively, overlap factor for pump and signal is represent as Γ, respectively and, the fiber loss of pump is marked as αp and signal is αs.

Amplifier gain is given by solving Eqs. (4, 5 and 6) analytical result in [1].

$$G = exp(-\alpha_s L) \times exp\left[\frac{hv_s}{P_{in}^s}\left(\frac{P_p(0) - P_p(L)}{hv_p} + \frac{P_s(0)}{hv_s}(G-1) - \frac{P_{ASE}^+(L)}{hv_s}\right)\right] \quad (7)$$

EDFA noise figure is given by following equation [22].

$$NF_{EDFA} = \frac{1}{G_{EDFA}} + \frac{P_{ASE}^0(\lambda_s)}{G_{EDFA}hv_s} - \frac{P_{ASE}^i(\lambda_s)}{hv_s} \quad (8)$$

3   Result and Discussions

An EDFA has been modeled using optsim 13 to allow various parameters of the system to be varied and simulated. The main criteria used to assess the performance of the EDFA amplifier are its gain, noise figure, input signal power, pump power and wavelength.

A 16 channel WDM system is carried out to evaluate the performance of co, counter and bidirectional pumping techniques with EDFA. The input wavelength range varies between 1546.12 nm to 1588.18 nm having channel spacing of 0.8 nm at data rate of 10 Gbps. 8 m length of EDFA is used with 980 nm pump wavelength at different pump power. Input signal power has been taken −10 dBm, −20 dBm and −30 dBm.

3.1   Analysis of Gain and NF for EDFA with Co Pumping

Figure 2 and 3 compares EDFA gain and noise figure configuration respectively with co directional pumping. Pump power varies between 100 mW to 500 mW at low input signal power of −30 dBm.

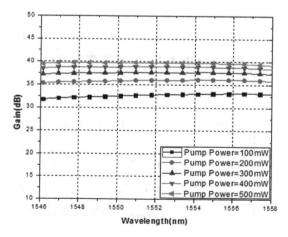

Fig. 2. Wavelength vs gain with different pump power @ co pumping

As illustrated in Fig. 2, gain increases with the rise in pump power and 39.5 dB maximum gain is achieved with 500 mW pump power. However, a strong pump provides a strong signal which permits efficient transfer of energy among the pump signal and input signal, without taking too much energy of the pump by ASE.

It can also be noticed that up to certain level the gain abruptly increases with pump power but after a particular point the increase of gain become smaller and the amplifier goes into saturation.

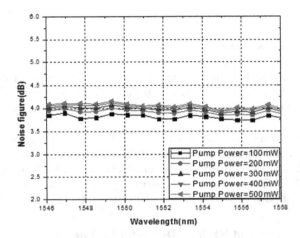

Fig. 3. Wavelength vs noise figure with various pump power @ co pumping

Figure 3 depicts that the noise figure slowly increases as pump power increases. 3.73 dB minimum and 4.15 dB maximum noise figure are obtained with 100 mW and 500 mW pump power respectively.

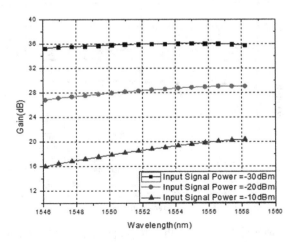

Fig. 4. Wavelength vs gain with different input signal power @ co pumping

From Fig. 4 it is concluded that the maximum gain of 36 dB is achieved at −30 dBm input signal power with 200 mW pump power. Gain decreases as input signal power increases due to the easy saturation of EDFA. As the input signal power increases stimulated emission occurs due to additional photons of EDFA which makes faster diminishing of metastable energy level as compared to filled. So ultimately no more amplification will take place which reduces the gain of EDFA.

3.2 Analysis of Gain and NF for EDFA with Counter Pumping

EDFA gain and noise figure configuration with counter directional pumping is shown in Fig. 5 and 6 respectively. Pump power varies between 100 mW to 500 mW at low input signal power of −30 dBm.

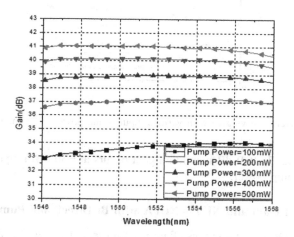

Fig. 5. Wavelength vs gain with different pump power @ counter pumping

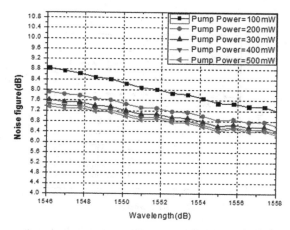

Fig. 6. Wavelength vs noise figure at various pump power @ counter pumping

It is observed from the Fig. 5 that the gain increases as the pump power increases and 41 dB maximum gain is obtained at −30 dBm input signal power with 500 mW pump power.

Figure 6 shows that the noise figure decreases as the pump power increases. 6.2 dB minimum and 8.8 dB maximum noise figure are obtained at −30 dBm input signal power with 500 mW and 100 mW pump power respectively.

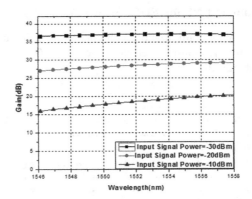

Fig. 7. Wavelength vs gain with various input signal power @ counter pumping

As seen in Fig. 7, 36.9 dB maximum gain occurs at −30 dBm input signal power with 200 mW pump power.

3.3   Analysis of Gain and NF for EDFA with Bi Directional Pumping

Comparison of EDFA gain and noise figure is represented in Fig. 8 and 9 respectively with bi directional pumping. Pump power varies between 100 mW to 500 mW at low input signal power of −30 dBm.

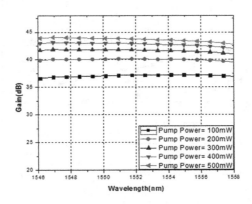

Fig. 8. Wavelength vs gain at various pump power @ bi directional pumping

Figure 8 concluded that the gain increases as the pump power increases and 44 dBdB maximum gain is achieved at −30 dBm input signal power with 500 mW pump power.

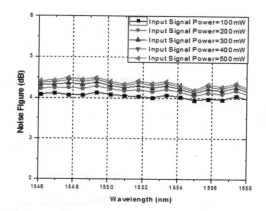

Fig. 9. Wavelength vs noise figure at various pump power @ bi directional pumping

It can be commented from the Fig. 9 that the noise figure is increasing as the pump power increases. 3.9 dB minimum and 4.5 dB maximum noise figure are obtained at −30 dBm input signal power with 100 mW and 500 mW pump power respectively.

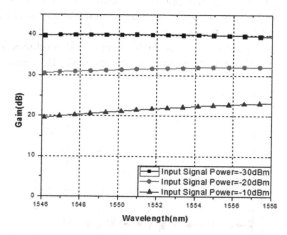

Fig. 10. Wavelength vs gain at various input signal power @ bi directional pumping

It is noted from the Fig. 10 that 40 dB maximum gain is attained at −30 dBm input signal power with 200 mW pump power.

3.4   Analysis of Gain and NF for EDFA with Co, Count and Bi Directional Pumping

Figure 11 and 12 shows comparison of gain and noise figure of three different pumping techniques.

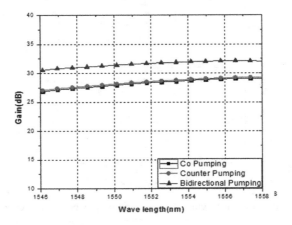

Fig. 11. Wavelength vs gain with different pumping

It is interesting to note that when comparison of gain has been made for co, counter and bi-directional pumping as shown in Fig. 11, the maximum gain of 32 dB at 200 mW pump power and −20 dBm input signal power is obtained with bidirectional pumping. It also represents that the gain of co and counter is almost the same due to the ASE pattern produced by the two pumps.

In the bidirectional pumping, situation is reversed, it produces a different ASE pattern when the gain of the same amount of pump power is compared with co and count pumping.

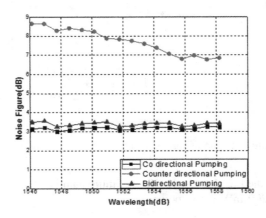

Fig. 12. Wavelength vs noise figure with different pumping

It has been perceived from the Fig. 12, on comparing noise figure for co, counter and bi directional pumping, the maximum noise figure of 8.7 dB at 200 mW pump power and −20 dBm input signal power is obtained with counter pumping.

From the graph of noise figure with different pumping configuration, it can be concluded that the noise figure of counter pumping is higher than other co and bi direction pumping.

Table 1. Summary of work done

Pumping analysis	Co pumping			Counter pumping			Bidirectional pumping		
	−30 dBm	−20 dBm	−10 dBm	−30 dBm	−20 dBm	−10 dBm	−30 dBm	−20 dBm	−10 dBm
Maximum Gain @ 200 mW pump power	36 dB	29.2 dB	20 dB	36.9 dB	29 dB	20 dB	40.1 dB	32 dB	23 dB
Maximum NF @ 200 mW pump power	4 dB	3.2 dB	3.5 dB	7.92 dB	8.65 dB	11.8 dB	4.2 dB	3.2 dB	3.5 dB

Table 1 shows the comparison of co, count and bi-direction pumping at various input signal power with 200 mW pump power. From the Table 1 it can be commented that, as the input signal power is increased, the gain begins to reduces due to the saturation. It also revealed that the noise figure of counter pumping is increased as increases in input signal power while the noise figure of co and bi-directional pumping are decreased as input signal power increases. Out of three pumping schemes, bi-direction pumping provides higher gain.

4 Conclusion

This paper presents, performance of EDFA in terms of pump power and input signal power with co, counter and bi-directional pumping configuration. It concludes that as the input signal power increases, the gain starts to reduces due to saturation. Also the maximum gain of 44 dB is obtained at −30 dBm input signal power and 500 mW pump power under bi-directional pumping. It has been also attended that as the input signal power is increased the noise figure of co and bi directional pumping decreases but for counter pumping it increases. Out of three pumping configurations, bi-direction pumping gives higher gain and co directional pumping has lowest noise figure for particular value of pump power and input signal power.

References

1. Bagga, P., Sarangl, H.: Simulation of 32 × 20 Gb/s WDM and DWDM system at different dispersion. Int. J. Advanced Res. Comput. Commun. Eng. **4**(3), 406–408 (2015)
2. Wasfi, M.: Optical fiber amplifiers-review. Int. J. Commun. Netw. Inf. Secur. **1**(1), 42–47 (2009)
3. Kour, A., Gupta, N.: Gain flattening of erbium doped fiber amplifier a review. Int. J. Sci. Eng. Technol. Res. **5**(12) (2016)
4. Cheng, C., Xiao, M.: Optimization of an erbium-doped fiber amplifier with radial effects. Opt. Commun. **254**(4–6), 215–222 (2005)
5. Mishal Singla, P., Kumar, S.: Comparative analysis of EDFA based 64 channel WDM systems f or different pumping techniques. Int. J. Sci. Eng. Res. **5**(6), 66–69 (2014)
6. Anthony, R., Lahiri, R., Biswas, S.: Gain clamped L-band EDFA with forward-backward pumping scheme using fiber Bragg grating. Optik **125**(11), 2463–2465 (2014)
7. Hamida, B.A., et al.: Flat-gain wide-band erbium doped fiber amplifier by combining two difference doped fibers. J. Eur. Opt. Soc. Rapid Publ. **10**, 15015 (2015)
8. Ismail, M.M., Othman, M.A., Zakaria, Z., Misran, M.H., Said, M.A.M., Sulaiman, H.A., Zainudin, M.N.S., Mutalib, M.A.: EDFA-WDM optical network design system. Procedia Eng. **53**, 294–302 (2013)
9. Dhokar, A., Deshmukh, S.D.: Design and performance analysis of dynamic EDFA. IOSR J. Eng. **5**(7), 23–33 (2015)
10. Amin, M.Z., Qureshi, K.K.: Er + 3-Er + 3; interaction effects and performance evaluation of Erbium Doped Fiber amplifiers. In: 2015 IEEE 28th Canadian Conference on Electrical and Computer Engineering (CCECE), pp. 1383–1386 (2015)
11. Dhokar, A., Deshmukh, S.D.: Overview of EDFA for the efficient performance analysis. IOSR J. Eng. **4**(3), 1–8 (2014)
12. Mahran, O., Aly, M.H.: Performance characteristics of dual-pumped hybrid EDFA/Raman optical amplifier. Appl. Opt. **55**(1), 22–26 (2016)
13. Yamashita, S., Nishihara, M.: L-band erbium-doped fiber amplifier incorporating an inline fiber grating laser. IEEE J. Sel. Top. Quantum Electron. **07**(1), 44–48 (2001)
14. Mishal Singla, P., Kumar, S.: Comparative analysis of EDFA based 32 channels WDM system for bidirectional and counter pumping techniques. Int. J. Emerg. Technol. Comput. Appl. Sci. (IJETCAS) **5**, 66–69 (2014)
15. Honde, V., Mhatr, A.: Performance analysis of WDM network based on EDFA amplifier with different pumping techniques. Int. J. Recent Innov. Trends Comput. Commun. **4**(4), 480–485 (2016)
16. Sivanantha, R., Vigneshwari, S., et al.: Novel high gain and wide band hybrid amplifier designed with combination of an EDFA and a discrete Raman amplifier. J. Opt. Technol. **83**(4), 69–79 (2016)
17. Jain, P., Gupta, N.: Comparative study of all optical amplifiers. Int. J. Sci. Eng. Res. **5**(11), 1522–1526 (2014)
18. http://nptel.ac.in/courses/117101002/26. Accessed 24 July 2017
19. Desurvire, Erbium Doped: Fiber Amplifiers, Principles and Applications. Academic Press, San Diego (1995)
20. Mahran, O., El-Samahy, A.E., Helmy, M.S., Abd El Hai, M.: Optoelectron. Adv. Mater. Rapid Comm. **4**(12), 1994 (2010)
21. Giles, C.R., Desurvire, E.: J. Lightwave Technol. Lett. **9**(2), 147 (1991)
22. Mahran, O.: Opt. Commun. **347**, 31 (2015)

Emerging Threats in Cloud Computing

Arjun Choudhary[1,3](✉) [ID] and Rajesh Bhadada[2]

[1] Department of Computer Science and Engineering,
MBM Engineering College, Jai Narain Vyas University, Jodhpur, India
[2] Department of Electronics and Communication Engineering,
MBM Engineering College, Jai Narain Vyas University, Jodhpur, India
rajesh_bhadada@rediffmail.com
[3] Department of Computer Science and Engineering,
Sardar Patel University of Police, Security and Criminal Justice, Jodhpur, India
a.choudhary@policeuniversity.ac.in

Abstract. In today's world cloud computing is being a new utility and its usage is growing day by day. This advancement in services being delivered is getting densely populated and complexed with some peculiar problems even with this advancement. This paper showcase the issues pertaining to cloud service consumers and the risks, threats identified by variety of international level organizations. This paper has also identified some new research areas which needs to be analyzed and some concrete solution are also discussed which needs to be provided. The material presented in this paper is in a lucid and simplified manner. It also covers the evolution and need of cloud computing technology to the current era.

Keywords: Cloud computing · Virtualization · Data security · Data localization

1 Introduction

In today's era, the information is the actual gold which can be useful to anyone having control of this information. Keeping this information from the *Infomongers*, has been getting difficult, as the ways through which information is being stolen are quite innovative and beyond imaginations to the security providers. Stuxnet malware [1, 2] has been a classical case study in this category. Probably this may be the reason due to which, still various organizations, even government organizations have been avoiding the adoption of Cloud Computing. Cloud Computing is viewed as utility just like gas, electricity, water etc., as initially mentioned by R. Buyya et al. [3]. Today, cloud has become a reality and an absolute necessity. Cloud computing is now a mainstream technology utilized by around 94% [4] of the total MNC (Multi National Companies) to efficiently increase the productivity as well provide the ease to the customers and employees. Almost half of the government organizations [8] are now coming over to utilize the cloud computing technology.

Cloud Computing as technology innovation is being adopted at every industry sector, due to fact that this technology is enabling them to reduce their capital investment and enabling them to look over other issues. Since the inception of Cloud

S. Gupta and J. N. Sarvaiya (Eds.): ET2ECN 2020, CCIS 1214, pp. 147–156, 2020.
https://doi.org/10.1007/978-981-15-7219-7_13

Computing in Gartner Hype Cycle in year 2008 [4], it has reached to new heights and currently more than 84% enterprises have multi-cloud strategy [4]. Due to this increasingly intake of cloud technology, the attacks are also looming and we can perceive that any technology which is claimed to be useful and being adopted by every enterprise will be primary target of the attackers. A classic example of using a single cloud environment was seen in US Department of Defense (DOD) JEDI project where Microsoft Azure was awarded $10Bn contract for next ten years, starting from 2019 [5]. This happened due to the fact that DOD does not want to have any issue with multi cloud strategy, as they will lose their secrecy and privacy by doing so, as claimed by media reports.

2 Cloud Security Current Issues Perceived by Cyber Security Agencies

In this research paper, we have found and discussed various cloud security issues from higher level to the granular level. Initially we have quantified all the security issues described by National Institute of Standards and Technology (NIST), CSA (Cloud Security Alliance) and ENISA (European Union Agency for Cybersecurity) Agencies in this section.

2.1 NIST Cloud Security Standards and Concerns

Multi-tenancy being the virtue of the optimal utilization of cloud computing is also an advantage for the evil doers, as misconfigured virtual machines, Application Programming Interface (API) designed for a service integration being not properly aligned with security measures required to keep service and its parameters abstract are some of the issues mentioned in this report.

In November, 2018 NIST published draft report of Trusted Cloud: Security practice guide for VMware Hybrid Cloud Infrastructure as a Service Environments [6] which in turn provided inputs to the NIST Cybersecurity framework. In this report, agency has shown major concerns over protection of information categorically and its consistent compliance and legal remedial requirements.

2.2 CSA Concerns Towards Cloud Security and Privacy

If we compare list of threats by CSA published during 2013 and 2019 in Table 1, then we can identify that there is a huge change among the threats in terms of the retaining the older one in the newest threat list. This omission is due to the fact that the traditional security issues, no more being considered under the responsibility of cloud service providers. Instead, newly added threats are more refined depicting the maturity level of consumers towards cloud.

2.3   ENISA Security Concern Towards Cloud Computing

In 2009, first time ENISA published a report cloud security risk assessment [7] which described the advantages security risk in cloud environment. This report also provided some criteria, to calculate the risk associated with adoption of cloud technology. Till the date there have been many research documents specifically been published by this organization related to cloud security area.

Table 1. Cloud computing top threats mentioned by Cloud Security Alliance [9–11].

The notorious nine [2013]	The treacherous 12 [2016]	The egregious eleven [2019]
• Data Breaches	• Data Breaches	• Data Breaches
• Data Loss	• Weak Identity, Credential and Access Management	• Misconfiguration and Inadequate Change Control
• Account or Service Traffic Hijacking	• Insecure APIs	• Lack of Cloud Security Architecture and Strategy
• Insecure Interfaces and APIs	• System and Application Vulnerabilities	• Insufficient Identity, Credential, Access and Key Management
• Denial of Service	• Account Hijacking	• Account Hijacking
• Malicious Insiders	• Malicious Insiders	• Insider Threat
• Abuse of Cloud Services	• Advanced Persistent Threats (APTs)	• Insecure Interfaces and APIs
• Insufficient Due Diligence	• Data Loss	• Weak Control Plane
• Shared Technology Vulnerabilities	• Insufficient Due Diligence	• Metastructure and Applistructure Failures
	• Abuse and Nefarious Use of Cloud Services	• Limited Cloud Usage Visibility
	• Denial of Service	• Abuse and Nefarious Use of Cloud Services
	• Shared Technology Issues	

3   Common Security Concerns by Cloud Consumer

In Sect. 2, we already had mentioned and discussed about the Cloud computing security issues. The main issue arises when we are dealing with a peculiar type of cloud i.e. it always depends on the cloud deployment type through which we can identify the security concerns. If we take the case of public cloud, only then the security and privacy concerns are always high for user side and the responsibility over the shoulders of CSP is more than the private or hybrid cloud. As, the sheer property of publicness/openness in cloud environment make it more vulnerable than the other non-disclosing or abstract cloud environments.

To access a threat we need to understand the attack vectors. Attack vectors are those entities through which the vulnerabilities are exploited and become threats for the environment. In cloud environment major attack vectors are *virtual machine, network layer, application layer, hypervisor, application program interface and legal & compliance unit/modules.*

3.1 Cloud Security Concepts

To understand the security concept of specifically cloud computing environment we need to understand the key aspects of cloud which are multi-tenancy, virtualization, federated services, service level agreement.

Multi-tenancy
Tenancy issue in cloud leads towards a safety hazard, the duty to verify the intentions of a user (be it a good or evil doer) in this multi-tenant system is quite difficult. Till the time CSP understands with the user behavior, attack could have already been done and exploited.

Through this variety of attacks like side channel attacks as discussed by Zhang et al. [12] in his paper where a new technique is being designed and implemented to detect real time side channel attacks.

Virtualization
Virtualization has been utilized as one of the conceptual aspects in Cloud computing technology. Based on customer requirement machine in a virtual environment will be ready to launch in no extra time.

The variety of major attacks in Virtual machines (VM) are:

1. VM Migration: During movement of VM from one physical server to another one, there are two kind of cases come across. Typical one is live migration when the VM is in running state and due to a certain reason like Energy Optimization algorithm directed to move this VM from Physical server PS_1 to Physical Server PS_k as discussed by Kapil et al. [13].
2. VM Escape: An attack performed through a native VM to a Virtual Machine Manager (VMM) and through this the attacker gains VMM and underlying host operating system [17]. If attacker is successful then he/she can monitor other VMs, shared resources. Attacker may also shut down or can take over all the VMs. Most notorious VM escape attacks are SubVirt [16], Bluepill [17] and Vitriol [18]. To mitigate the risks posed by the attacks mentioned above, cloud admin must prefer deployment option with the strong isolation, all the library calls and access must be checked and logged properly [15].
3. VM Hopping: This attack was previously very common in virtualization where an attacker attempts to acquire another VMs in the same hypervisor based on one VM gain [14].

Although there are many more attacks strategy being run over by attackers regularly few of them are VM rollback [19], VM Sprawl [20], VM Poaching [21], VM DoS attacks, VM cloning. Other than above discussed attacks there are attacks which fall in the category of legacy system related attacks but some of them are still applicable over the cloud environment like Malware, Ransomware, Virus, Trojan Horse, etc.

For the attacks mentioned cloud providers must utilize the principle of least privilege and defense in depth strategy [15].

3.2   Common Cloud Security Threats

Data Level Security Issues

Data is the backbone of any business today across the world, most of the attacks being performed and targeted over data theft only. Data level security can be divided into two main categories i.e. Data in Transit and Data at Rest. Few of the data security issues have been discussed over here.

1. Data at Rest
   a. Data Encryption: In coming years, data producing rate has been manifolds and different type of data encryption is needed as per the size and type of data. For example Block Level Data, AES or DES encryption mechanism will be better, for authentication RSA or ECC encryption mechanism may be implemented based on severity of the data. In 2020, we are talking about the post quantum cryptography era [22], this means that the current level of encryption will become obsolete as soon as Quantum computers are commercialized.
   b. Data Location: As data location is not known to the user, it is imperative that User is not able to identify its data location exactly which in turn provides insecurity to the user. As well there are laws and very variety of the countries which states that the data should be stored locally and should be in proper legal compliances held by that nation.
2. Data in Transit: The data in transition is important from the perspective of receiving user which be an individual or a cloud service provider. As services also interact with each other with the help of data. The communication takes place the help of secure authentication done by Transport Layer Security.
   a. Data Lineage: Data lineage is related with the origin of the data from where it first originated and moved over a time period. It is quite helpful during the editing part and one of the most challenging and arduous issue involving the tracing due to the dynamic nature of cloud environment in cyber forensics.
   b. Data Leakage: Once the data is being utilized by multitenant users the data leakage issue arises and we never know when there is a leakage of the data as the data has not been modified, has not been destroyed. It has only been copied or created a new replica of the same data. The data leakage issue is quite severe and untraceable most of times.

To avoid these kind of situations, cloud providers must schedule Security Audits like ISO 27001 ISMS each trimester or by half year by their internal auditors and once a year by external auditors. This in turn will ensure that the organization is serious towards the security and in this way will try to get the vulnerabilities in the existing system procedure. Organizations may also opt for Red and Blue team internal/external competitions or bug bounty competitions (Fig. 1).

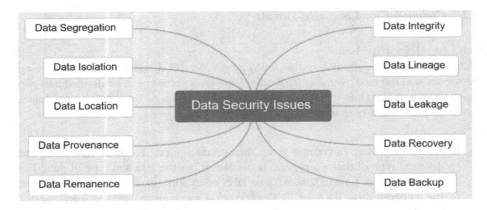

Fig. 1. Data security issues.

Application Level Security Issue

Application layer is one of most busy and targeted layer at which all the applications interact with the end user.

3. Authentication and Authorization of Cloud Users: Authentication is the process of verifying the user whether he/she is the rightful owner of the service or not. For this, variety of authentication services are being implemented in cloud environment with the help of Identity and Access Management module. Some of the services are Active Directory (AD), Lightweight Directory Access Protocol (LDAP), Kerberos, Token management, Session management, Identity Providers etc. As well services are also being authenticated with the help of a API tokens. Multifactor authentication is also being utilized for identity and access management.

To avoid the risks posed during authentication process, secure and sanitized APIs need to be used along with currently standardized TLS and JSON security standards should be used while doing authentication or any communications.

4. Secure development of Cloud Application: With the exponential growth of digital platforms in complex manner its getting difficult to manage, develop, test and secure the service. Erstwhile used Software Development Lifecycle (SDLC) which was the base of modern software, can never be the base of cloud based application development due to the sheer nature of the application being accessed and provided to a large base.

Security and privacy has become a new norm and needs to be implemented with utmost care and diligence. Due to which, a newly adapted SDLC is being offered and popularly used by cloud application developers which usually checks and verify the validity of the offered service using risk centric approach for development and maintenance of applications and systems [24–26]. This includes mainly static and dynamic code analysis with proper input validation and error/exception handling. This mainly concentrates over the issue of security being the guiding principle during application development at each stage and due to the peculiar characteristics of cloud computing the usual SDLC cannot be followed.

4 Research Challenges in Cloud Computing

Research in any field paves a way to upgrade the requirements of next generations technological advancements. Cloud Computing is very much adopted technology in all over the world, but still it is in development stage and needs research to be done in this field. We have identified some of the issues pertaining to the research in cloud computing area, which need to be fully addressed, while new challenges keep on emerging as this technology reaches to the maturity.

4.1 Audit Trail

Cloud Computing environment is such a complex platform where if an auditor is trying to find certain case related evidence then due to the sheer nature of scalability, it is quite difficult that auditor is able to identify the motive and path of crime. In current times also there have been evidence in which CSP running their infrastructures, in those nations, where law always allow them to avoid with all the complexity and requirements of keeping logs of everything as proof. These nations have been proven heaven for the attackers.

Due to this reason, there is an urgent requirement of a universal standardized Audit platform which provides interoperability, universally tried and tested Audit tools.

4.2 Cloud Forensics

Tools and techniques for digital forensics in mobile phones and other earlier digital systems like PC, Servers, etc. have been streamlined and the software needed to run the forensic examination are coming to a saturation stage. Only after any upgradations or any new zero day vulnerability emerges, forensics tools need to be updated. Cloud computing being current era innovative technology, needs to yet develop and streamline the standard operating procedure for its forensic examination [23]. This is also due to the very fact that there is no International committee or task force, yet acclaimed and supported by each CSP group across the world for making international standards for cloud computing and its related services.

4.3 Legal and Compliance

"Cloud Technology is not having any bar or restriction to not to provide their service in a specific part of the world". This statement made by many in 2009 would have probably influenced and asserted many enterprises. But, in today's scenario after the implementation of laws like General Data Protection Regulation (GDPR) by European Union (EU) [27] it has been a mandate with most of the countries that the data obtained or created by a nation's citizen, then it should be localized locally instead of any overseas country which further can utilize the value of data. This also creates a lot of problems including Data Jurisdiction, Extradition treaty and many more to name them. Data localization has been in the past five years the most hot topics if we say in context with cloud computing technology.

In India, recently **RBI**, equivalent of Federal Reserve in US has ordered to *VISA* and *MasterCard* enterprises to store all Indian citizens data and transaction in India for supervision purpose, as mentioned in the order [28]. Due to very fact that this data should be coming under the law of Indian Government. It will also help Indian government to access data and conduct investigations/research as and when needed. If we will see to the time consumed to receive any response of any Law Enforcement Agency to acquire any information related to any incident which involve a cloud firm, then it will reach to more than one month time, which in turn will slow the pace of an investigation as well dilute the severity of the act.

4.4 Open Source Issues in Cloud Computing Environment

The use of open source software on the cloud platform is increasing day by day. The major obstacle for the enterprises to adopt the cloud platform is the vendor lock-in. The vendor lock-in arises due to use of closed source software, data formats and protocols. The open source software make available the source code and freedom to modify the original code as per the needs of the user. These opensource projects have support of development community having self-motivated and creative persons.

The open source projects on cloud offer various advantages and disadvantages as explained below:-

1. Modularity: The modular approach of the application lets you customize, rearrange or change the modules as per your needs. It also offers the ability to start from the scratch or rollback.
2. Security: The open source software are developed by experts of the domain and further tested and scrutinized by a large community members working on the same field. This makes the discovery and fixing of bugs easier and fast in open source software.
3. Resource efficiency: Due to modular nature of the open source software, all the component of the software are not required to be installed as against the case in closed source software. This avoids unnecessary use of compute resources.
4. Technical Know-How: The unique selling proposition of the open source software is the customization. To implement these customizations, the user need to have technical know-how of the field.

5 Conclusion

In this paper we have provided a novel and different insights into the current issues of the cloud computing technology and concerns shared by different security organizations across the world. Currently if we see and compare the security requirements from the native computing devices, cloud computing does require quite different approaches and thus the attacks also vary. In this research paper we tried to showcase concerns of a cloud consumer related to security, other than the regular ones. Cloud computing being the most utilized technology by variety of enterprises not only in the IT sectors, but also in other sectors. There are problems in cloud computing environment which make difficult for researchers in current time, these are being discussed with possible solutions as well. In the end multiple directions for further research improvements in private, public, or in new federated cloud computing environments.

References

1. Langner, R.: Stuxnet: dissecting a cyberwarfare weapon. IEEE Secur. Privacy **9**(3), 49–51 (2011)
2. Falliere, N., Murchu, L.O., Chien, E.: W32. Stuxnet dossier. White Paper Symantec Corp. Secur. Response **5**(6), 29 (2011)
3. Buyya, R., Yeo, C.S., Venugopal, S., Broberg, J., Brandic, I.: Cloud computing and emerging IT platforms: vision, hype, and reality for delivering computing as the 5th utility. Future Gener. Comput. Syst. **25**, 17 (2009)
4. RightScale 2019 State of the Cloud Report, January 2019. https://info.flexera.com/SLO-CM-WP-Gartner-Magic-Quadrant-Cloud-Management-Platform-2019. Accessed 10 Nov 2019
5. U.S. Department of Defense: Contracts for 25 October 2019. https://www.defense.gov/Newsroom/Contracts/Contract/Article/1999639/. Accessed 4 Nov 2019
6. Bartock, M., et al.: Trusted Cloud: Security Practice Guide for VMware Hybrid Cloud Infrastructure as a Service (IaaS) Environments (No. NIST Special Publication (SP) 1800-19 (Draft)). National Institute of Standards and Technology (2018)
7. Catteddu, D., Hogben, G.: ENISA Cloud Computing Risk Assessment. ENISA (2009)
8. Understanding Cloud Adoption in Government, 11 April 2018. https://www.gartner.com/smarterwithgartner/understanding-cloud-adoption-in-government/. Accessed 10 Nov 2019
9. Los, R., Shackleford, D., Sullivan, B.: The notorious nine cloud computing top threats in 2013. Cloud Security Alliance (2013)
10. Top Threats Working Group: The treacherous 12: cloud computing top threats in 2016. Cloud Security Alliance (2016)
11. Top threats to cloud computing the egregious 11, Cloud Security Alliance (2019)
12. Zhang, T., Zhang, Y., Lee, R.B.: CloudRadar: a real-time side-channel attack detection system in clouds. In: Monrose, F., Dacier, M., Blanc, G., Garcia-Alfaro, J. (eds.) RAID 2016. LNCS, vol. 9854, pp. 118–140. Springer, Cham (2016). https://doi.org/10.1007/978-3-319-45719-2_6
13. Kapil, D., Pilli, E.S., Joshi, R.C.: Live virtual machine migration techniques: survey and research challenges. In: 2013 3rd IEEE International Advance Computing Conference (IACC), pp. 963–969. IEEE, February 2013
14. Inci, M.S., Gülmezoglu, B., Apecechea, G.I., Eisenbarth, T., Sunar, B.: Seriously, get off my cloud! Cross-VM RSA Key Recovery in a Public Cloud. IACR Cryptology ePrint Archive, 2015(1-15) (2015)
15. Otterstad, C., Yarygina, T.: Low-level exploitation mitigation by diverse microservices. In: De Paoli, F., Schulte, S., Broch Johnsen, E. (eds.) ESOCC 2017. LNCS, vol. 10465, pp. 49–56. Springer, Cham (2017). https://doi.org/10.1007/978-3-319-67262-5_4
16. King, S., Chen, P.: SubVirt: implementing malware with virtual machines. In: IEEE Symposium on Security and Privacy, Washington, DC, USA, pp. 314–327. IEEE Computer Society (2006)

17. Shoaib, Y., Das, O.: Pouring cloud virtualization security inside out. arXiv preprint arXiv: 1411.3771 (2014)
18. Zovi, D.D.: Hardware Virtualization Rootkits, Black Hat USA 2006 Briefing & Trainings (Presentation), 29 July–3 August 2006. Accessed 14 Mar 2013
19. Xia, Y., Liu, Y., Chen, H., Zang, B.: Defending against vm rollback attack. In: IEEE/IFIP International Conference on Dependable Systems and Networks Workshops (DSN 2012), pp. 1–5. IEEE, June 2012
20. Krishna, E.P., Sandhya, E., Karthik, M.G.: Managing DDoS attacks on virtual machines by segregated policy management. Glob. J. Comput. Sci. Technol. (2014)
21. Subramanian, N., Jeyaraj, A.: Recent security challenges in cloud computing. Comput. Electr. Eng. **71**, 28–42 (2018)
22. Chen, L., et al.: Report on post-quantum cryptography. US Department of Commerce, National Institute of Standards and Technology (2016)
23. Joshi, R.C., Pilli, E.S.: Cloud forensics. In: Fundamentals of network Forensics. CCN, pp. 187–202. Springer, London (2016). https://doi.org/10.1007/978-1-4471-7299-4_10
24. Muni Sekhar, V., Gopal Rao, K.V., Rao, N.S.: Convention cloud application development: SOA. Int. J. Adv. Comput. **3**(3), 108–112 (2011)
25. Vijayakumar, K., Arun, C.: Continuous security assessment of cloud based applications using distributed hashing algorithm in SDLC. Cluster Comput. 1–12 (2017)
26. Sadler, H.: ER 2 C SDMLC: enterprise release risk-centric systems development and maintenance life cycle. Softw. Qual. J. 1–33 (2019)
27. Protection Regulation: General data protection regulation (GDPR) (2018)
28. Reserve Bank of India (RBI): Directive on storage of payment system data (2018). https://rbidocs.rbi.org.in/rdocs/notification/PDFs/153PAYMENTEC233862ECC4424893C558DB-75B3E2BC.PDF. Accessed 9 Nov 2019

Reduction in Complexity of Anti-jamming with Interference Approximation and Classification Algorithm

Sheetal M. Ruparelia[✉] and Priyanka L. Lineswala

Department of Electronics and Communication, CKPCET, Surat, India
sheetal.ruparelia@ckpcet.ac.in, rup.sheetal@gmail.com

Abstract. Interference Approximation and Classification (IAC) is a modified frequency estimation technique for narrowband interference. Improvement in the performance of an anti-jamming with ICA is presented especially for GPS L1 and NavIC L5 band under Continuous Wave (CW) and chirp jamming scenario. IAC is implemented by dual approximation of interference in which frequency and sweep period are calculated using the Adaptive Line Enhancer (ALE) and Low Pass Differentiator (LPD). However, a Pattern Enhancement Technique (PET) is used to classify interference. After classification, only the chirp type jamming signal is further refined by the Kalman filter. As Kalman filter is activated only for chirp, the execution time and so complexity is reduced. The advantage of such an algorithm is to effectively classify the interference, and remove it by adjusting the optimal width of the notch filter.

Keywords: GPS · NavIC · Jammer · Notch filter · Kalman filter

1 Introduction

The market for navigation receivers has huge potential and is growing exponentially with increasing demand for a wide variety of navigation applications [1]. The requirement is ever growing so the threat. The receiver design should consider the safety features like anti-spoofing and anti-jamming margins, which are the need of the day.

The prime objective of this work is to provide a powerful signal processing algorithm which can act as an anti-jamming in Global Navigation Satellite System (GNSS) receivers. Here, proposed anti-jamming algorithm with Interference Approximation and Classification (IAC) performs detection of interference, estimation of interference frequency and mitigation. The IAC algorithm is performed by dual frequency estimation, sweep period estimation and identification of interference with reduced complexity. In this paper, Global Positioning System (GPS) L1 and Navigation through Indian Constellation (NavIC) L5 band with Continuous Wave (CW) as well as chirp jamming signals are considered to implement the proposed algorithm.

In prior work of [2], the GNSS interference (jamming) frequency is estimated by using the properties of the trigonometric functions. These values contain some errors caused by noise measurement and interference-related frequency changes. Again, both

S. Gupta and J. N. Sarvaiya (Eds.): ET2ECN 2020, CCIS 1214, pp. 157–169, 2020.
https://doi.org/10.1007/978-981-15-7219-7_14

the CW and chirp jamming signal are processed by Kalman filter which makes the design of algorithm quite complex.

In the proposed algorithm, the Adaptive Line Enhancer (ALE) is used to provide better first stage frequency approximation of the interference. The ALE as the prior frequency estimator is already being proposed in the literature like [3–5] for CW interference. But, the chirp interference requires proper estimation of the sweep period along with its frequency. So, here Low Pass Differentiator (LPD) and Pattern Enhancement Technique (PET) is used for secondary estimation. The results of estimation are again refined by Kalman filter which gives accurate parameters for chirp jamming and then mitigated by adaptive notch filtering. Whereas, the CW jamming directly mitigated by adaptive notch filtering reduces the complexity in signal processing.

The rest of this paper is organized as follows. The GNSS signal model and the interference model are briefed in Sect. 2 with the implementation steps of the IAC algorithm. Section 3 includes the resultant analysis of the proposed algorithm with two different scenarios: the proposed algorithm on GPS L1 band signal and NavIC L5 band signal. Finally, the last part summarizes the work.

2   System Model

Generally, the received navigation signal from the satellite is first pre-amplified, filtered and down-converted to Intermediate Frequency (IF). Detection of interference is the first step of the mitigation process. The presence of interference in the receiver can be identified by two methods: Automatic Gain Control (AGC) monitoring; Variation in Carrier to Noise Density Ratio (C/N$_0$) [6]. The Analog to Digital Conversion (ADC) produces streams of digitized signal samples that are further used for Position, Velocity and Time (PVT) calculations by baseband processing [7]. Here, the proposed IAC algorithm is applied at digital IF (highlighted) stage of the receiver as shown in Fig. 1.

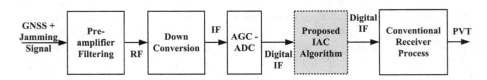

Fig. 1. Conceptual receiver architecture for proposed algorithm

2.1   GNSS Signal and Interference Models

The MATLAB based GPS L1 signal and interference model is used to produce an IF signal. The received GPS L1 signal in the existence of interference [15] can be modelled as

$$r_n = \sqrt{2P}D_{n-\tau}C_{n-\tau}\cos(2\pi(f_{IF}+f_d)n+\theta)+v_n+i_n \tag{1}$$

Where, P denotes the IF signal power, D_n represents the navigation data, C_n is the Coarse/Acquisition (C/A) code used, f_{IF} denotes the IF, f_d denotes the Doppler frequency shift, v_n represents the noise, i_n is the interference, τ is the code phase of the received signal and θ is the phase. Also $n = t/f_s$, where, t is the time instant and f_s is the sampling frequency. The chirp-type GNSS interference used here is shown as per [2],

$$i_{chirp,n} = \sqrt{2P_i}\cos(2\pi S_{tn}n + \varphi_i)$$ (2)

Where, P_i is the power of interference signal and φ_i represents the initial phase. S_{tn} is expressed as

$$S_{tn} = f_0 + \frac{\Delta f}{2}n$$ (3)

f_0 is the initial frequency and the Δf is expressed to indicate the deviation in the digital frequency. Moreover, n varies inside the margin T, which is the sweep period of the chirp-type interference.

The single-tone CW jamming is exhibited as:

$$i_{CW} = \sqrt{2P_i}\cos(2\pi f_i n + \varphi_i)$$ (4)

Where, f_i is the interference frequency.

2.2 Design Flow of Proposed IAC Algorithm

Anti-jamming using jammer characterization and cancellation is a standard mitigation method. Here, the jammer is characterized using ALE, LPD and PET stage. As it is very obvious that the chirp interference needs proper estimation of frequency and sweep period for characterization, whereas CW interference can be directly mitigated by notch filtering once its frequency is identified. Hence, at the LPD and PET stage interference are classified and diverted to own ways towards the mitigation as shown in Fig. 2. As the Kalman filter has to be activated only for the chirp type interference, the operation time and so complexity can be minimized. The design of the proposed algorithm with actual process flow is shown in Fig. 2.

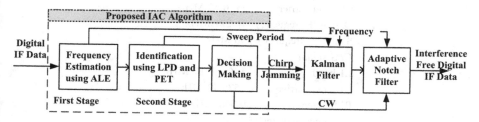

Fig. 2. Process flow of jamming mitigation with proposed IAC algorithm

The processing steps are as follow:

- The amendment proposed in this work is to estimate the preliminary frequency of interference using ALE rather than frequency calculation using trigonometric functions as per [2]. The output of ALE for chirp interference and for CW interference is given to LPD stage.
- Then, the measurement passing through the LPD is enhanced by PET and provides a better sweep period estimation. This helps to classify the type of interference for the decision stage.
- If the classification logic generates a pulsed signal at certain fixed interval which reveals the existence of chirp interference and will be further refined by the Kalman filter. Otherwise, directly applied to notch filter for mitigation operation.
- The role of the Kalman filter is to give a proper estimation of frequency and sweep period. These parameters help to set the width of the notch and accordingly they are mitigated by the adaptive notch filter.
- As Kalman filter is the best-suited estimator for chirp type interference, the signal which is CW interfered need not go through it which reduces the extra burden in the signal processing unit of the receiver and so computational complexity is reduced.

3   Results Analysis

The effectiveness of an algorithm is being tested on NavIC receiver provided by SAC, ISRO, Ahmedabad. Some of the features of this receiver are as per [8] and listed in Table 1. The receiver provides real IF samples at the output of the front end, which is required to apply the proposed algorithm. To create interfered environment, the antenna of the receiver was targeted using CW and chirp signals as per [9, 10].

Table 1. Parameter consideration for navigation signals

Parameter	Value
NavIC signal	
L5-band	1164.45–1188.45 MHz
L5-band carrier	1176.45 MHz
Digital IF frequency	16.221 MHz
Sampling frequency	56 MHz
GPS signal	
L1-band	1563–1587 MHz
L1-band carrier	1575.42 MHz
IF frequency	9.548 MHz
Sampling frequency	38.192 MHz

The IF data of both GPS and NavIC signals are considered in the analysis of results and analyzed at each stage of jamming mitigation described in Sect. 2. The parameter considered for the navigation signals and implementations is shown in Table 1. The original signals of NavIC and GPS are interfered either by CW or by chirp jamming so that the Power Spectral Density (PSD) of the signal gets changed as shown in Fig. 3 and Fig. 4, respectively.

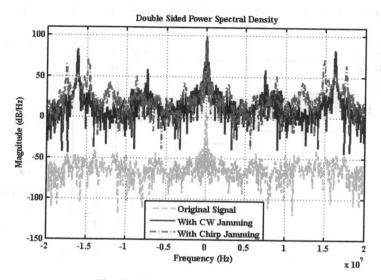

Fig. 3. PSD analysis of NavIC signal

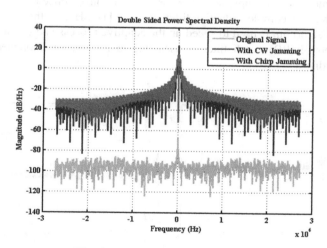

Fig. 4. PSD analysis of GPS signal

3.1 Analysis at ALE Stage

To estimate the frequency of interference, an old but very effective method called ALE is used. ALE is an adaptive self-tuning filter capable of separating the narrowband and broadband (noise) signals [2–5]. The ALE becomes an interesting application in noise reduction because of its simplicity and ease of implementation. Figure 5 shows the block diagram of ALE used for first stage approximation. It is comprising of a particular sensor and delay Δ to yield a delayed form of $d(n)$ denoted by $x(n)$ which correlates the target signal component while leaving the noise uncorrelated.

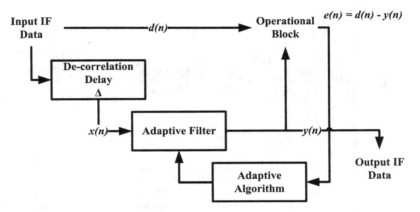

Fig. 5. Block diagram of adaptive line enhancer [11]

On the other hand, to achieve the best performance w.r.t. computational process, the optimum method is to implement ALE on a better convergence rate of an adaptive algorithm with a less complex adaptive filter structure [11]. Hence, the Recursive Least Square (RLS) algorithm is used to speed up the adaptive process and the lattice Infinite Impulse Response (IIR) notch filter is used due to its ease of implementation and straightforwardness.

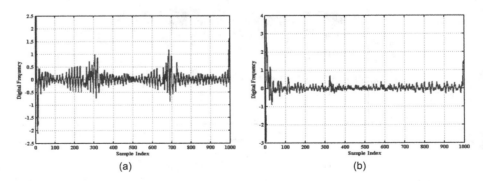

Fig. 6. Frequency measurement by ALE for the NavIC signal with (a) chirp jamming and (b) CW jamming

For implementing this algorithm, 1000 real IF samples are taken for observation of which initial 50 samples are ignored due to settling time. The preliminary frequency estimation obtained for NavIC with a chirp and CW interference is quite justifiable and shown in Fig. 6(a) and Fig. 6(b) respectively. In Fig. 6(a) the frequency gets changed for each sample index, not in a linear manner, but still provides frequency variation at a certain sweep period of chirp jamming. Whereas, in Fig. 6(b) as expected for CW jamming, the frequency remains almost constant.

3.2   Analysis at LPD and PET Stage

In order to eliminate the effect of interference effectively, it is necessary to classify the types of interference. In general, the single-tone CW jamming has a stationary or single frequency. Whereas, in chirp-type interference, frequency changes periodically in a sweep [12]. Thus, appropriate estimations of the jammer's initial frequency, the sweep rate and the sweep period of the chirp signal are very essential to identify the type of interference. The implementation parameter for the LPD and PET are as described in Table 2.

Table 2. Classification logic parameters

Parameters	Values
NavIC system	
β_{en}	5
f_{max}/f_s	0.285
f_{min}/f_s	0.1832
GPS system	
β_{en}	9
f_{max}/f_s	1.334
f_{min}/f_s	1.245

The signal measurement changes intensely at the end of the sweep period and the alteration of frequency is converted by differentiator into a peak. The filter has quite easy structure for improving the tracking speed of the filter. A chirp signal has a peak at the starting of the sweep period, and the interference frequency changes drastically. The sweep period can be estimated once, the time index at the peak is measured. The peak does not exist in case of the single-tone CW jamming because there is no frequency change and so it is possible to differentiate among the two types. However, the peak of LPD output (Z_{Gn}) cannot be easily predictable by a certain threshold as Z_{Gn} has a significant amount of noise due to the error in measurement. So, a pattern enhancement algorithm [13–15] is used to identify the peak effectively by reducing the noise effect. The complete algorithm works as follows:

LPD and PET Algorithm

```
Set Forgetting Factor   γ = 0.9
For   i = 1:N
Compute Normalization Factor from logic parameters:
```
$$\lambda_z = \beta_{en} \times [(f_{max} - f_{min}) \div f_s]$$
```
Compute Normalized Z_Gn by:
```

$$Z_{Gn} = \gamma \, Z_{G(n-1)} - (1 - \gamma)\left(\frac{Z_n - Z_{n-6}}{\lambda_z}\right)$$

```
Compute Enhancement Pattern Z_AR:
```
$$Z_{AR} = E_n^T r_n \quad ; r_n = \text{AR co-efficient}, E_n^T = \text{transpose of } Z_{Gn}$$
```
end for
```

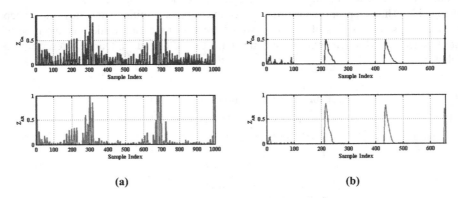

(a)   (b)

Fig. 7. LPD and PET stage results for chirp jamming (a) NavIC signal (b) GPS signal

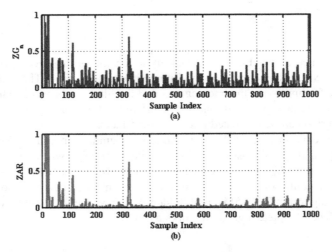

Fig. 8. Results for NavIC with CW jamming (a) normalized LPD output (b) enhanced pattern at PET stage

Here, the results obtained are as expected and shown in Fig. 7 and Fig. 8 when measured from ALE passes through the LPD and PET for chirp and CW interference respectively.

3.3   Analysis of the Decision Making Stage

The proposed IAC algorithm is based on the exclusive pattern of Z_{Gn}. As stated previously, peaks of Z_{Gn} is produced only if chirp interference is received. The type of interference is decided according to the characteristic of Z_{AR}, which is an enhanced value of Z_{Gn}. The results obtained in Fig. 9 and Fig. 10 from classification logic, can clearly show the chirp and CW interferences are classified. The algorithm to generate the decision is as follows:

Decision-Making Algorithm

```
Get (Z_AR)
Calculate Threshold (T_H) by:
```
$$T_H = \gamma \times [(f_{max} - f_{min}) \div f_s]$$
```
for i = 1:N
if (Z_AR ≥ T_H)
     S_Pn = 1
else
     S_Pn = 0
end if
end for
-- Calculate Sweep Period using a difference in two con-
secutive time index.
```

3.4   Analysis of Kalman Filter

If the signal is chirp interfered, identified by the proposed algorithm, it has to pass through the Kalman filter for better estimation of the frequency. Here, the role of the Kalman filter is to estimate or track the frequency of interference of receiving samples [16, 17]. Hence it is important to note that, the initial frequency and the error covariance must be known before processed through Kalman filter. This shows the importance of the proper preliminary frequency estimation which is, proposed in this work.

In the filter design, the state and covariance are initialised at the beginning of the estimated sweep period to improve the tracking performance. These covariance are of two types: process noise covariance (Q); measurement noise covariance (R) and their values are set as $Q = 1 \times 10^{-6}$ and $R = 0.05$. Even in this case, Kalman checks the chirp frequency very well and the results are shown in Fig. 10.

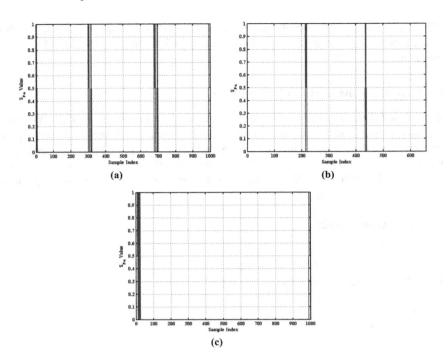

Fig. 9. Decision stage results for (a) NavIC chirp jamming (b) GPS chirp jamming (c) NavIC CW jamming

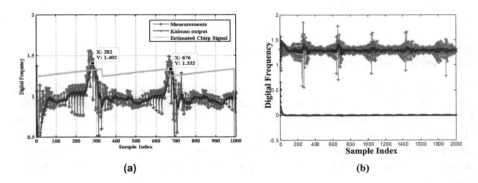

Fig. 10. Interference (chirp jamming) tracking by Kalman filter (a) NavIC signal and (b) GPS signal

In the final step, the notch filter is used in the mitigation process as all the interference spectrum fall under the narrow band. Also, notch filtering has been proven to be an efficient mitigation algorithm for a family of interfering signals, pure sinusoids, which appears as a spike in the spectral domain [18, 19]. The notch filter is now able to place a deep null based on the interference frequency that is properly updated with the results of the Kalman filter.

3.5 Summary

The proposed algorithm is applied on GPS L1 signal and to the NavIC L5 signal. The results obtained from both systems are compared with the results of existing systems as per [2]. Executions of the standard Kalman filter require $O(d^3)$ time and $O(d^2)$ space per time step, where d denotes the measurement of the system state variable [16]. Therefore, many of these calculations will not be performed when CW is received. As a result, the complexity of the system is reduced and becomes more robust and reliable.

The simulation results are shown in Table 3 and Table 4. The true values show the frequency at the sweep period and number of sweep period samples where frequency suddenly reduces. The initial frequency has not been considered as Kalman is unable to reach that frequency. The % Error shows that the estimation of chirp signal is quite good.

Table 3. Results of Kalman estimation of proposed algorithm on GPS L1 signal

Sweep period	Estimation parameter	I	II
True	Frequency	0.286	0.286
	Sweep period samples	150	300
Simulated	Frequency	0.2827	0.2725
	Sweep period samples	153	300
% Error	Frequency	1.1	4.7
	Sweep period samples	2	0

Table 4. Results of Kalman estimation of proposed algorithm on NavIC L5 signal

Sweep period	Estimation parameter	I	II
True	Frequency	1.402	1.332
	Sweep period samples	282	676
Simulated	Frequency	1.333	1.333
	Sweep period samples	330	660
% Error	Frequency	5.17	0.075
	Sweep period samples	15	1.06

4 Conclusion

Finally, we can say that we cannot eliminate intentional and unintentional interference signals, but we must learn to coexist with them. The proposed algorithm in this work clearly illustrates the innovative interference identification and mitigation technique, which considerably improves the GNSS performance in terms of sensitivity and accuracy in a noisy environment. Compared with the existing algorithms, the percentage error found in the case of the proposed algorithm is slightly higher, but the main advantage of the algorithm is that the computational burden of the system is reduced. Various advanced versions of the Kalman filter can be used, such as the Adaptive Fading Kalman filter. In addition, some alternatives can be applied that will not only mitigate interference, but also retrieve interfered GNSS data.

References

1. GNSS Market Report Issue 2, EGSA, European GNSS Agency (2018)
2. Kang, C.H., Kim, S.Y., Park, C.G.: Global navigation satellite system interference tracking and mitigation based on an adaptive fading Kalman filter. IET Radar Sonar Navig. 9(8), 1030–1039 (2015)
3. Cho, N.I., Choi, C.H., Lee, S.U.: Adaptive line enhancement by using an IIR lattice notch filter. IEEE Trans. Acoust. Speech Signal Process. 37(4), 585–589 (1989)
4. Cho, N.I., Lee, S.U.: Tracking analysis of an adaptive lattice notch filter. IEEE Trans. Circuits Syst. II Analog Digit. Sig. Process. 42(3), 186–195 (1995)
5. Choi, J.W., Cho, N.I.: Suppression of narrow-band interference in DS-spread spectrum systems using adaptive IIR notch filter. Sig. Process. 82(12), 2003–2013 (2002)
6. Ruparelia, S., Lineswala, P., Jagiwala, D., Desai, M.V., Shah, S.N. Dalal, U.D.: Study of L5 band interferences on IRNSS. In: Proceedings of International GNSS (GAGAN-IRNSS) User Meet, Bengaluru, pp. 1–10 (2015)
7. Kaplan, E., Hegarty, C.: Understanding GPS: Principles and Applications, 2nd edn. Artech House, Boston (2005)
8. Signal in space ICD for Standard Positioning Services, Version 1.0, ISRO, IRNSS, August 2017
9. Lineswala, P.L., Shah, S.N.: Jamming: the probable menace to NavIC. IET Radar Sonar Navig. 13(6), 1039–1044 (2019)
10. Lineswala, P.L., Shah, S.N.: Performance analysis of different interference detection techniques for navigation with Indian constellation. IET Radar Sonar Navig. (2019). https://doi.org/10.1049/iet-rsn.2019.0091
11. Ramli, R.M., Noor, A.A., Samad, S.A.: A review of adaptive line enhancers for noise cancellation. Aust. J. Basic Appl. Sci. 6(6), 337–352 (2012)
12. Dovis, F.: GNSS Interference Threats and Countermeasures, 1st edn. Artech House, Boston (2015)
13. Oikonomou, V.P., Tzallas, A.T., Fotiadis, D.I.: A Kalman filter based methodology for EEG spike enhancement. Comput. Methods Programs Biomed. 85(2), 101–108 (2007)
14. Arnold, M., Milner, X.H.R., Witte, H., Bauer, R., Braun, C.: Adaptive AR modeling of nonstationary time series by means of Kalman filtering. IEEE Trans. Biomed. Eng. 45(5), 553–562 (1998)
15. Grenier, Y.: Time-dependent ARMA modeling of non-stationary signals. IEEE Trans. Acoust. Speech Signal Process. 31(4), 899–911 (1983)
16. Pnevmatikakis, E.A., Rad, K.R., Huggins, J., Paninski, L.: Fast Kalman filtering and forward–backward smoothing via a low-rank perturbative approach. J. Comput. Graph. Stat. 23(2), 316–339 (2014)
17. Bishop, G., Welch, G.: An introduction to the Kalman filter. In: Proceeding of SIGGRAPH, Course, 8(27599-23175), p. 41 (2001)

18. Borio, D., Camoriano, L., Presti, L.L.: Two-pole and multi-pole notch filters: a computationally effective solution for GNSS interference detection and mitigation. IEEE Syst. J. **2**(1), 38–47 (2008)
19. Varshney, N., Jain, R.C.: An adaptive notch filter for narrow band interference removal. In: 2013 National Conference on Communications (NCC), pp. 1–5. IEEE (2013)

Networking

Effect of EEG Dual-Channel Acquisition and Gender Specification Subjects on the Classification of Sleep Stages Using Machine Learning Techniques

Santosh Kumar Satapathy[1(✉)], D. Loganathan[1], and Anirban Mitra[2]

[1] Pondicherry Engineering College, Puducherry, India
{santosh.satapathy, drloganathan}@pec.edu
[2] Amity University, Kolkata, India
mitra.anirban@gmail.com

Abstract. Nowadays sleep staging is considered one of the major issues in all age groups. Proper sleep scoring of sleep stages can give clinical information for selecting a suitable diagnosing of sleep disorder. Since the manual visual scoring of sleep stage classification is highly time-consuming and it also depends on expert experiences. To overcome this problem automatic sleep stage classification obtained to diagnosis sleep disorder. The main objective of this study is to automatic sleep stage classification on dual channels of EEG signals in gender-specific subjects. This study round up a wide range of research findings concerning sleep stage classification. Here we have combined the NREM and REM stage into one stage, called the sleep stage. Basically here we have proposed two-state classification and practically implemented on public available sleep dataset. In this study, we have considered two channels of EEG signals with different sex subjects. Feature selection and classifiers are assessed the accuracy level of which channel recordings and which classification algorithm is more suitable to discriminating the different sleep stages in subject-gender specific accurately. According to our achieved results from both the gender-specific subjects from dual channels of EEG signal, subject male category with F3-A2 channel and Ensemble classifier are chosen as the best channel and classifier. The mentioned channel and classifier have reached 90.7% accuracy, in the same manner for the female subject category with the C3-A2 channel and LSVM classifier are chosen as the best channel and classifier and have reached 91.5% accuracy levels in discriminating the different stages of sleep. This study shows that gender-specific and channel-specific recordings can be classifying sleep stages with a level accuracy that makes it more suitable for scientific and clinical sleep disorder assessment.

Keywords: Automatic sleep stage classification · EEG · Feature selection

1 Introduction

Sleep is a fundamental biological requirement of human health. Over the past 20 years, there have been increased sleep diseases and its associated diseases in all age groups across the world. As per the data from the National Health Interview survey 2013-14

© Springer Nature Singapore Pte Ltd. 2020
S. Gupta and J. N. Sarvaiya (Eds.): ET2ECN 2020, CCIS 1214, pp. 173–188, 2020.
https://doi.org/10.1007/978-981-15-7219-7_15

and the survey conducted in the United States. Overall it has found that single parents with children under age 18 years were more likely to have shorter sleep duration than adults in two-parent families with children below 18 and adults living without children under age 18 [1]. Accordingly, the National Sleep Foundation report of the year 2014, 45% of Americans affected by low quality sleep and its associated diseases [2]. The Sleep Health Foundation (SHF) 2016 survey in Australia has found that the average sleep time is 7 h but according to survey report, we have observed that 76% who sleep less than 5½ h and also reported that maximum they have day time impairment and other sleep-related symptoms [3]. Sleep is one of the resting states for humans.In this state generally humans are unconscious towards major activities happening in their surrounding environment. Investigation has been conducted to understand the different sleep processes for various purposes. Some sleep disorder causes to threat of like in later part of our life such as obstructive sleep apnea, insomnia and narcolepsy [4]. For that reason, sleep stage classification is taken one of the important steps for deciding the proper diagnosing of sleep diseases [5]. The standard procedure to identify the sleep disorder is analysis the sleep cycle and its sleep quality and for that one of the standard techniques is sleep scoring, this score to be extracted from subjects during sleep from fixed electrodes associated with the brain. This total procedure to be called as sleep test or PSG (polysomnography) test where we have considered multiple channels which include electroencephalogram (EEG), electromyogram (EMG), and electrooculogram (EOG), electrocardiogram (ECG), respiratory signals, blood oxygen saturation, and other measurements. These recordings are generally divided into epochs and as per our proposed study, we have also taken 30 s no overlapping epochs for measuring the different sleep stages. All these recording procedures have to monitored through a set of sleep experts and technicians followed by some standard guidelines based on Rechtschaffen & Kales(R&K rules) manuals and the latest documented sleep rules of the American Academy of Sleep Medicine (AASM). In early 1957, the sleep technicians have observed practically two phases of sleep that have to be identified such as the Non-Rapid Eye Movement (NREM) and the Rapid Eye Movement (REM) [6]. In 1968, R&K has introduced a new sleep manually, with accordingly the NREM stage consisted of four sub sleep stages such as NREM-1(N-1), NREM-2(N-2), NREM-3(N-3), NREM-4(N-4). Since 2007 the American Academy of Sleep Medicine redefined the sleep stages and re-declared new rules in sleep stage classification. Currently, all sleep-related analysis research work followed as per AASM manuals. For the proper diagnosing of sleep stages, the most appropriate signal for sleep is to EEG from PSG [7, 8]. Most of the sleep experts considered that EEG is appropriate for proper sleep scoring because the signals extracted directly from electrodes which have to be fixed on brains. Thus in this study, we have considered the EEG signals and its extracted features for sleep scoring and also we have a deal with 30-s segment epochs for this research work.

In the diagnosis approach of sleep disorder, PSG was used to classify the sleep stages. Sleep stages are cyclically repeated during sleep. The PSG test considered the bio-signals from placed electrodes attached in the brain of patients. The electrodes include a combination of EEG, ECG, EMG, and EOG [9]. Besides here, we have also mentioned the possible different sleep stages in Table 1 but in this study, we have considered the two-state sleep stage classification to detect the sleep disorder.

Table 1. Possible different pattern of six sleep stages

Sleep states	Sleep stages
Six-state	Wake, N-1, N-2, N-3, N4, REM
Five-state	Wake, N-1, N-2, N-3, REM
Four-state	Wake, N-1, [N-2 + N-3], REM
Three-state	Wake, [N-1 + N-2 + N-3], REM
Two-state	Wake, Sleep [N-1 + N-2 + N-3 + REM]

The traditional sleep staging process completely depends on sleep expert's visual interpretations of extracted signals. In this visual interpretation approach, certain disadvantages occurred due to huge bulks of data to monitor and it takes more time to visualize the recorded wave patterns which lead overburden to the clinician and it becomes results in poor accuracy in sleep analysis [10]. In this research work, we have also obtained the automatic sleep stage classification followed by AASM manuals for our experimental work.

This paper is organized as follows: Sect. 2 is described the related work of the proposed method. Section 3 explains about data description. Section 4 described methods obtained for experimental work. Section 5 described the experimental details and related discussion on results of the proposed study. Finally, concluding remarks of this paper in Sect. 6.

2 Related Work

Automatic sleep staging has become one of the emerging technologies in the field of sleep study. Most of the researchers have used these approaches for their novel research work. It was observed that most of the proposed study or contribution in a combination of mathematical theories and machine learning techniques. The maximum work has done regarding sleep stage classification to analyses the sleep disorder effectively. Some of the contributed research focused on different classifier selection for classification in between different sleep its accuracy with different classifications algorithms. Some authors have emphasized different features extracted from preprocessed signals and have observed that which features made more effectively to discriminate between different signal patterns. Some of the contributed papers have also used different datasets for their experimental work. As we have observed the most of the researchers used the physio-net SLEEP-EDF (Expanded) dataset used for sleep stage scoring and some other datasets also have used by certain researchers such as ISRUC-SLEEP and Dream Sleep Apnea datasets.

Z.H. Geand and Y.F. Sun [11] has considered the multiple channels of EEG and extracted the power spectral density features from that multiple channels and those features input in multiple feed-forward neural network classifiers and the system achieved classification accuracies above 90% for different possible sleep criterions. In [8] the authors have considered the SLEEP-EDF datasets for sleep scoring and obtained visibility graph features were extracted from acquired signals and forwarded to a classifier to distinguish between different sleep stages and the classification accuracy has achieved 87%. In [12] the authors considered EEG signal and extracted nonlinear features from the raw signal and adopted iterative filtering mechanisms are obtained for automatic classification in between different sleep stages. Diykh et al. [13] have extracted static features from different sub-segments of the EEG signal and the size of sub-segments is determined empirically. In this study, the authors have considered the K-means classifier for discriminating between different sleep stages. Liang et al. [14] proposed an automatic sleep stage classification in which the author has extracted entropy features from input channel signals and has achieved overall sleep stage classification accuracy are 83.49%. Khalighi, S. et al. proposed an improved automated sleep stage classification based on subject independent method with application in sleep-wake detection and multi-class sleep stage classification. The authors have extracted features from temporal, time and time-frequency domains. The extracted features are validated through a two-step method such as histogram analysis method followed by an automatic feature selector. The selected feature set is classified using SVM classifier. The system achieved a good performance by combining with 6 channels 9 channels of multi-class sleep staging [15]. The authors proposed automatic identification of sleep related disorders by analyzing the EEG signals and here for experimental work the authors have considered two different types of subjects such as one from healthy category and other category from subject who effected with sleep related disorders like bruxism. In this study mainly focused with two classes sleep stage classification. Features extracted by using welch techniques and forwarded through DT classifier for classifying sleep stages and reached overall classification accuracy for C4-P4 and C4-A1 channels were 81.70% and 74.11% [16]. In [17] the authors have proposed an automated sleep stage classification using machine learning techniques based on EEG signal. Here author has compared the classification performances of two conventional classification techniques such as ANN and SVM based on wavelet based features and neighboring component analysis. It has reported that the overall classification accuracy achieved for ANN and SVM were 90.30% and 89.93% respectively. Ebrahimi et al. [18] has considered the physio net dataset and the author has considered NREM-1 and REM as a single-stage due to some similar characteristics found in the wave patterns in both the stages. Here the author also implemented the wavelet concept for segmenting into different sub-bands. They achieved an overall accuracy of 93% in sleep stage classification. Anna Krakovska and Kristına Susmakova [19] have proposed a combination of optimal features for classification of sleep stages and he has obtained quadratic discriminate analysis for sleep scoring and they obtained the overall accuracies of 74%. Sharma et al. [20] has proposed a work on sleep stage classification using single channel of EEG and he has used a wavelet bank and three band time frequency localized for feature extraction from input signal. In this study he has classified the five state sleep stage classifications. He has reached overall classification accuracies of 91.5–93% in order to classification among different sleep stages.

3   Data Description

In this study, we have considered the ISRUC-Sleep Subgroup I dataset. This dataset was derived from the ISRUC-SLEEP database, It is publicly available for researchers those who are research in sleep disorder [21]. This dataset was collected from the Sleep Medicine Centre of the Hospital of Coimbra University (CHUC) in Portugal. This dataset contains 100 subject information basically; the subjects are in the adult category, including both healthy and with some effected sleep problem. Out of 100 human adults, 53 males, 42 female subjects are there and the rest of the 5 subject's sex is not specified in the database. The average age of 100 subjects are 51 ± 16 yrs., height 1.35 ± 6.63 m, and weight 65.09 ± 34.97 kg, and BMI 23.53 ± 12.83 kg/m^2. Data collection was taken from subjects around 8–9 h a full night for individual subjects. This dataset collected signals from 11 electrodes that have placed in the subjects different parts of the body and those electrodes are extracted signals like EEG, EMG, ECG, and EOG. For this proposed study here we have used two-electrode signals from EEG such as F3-A2 and C3-A2. Here, we have considered only two subjects with different gender for our experimental work. The sampling frequency of the EEG signals is 200 Hz and segmented into 30 s epoch length. For our research work for sleep stage classification we have followed the standard AASM manuals and the concerned EEG recordings and its annotations done through sleep experts. Here we have extracted 750 epochs with 6000 samples from each subject for both the channels such as F3-A2 and C3-A2. Table 2 and Table 3 show some EEG signals segments of all sleep stages of both the subjects-15 and subjects-23 respectively.

Table 2. Subject-15 EEG (F3-A2/C3-A2) signal segments of all sleep stages

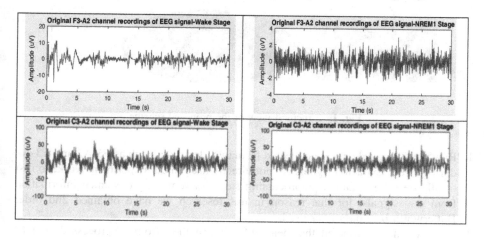

Table 3. Distribution of sleep stages in each subject used in this study

Subject no/gender stages	Wake	NREM-1	NREM-2	NREM-3	REM	Total
Subject-15/male	189	80	151	181	149	750
Subject-23/female	212	99	270	65	104	750
Total	401	179	421	246	253	1500

4   Methods

In this proposed study, we have dealt with two state classifications and also evaluate the performances of gender-specific sleep stage classification. Figure 1 represents a structural view of our proposed scheme. The simplified layout of the execution process is shown as follows:

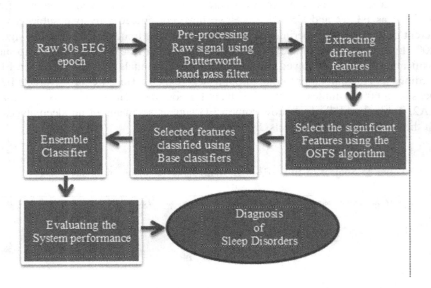

Fig. 1. Structural view of the proposed scheme

1. Raw physiological data are collected from two electrodes such as F3-A2 and C3-A2 during sleep. Extracted signals are not directly used in our experiment work, so first of all, we have obtained preprocessing steps for removing unwanted information from raw signals, for that reason in this research we have obtained 2nd order Butterworth bandpass filter used.
2. Next, we have extracted the meaningful information from preprocessed signals, which is supporting to discriminate the different characteristics of signals on different time instant and frequency instant. In this experimental work, we have

considered both the time domain and frequency domain features for our research work. In total of 38 features, we have extracted from considered two channels such as F3-A2 and C3-A2.

3. After feature extraction, we have implemented feature selection techniques where we are trying to find the best feature combination for different classifiers for classifying different sleep stage identification.

4. Next, the classification mechanism used where we have given the input as the best combination features to different classifiers adopted by our study.

5. The improved classifier's results are used to analyze the different sleep stages. Finally, the results of the sleep score from different stages will be used to assist sleep experts/clinicians in the diagnosis of sleep disorder.

4.1 Data Pre-processing

After signal acquisition from different channels, signals must be preprocessed before proceeding further analysis in related to experiment work. The collected raw signals are contaminated with certain noise factor and artifacts. The artifacts may be eye movements, heartbeat. In addition some more artefacts such muscle movement during sleep and communication interference due to high voltage in powerlines observed in raw signals which may not be suitable for further processing. For that reason, we have obtained the data pre-processing in our experiment work as an initial step. For preprocessing the signals we have adopted the Z score normalization was applied. In Eq. (1) we have mentioned the Z score normalization technique.

$$V' = (V - \bar{A})/\sigma_A \qquad (1)$$

V', V is the new and old of each entry of data respectively. σ_A, A is the standard deviation and mean of A respectively. Next to Z score normalization, we have also used the 2nd order butter worth filtering techniques to remove the muscle artifacts from the raw signal.

4.2 Feature Extraction

After obtaining the noise-free signal from the signal enhancement phase, essential features are extracted from the brain signals. In this phase, we are trying to find the essential characteristics of the processed signal. Though the considered signals are non-stationary and its characteristics changed with different time instants. This means that only time-domain features are not sufficient for generating the best features from preprocessed signals. Thus in this study, we have focused time domain, frequency domain, time-frequency domain features for our experimental work. In this experimental work, we have only extracted the linear features from the input channels such as F3-A2 and C3-A2. In total we have extracted 38 features from both the input channels. Table 4 briefly described the features extracted for this proposed study.

Table 4. List of extracted features

Label	Short description (EEG frequency domain feature)	Label	Short description (EEG time domain)
F1	Power	F25, F26, F27	Signal Activity, Complexity, Mobility
F2, F3, F4, F5	Band power in δ, θ, α, β sub band	F28, F29, F30	Mean, Maximum, Minimum
F6, F7, F8, F9	Relative spectral power in δ, θ, α, β sub band	F31, F32, F33	Standard Deviation, Median, Variance
F10, F11, F12, F13, F14, F15	Power ratios: α/δ, δ/β, δ/θ, θ/α, θ/β, α/β	F34, F35	Zero crossing rate, 75 Percentile
F16	$(\theta + \delta)/(\alpha + \beta)$	F36	Skewness
F17, F18, F19, F20	Centre frequency in δ, θ, α, β sub band	F37	Kurtosis
F21, F22, F23, F24	Maximum power in δ, θ, α, β sub band	F38	Energy

4.3   Feature Selection

In this study, we have considered the Online Streaming Feature Selection (OSFS) techniques for selecting suitable features for the classification tasks. OSFS divides features into different categories such as i. strongly relevant ii. weakly relevant iii. irrelevant features. With this approach the total features analyzed to find the optimal features set for classification with help of two phases i) online relevance analysis ii) online redundancy analysis. In the relevance analysis phase, OSFS discriminating between strongly and weakly features and add into a set named as Best Candidate Feature (BCF). When any new feature arrives, OSFS has to verify either the feature relevant as per class label value or not, if it satisfies it included with BCF set or simply discarded. When any new feature adds into the BCF set then the redundancy phase performed and it ultimately removed the redundant features from the BCF [22]. Finally, we have extracted in a total of 38 features for this experimental study on two-state classifications. In this proposed research work, we have adopted min-max normalization techniques to avoid the effect of EEG features and any abnormal values in the classification process. We made bring all features values in a range between 0 to 1 only [23]. In Eq. (2) we have mentioned min-max normalization techniques.

$$XNorm = [X - \min(X)]/\max(X) - \min(X) \qquad (2)$$

Where XNorm represents the feature values after normalization is the initial set of feature value, min and max are the minimum and maximum values in the X feature set.

4.4   Classification

SVM: It is a binary classification technique through which we have analyzed the data and recognize its patterns. SVM considers a set of training samples and designed a model when any new samples test through this trained model then the classifier assigns to one class as per its matched characteristics out of the two classes. This condition is only applicable in case the problem is linear separable condition [23].

DT: In our proposed study, we employed decision tree classifier techniques to measure the performances of sleep stage classification. DT contains two attributes one is an explanatory attribute and another one is the target attribute. The decision tree classifiers generate the tree to classify the objects according to the target attribute values. DT classifier considering some points during classification process i) Attribute Selection ii) Pruning iii) Selection of continuous attributes [24].

KNN: It is one of the base classifiers; this technique generally obtained in multi-modal distribution oriented problems only. Though our proposed work is the same nature where the same class of epochs is distributed in different locations in feature vector space. With the help of KNN techniques, we are assigning the labels to those input epochs based on the majority vote of its k-nearest samples [25].

ENSEMBLE: It is one of the standard paradigms of machine learning concept. The main idea is to include in our study is that to promote weak learners into stronger learners by assigning some more weight factors in the model. And it ultimately improves the accuracy factor of the model. The main advantage of this ensemble learner is to reduce the variance and bias values so that to predict the target variables is more closely. Here we have approached boosting methods, in which we are trying to give more focus on slow learners and in each step we have put some weights till that points are not accurately recognized properly.

5 Experiment and Discussions

The main contributions of the proposed study are exploiting gender-specific two-stage classification. For this implementation work, we have considered two channels for two different gender subjects one from the male category and the other from the female category. Here we have obtained the data from two channels of EEG signals such as F3-A2 and C3-A2 for both the category. This study deduced that the wake stage can be distinguished from sleep stages. This complete experiment worked upon the ISRUC-Sleep dataset, which is briefly described in Sect. 3. The main objective here is to discriminate in between wake stage versus sleep stage (NREM + REM). The complete work of this proposed study is followed by AASM standard rules to recognize the different patterns of sleep. Next to this work of this research, we have extracted both frequency and time domain-related features for this experimental work. With the use of 38 features extracted from the obtained input channels. Out of these features, some selected effective features selected through the online streaming feature selection technique to each classifier. In this experimental work, we have used three base classifiers like SVM, DT, KNN along with we have also employed ensemble classifiers for discriminating between wake stage and sleep stage. The major outcome expecting from this contribution are (1) To find an effective classification algorithm is subject to best discriminating in between two-stage classification, (2) To choose the best effective classifiers for classification, we have computed seven index parameter from both the gender-specific patients, (3) To compare in between channel acquisition effectiveness towards how best to recognize the different sleep stages (4) To compare the accuracy in between different classifiers to different index metric to make finalize that which classification algorithm is more appropriate for detecting the different sleep stages accurate levels. In this study, we have calculated five indicators of performance evaluation involved in this experiment include the following (1) Accuracy is defined as TP + TN/(TP + TN + FP + FN) (2) Sensitivity (True Positive Rate) is defined as TP/(TP + FN) sometimes it is also called the recall. (3) Specificity (True Negative Rate) is defined as TN/(TN + FP). (4) Precision defined is defined as TP/(TP + FP). (5) F1-score is defined as 2 * Precision * Recall/(Precision + Recall). For this proposed study all the experiments have been conducted using the Inteli7-6700 processor with 24 GB RAM. The software is Mat lab R2017a on windows10 OS.

To compare and analyses the results of different classifiers, a standard experiment was carried out through Mat lab coding. Figure 2, 4, 6 and 8 illustrates the overall classification accuracy of different classifiers for two-state sleep stages. It has found that results of different classifiers have varied with subjects to channel selection and subject gender. We have seen that some small differences found in results from different classifiers with the above-mentioned condition one is channel selection and other is gender. With our observation, these small differences have less effect on the results of sleep stages. To confirm the experiment result from different classifiers we have also computed the six index parameter such as accuracy, sensitivity, specificity, precision, area under curve and F1-score. Figure 3, 5, 7 and 9 illustrate the overall performances of different evaluation metric used for this study. Table 5 and Table 6 shows the various performance evaluation parameters for the male subject data of the model for two sleep classes using dual channel and for female subject the same performance evaluation parameters presents in Table 7 and Table 8 for individual channel. It was observed that from our experimental result we found the higher values for sensitivity, precision, F1score and lower values for specificity it signifies that our proposed study proposes a better classification of sleep stages.

Table 5. Performance metric evaluation (subject-15, male, C3-A2 channel)

C3A2	Accuracy	Area under curve	Precision	Recall	F1-score	Error rate	Specificity
LSVM	0.872	0.933	0.897	0.935	0.915	0.128	0.682
DT	0.851	0.88	0.934	0.86	0.893	0.149	0.82
KNN	0.875	0.819	0.904	0.93	0.916	0.125	0.708
ENSEMBLE	0.887	0.952	0.899	0.955	0.926	0.113	0.682

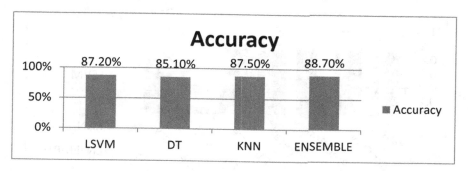

Fig. 2. Overall accuracy of subject-15 (male) for C3-A2 channel

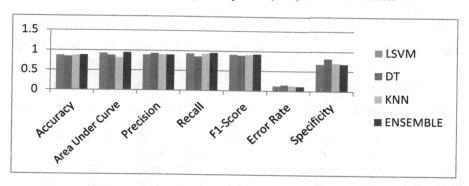

Fig. 3. Overall accuracy, AUC, precision, recall, F1-score, error rate, specificity for C3-A2

Table 6. Performance metric evaluation (subject-15, male, F3-A2 channel)

F3A2	Accuracy	Area under curve	Precision	Recall	F1-score	Error rate	Specificity
LSVM	0.903	0.963	0.937	0.932	0.934	0.097	0.814
DT	0.903	0.914	0.95	0.921	0.935	0.094	0.857
KNN	0.891	0.854	0.926	0.926	0.926	0.109	0.783
ENSEMBLE	0.907	0.96	0.964	0.909	0.467	0.093	0.769

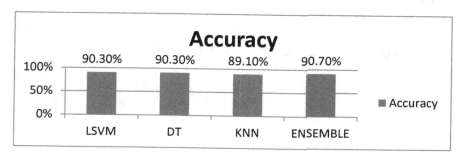

Fig. 4. Overall accuracy of subject-15 (male) for F3-A2 channel

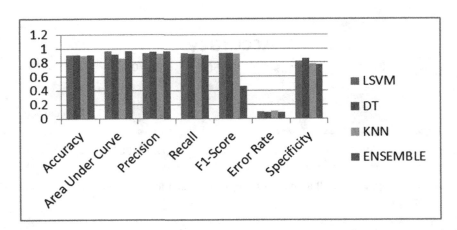

Fig. 5. Overall accuracy, AUC, precision, recall, F1-score, error rate, specificity for F3-A2

Table 7. Performance metric evaluation (subject-23, female, F3-A2 channel)

F3A2	Accuracy	Area under curve	Precision	Recall	F1-score	Error rate	Specificity
LSVM	0.913	0.967	0.929	0.951	0.469	0.086	0.816
DT	0.912	0.923	0.919	0.96	0.919	0.469	0.787
KNN	0.897	0.856	0.91	0.949	0.929	0.102	0.764
ENSEMBLE	0.912	0.969	0.919	0.96	0.469	0.088	0.787

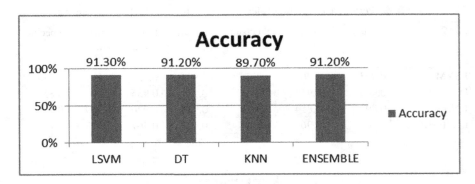

Fig. 6. Overall accuracy of subject-23 (female) for F3-A2 channel

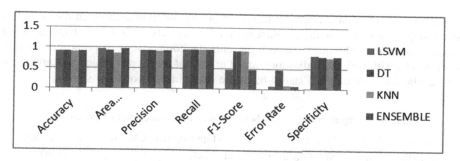

Fig. 7. Overall accuracy, AUC, precision, recall, F1-score, error rate, specificity for F3-A2

Table 8. Performance metric evaluation (subject-23, female, C3-A2 channel)

C3A2	Accuracy	Area under curve	Precision	Recall	F1-score	Error rate	Specificity
LSVM	0.915	0.965	0.932	0.949	0.94	0.085	0.825
DT	0.907	0.929	0.92	0.951	0.935	0.093	0.792
KNN	0.895	0.859	0.915	0.94	0.927	0.105	0.778
ENSEMBLE	0.903	0.967	0.91	0.959	0.933	0.097	0.759

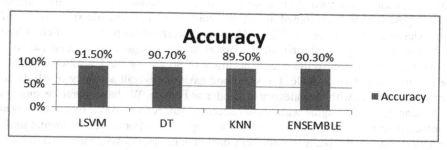

Fig. 8. Overall accuracy of subject-23 (female) for C3-A2 channel

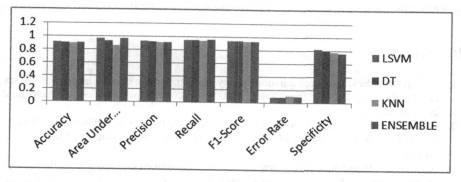

Fig. 9. Overall accuracy, AUC, precision, recall, F1-score, error rate, specificity for C3-A2

Many of studies have been conducted earlier by different authors on the two class sleep stage classification using different public datasets with EEG channels using machine learning techniques. Table 9 presents the comparisons of proposed research work results with various studies mentioned in state of the art part which are carried out on the classification of sleep stages based on dual channels of EEG signals.

Table 9. Comparison of results between previous studies and proposed study

Study	Year	Detection	Input signals	Classifier used	Accuracy
Ref [15]	2019	Sleep disorder bruxism	EEG	DT	81.70%
Ref [16]	2018	Sleep disorder	EEG	LSVM	89.93%
Proposed	**Present**	**Sleep disorder**	**EEG**	**LSVM**	**91.50%**

6   Conclusion

Sleep scoring is one of the important methods to classifying sleep disorders for sleep stage classification from over the years automatic sleep stage classification techniques approached. ASSC usually designed from statistical methods and machine learning techniques. In this proposed study we have established the usefulness of ASSC scoring based on an in brain EEG sensor. For accuracy, this has been achieved for two scenarios: scenario1 examined sleep score for individual channel to classification among sleep stages.scenario2: examined automatic score for gender-specific subjects for different channels of brain signals (EEG). Here we performed sleep stage prediction from dual channel with gender-based for the two-state sleep stage classification (wake vs sleep). For scenario1 gave the overall accuracy of 90.7% for the F3-A2 channel with the category of gender as male. For scenario2 gave the overall accuracy of 91.5% for the C3-A2 channel with the category of gender as Female. We have therefore sure that dual channels of EEG signal with gender specified subject's carries a sufficient amount of information to accurately represent human sleep pattern. For this experimental study, we have extracted the brain signals from dual-channel from two gender-specific subjects and future application studies will consider a larger group of subjects include the number of channels of EEG, EOG, and EMG signals and consider different time frame segmentation for proper diagnosis of sleep stage classification.

References

1. Nugent, CN. Black, LI.: Sleep duration, quality of sleep, and use of sleep medication, by sex and family type. NCHS Data Brief. **230**, 1–8 (2016).https://www.cdc.gov/nchs/data/databriefs/db230.pdf
2. National Sleep Foundation [NFS]: Lack of Sleep is Affecting Americans. https://www.sleepfoundation.org/press-release/lack-sleep-affecting-americans-finds-national-sleep-foundation
3. Sleep Health Foundation [SHF]. https://www.sleepfoundation.org/press-release/lack-sleep-affecting-americans-finds-national-sleep-foundation

4. American Academy of Sleep Medicine, et al.: International Classification of Sleep Disorders, Diagnostic and Coding Manual, pp. 148–152 (2005). https://doi.org/10.1378/chest.14-0970
5. Boostani, R., Karimzadeh, F., Nami, M.: A comparative review on sleep stage classification methods in patients and healthy individuals. Comput. Methods Progr. Biomed. **140**, 77–91 (2017)
6. Jafari, B., Mohesenin, V.: Polysomnography. Clin. Chest Med. **31**(2), 87–97 (2010)
7. Liang, S.F., Kio, C.E., Hu, Y.H., Pan, Y.H., Wang, Y.H.: Automatic stage scoring of single-channel sleep EEG by using multiscale entropy and autoregressive models. IEEE Trans. Instrum. Measur. **61**(6), 1649–1657 (2012)
8. Sharma, R., Pachori, R.B., Upadhyay, A.: Automatic sleep stages classification based on iterative filtering of electroencephalogram signals. Neural Comput. Appl. **28**(10), 2959–2978 (2017)
9. Berry, R.: Fundamentals of Sleep Medicine. Elsevier Saunders, Philadelphia (2012)
10. Zhu, G.H., Li, Y., Wen, P.P.: Analysis and classification of sleep stages based on difference visibility graphs from as single channel EEG signal. IEEE J. Biomed. Health Inform. **18**(6), 1813–1821 (2014)
11. Geand, Z.H., Sun, Y.F.: Sleep stages classification using neural networks with multi-channel neural data. In: Lecture Notes in Computer Science, pp. 306–316. Springer (2015)
12. Diykh, M., Li, Y.: Complex networks approach for EEG signal sleep stages classification. Expert Syst. Appl. **63**(11), 241–248 (2016)
13. Liang, S.F., Kuo, C.E., Hu, Y.H., Pan, Y.H., Wang, Y.H.: Automatic stage scoring of single-channel sleep EEG by using multiscale entropy and autoregressive models. IEEE Trans. Instrum. Meas. **61**(6), 1649–1657 (2012)
14. Khalighi, S., Sousa, T., Pires, G., Nunes, U.: Automatic sleep staging: a computer assisted approach for optimal combination of features and polysomnographic channels. Expert Syst. Appl. **40**(17), 7046–7059 (2013)
15. Heyat, M.B.B., Lai, D., Khan, F.I., Zhang, Y.: Sleep bruxism detection using decision tree method by the combination of C4-P4 and C4-A1 channels of scalp EEG. IEEE Access **7**, 102542–102553 (2019)
16. Alizadeh, S., et al.: Performance comparison of machine learning techniques in sleep scoring based on wavelet features and neighboring component analysis (2018)
17. Ebrahimi, F., Mikaeili, M., Estrada, E., Nazeran, H.: Automatic sleep stage classification based on EEG signals by using neural networks and wavelet packet coefficients. In: Proceedings of 30th Annual International IEEE EMBS Conference (2008)
18. Krakovska, A., Mezeiova, K.: Automatic sleeps scoring: a search for an optimal combination of measures. Artif. Intell. Med. **53**, 25–33 (2011)
19. Sharma, M., Goyal, D., Achuth, P.V., Acharya, U.R.: An accurate sleep stages-classification system using a new class of optimally time-frequency localized three-band wavelet filter. Comput. Biol. Med. **98**, 58–75 (2018)
20. Khalighi, S., Sousa, T., Santos, J.M., Nunes, U.: ISRUC-Sleep: a comprehensive public dataset for sleep researchers. Comput. Methods Programs Biomed. **124**, 180–192 (2016)
21. Acharya, U.R., Chua, E.C., Chua, K.C., Min, L.C., Tamura, T.: Analysis and automatic identification of sleep stages using higher order spectra. Int. J. Neural Syst. **20**(6), 509–521 (2010)
22. Lauer, F., Guermeur, Y.: MSVMpack: a multi-class support vector machine package. J. Mach. Learn. Res. **2**, 2293–2296 (2011)
23. Hanaoka, M., Kobayashi, M., Yamazaki, H.: Automated sleep stage scoring by decision tree learning. In: Proceedings of the 23rd Annual EMBS International Conference, Istanbul, Turkey, 25–28 October 2001 (2001)

24. Gunes, S., Polat, K., Yosunkaya, S.: Efficient sleep stage recognition system based on EEG signal using k-means clustering based feature weighting. Expert Syst. Appl. **37**, 7922–7928 (2010)
25. İlhan, H.O., Bilgin, G.: Sleep stage classification via ensemble and conventional machine learning methods using single channel EEG signals. Int. J. Intell. Syst. Appl. Eng. **5**(4), 174–184 (2017)

Hyperspectral Endmember Extraction Algorithm Using Convex Geometry and K-Means

Dharambhai Shah, Tanish Zaveri[✉], and Rutvik Dixit

Institute of Technology, Nirma University, Ahmedabad, Gujarat, India
shahdharam7@gmail.com, ztanish@gmail.com, dixit.rutvik20@gmail.com

Abstract. Hyperspectral unmixing is a technique of approximating spectral signatures of pure types and their corresponding combined proportions at all pixels in the hyperspectral data. Hyperspectral unmixing is a noteworthy task for understanding, study and visualization of hyperspectral image. In this task, extracting pure spectral signatures is very challenging. In this paper, a novel approach, using convex geometry and k-means concepts, is proposed for endmember extraction. The majority of existing techniques of endmember extraction uses only convex geometry. Using K-means with convex geometry improves the accuracy of the extraction process. The proposed algorithm is compared with other state-of-art algorithms using simulated and real-world datasets. Based on simulation results, it is seen that the proposed algorithm outperforms other state-of-art algorithms.

Keywords: Convex geometry · Covariance · Endmember extraction · Hyperspectral image · Kmeans

1 Introduction

Hyperspectral remote sensing is associated with the abstraction of data from substances or sights lying on the surface of the ground, based on their radiance value captured from sensors of airborne or space-borne types. In the remote sensing technology, the hyperspectral sensor is a remarkable sensor that acquires images of visible, short wave infrared and mid-wave infrared. The main advantage of the hyperspectral sensor is it captures images at a very high spectral resolution which helps to identify very minute details of many objects. Due to this advantage, hyperspectral sensors are used in many applications [5,12,15] of agriculture, water, vegetation and urban. However, this hyperspectral sensors comes with many challenges [5,15,17]. The major limitation of the hyperspectral sensor is its low spatial resolution. Due to low spatial resolution, many pixels are of mixed types in the hyperspectral image. These mixed pixels are not only due to low spatial resolution but also due to intimate mixing and multiple scattering.

Extracting pure materials with their abundances in the mixing is called as unmixing. Hyperspectral Unmixing (HU) decomposes mixed type of pixels into

© Springer Nature Singapore Pte Ltd. 2020
S. Gupta and J. N. Sarvaiya (Eds.): ET2ECN 2020, CCIS 1214, pp. 189–200, 2020.
https://doi.org/10.1007/978-981-15-7219-7_16

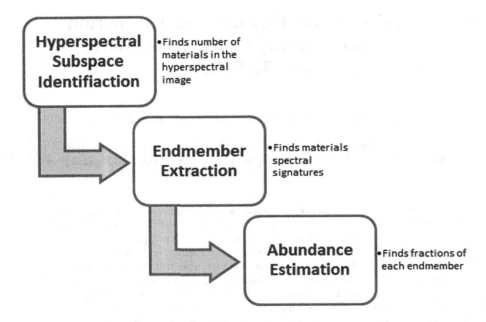

Fig. 1. Hyperspectral Unmixing chain

pure components along with their portions. Hyperspectral Unmixing is basically considered as a three-stage problem in a chain [1], as shown in Fig. 1. The first stage is hyperspectral subspace identification, which finds the number of materials in a given hyperspectral image. Hyperspectral subspace identification is addressed by many researchers [2,16]. The second stage is endmember extraction, which extracts pure material signatures from the image. The third stage is abundance estimation, which finds the proportion of material in mixing. There are various abundance estimation approaches in the literature [2,11].

Hyperspectral Unmixing (HU) is of two types: Linear or Non-linear. Linear Hyperspectral Unmixing (LHU) is a linear combination of all pure material's spectral signatures in a mixed type of pixel. Low spatial resolution is the major reason for LHU. Non-Linear Hyperspectral Unmixing (NLHU) is a non-linear combination of all pure material's spectral signatures in a mixed type of pixel. Multiple scattering and intimate mixing are the main reasons for NLHU.

In this paper, endmember extraction is addressed. Endmember extraction is approached using convex geometry and k-means concepts. Convex geometry is the conventional approach of endmember extraction. The major contribution in this paper is the application of k-means with convex geometry. A novel approach is proposed for improving the accuracy of endmember extraction. The organization of the remaining paper is as follows. Section 2 defines the problem statement with a brief introduction to existing literature. Section 3 explains the proposed algorithm. Section 4 elaborates evaluation indices and datasets. Section 5 demonstrates the comparison results. The paper ends with closing notes at the end.

2   Problem Statement and Literature

LHU is a widely accepted unmixing technique as compared to NLHU because of its simplicity and tolerable estimate to the real-world situation. Before explaining the proposed work, it is necessary to define the problem statement mathematically. In this section, the problem statement is defined mathematically first and then a brief introduction to the existing techniques.

Let mixed pixel ($\mathbf{r}$) of size $L \times 1$ be,

$$\mathbf{r} = \mathbf{M} \times \alpha + \mathbf{n} \tag{1}$$

where $\mathbf{M}$ is pure materials array of size $L \times Q$. $\alpha = [\alpha_1, \alpha_2, ..., \alpha_Q]$ is the abundance vector of size $Q \times 1$. $\mathbf{n}$ is noise vector of size $L \times 1$ due to perturbation and error. In LHU jargon, an abundance vector usually follows two constraints.

1. ASC: Abundance Sum-to-One Constraint

$$\sum_{i=1}^{Q} \alpha_i = 1 \tag{2}$$

2. ANC: Abundance Non-negativity Constraint

$$\alpha_i \geq 0, \forall i \tag{3}$$

As per Fig. 1, the unmixing problem can be defined as the following three problems mathematically.

1. Hyperspectral subspace identification finds number of materials Q for given mixed pixel $\mathbf{r}$
2. Endmember extraction finds pure material matrix M for the given value of Q and $\mathbf{r}$
3. Abundance estimation estimates α for the given value of Q, $\mathbf{M}$ and $\mathbf{r}$

There are various hyperspectral subspace identification algorithms [6] to find the number of pure materials in the hyperspectral data. Using these algorithms and for the given image, various endmember extraction algorithms [2] are developed. The most popular endmember extraction algorithms are N-point FINDer (NFINDR) [22], Simplex Growing Algorithm (SGA) [4], Successive Volume MAXimization (SVMAX) [3], Alternating Volume MAXimization (AVMAX) [3], Vertex Component Analysis (VCA) [13], Pixel Purity Index (PPI) [7], Independent Component Analysis (ICA) [21], Automatic Target Generation Process (ATGP) [14]. Four algorithms (NFINDR, SGA, SVMAX and AVMAX) are based on Winter's fact [22]. PPI generates random vectors and calculates the score of purity. Depending on the score, pure pixels are decided. ICA is a well-known algorithm for source separation from the last three decades. VCA and ATGP algorithms are based on the similarity between spectral signatures. Based on different similarity scores, both algorithms find pure pixels.

3   Proposed Work

In the hyperspectral image analysis, it is very common to convert three dimensional image $\mathbf{X}$ of size $M \times N \times Z$ to two dimensional image $\mathbf{R}$ of size $Z \times L$. In this conversion, M, N are height, width of hyperspectral image and $Z = M \times N$ is the number of pixels in the hyperspectral image. $\mathbf{R}$ can be represented as,

$$
\begin{aligned}
\mathbf{R} &= [\mathbf{r_1}, \mathbf{r_2}, ..., \mathbf{r_L}] \\
&= [\mathbf{r^1}, \mathbf{r^2}, ..., \mathbf{r^Z}]^T \\
&= \begin{bmatrix} r_1^1 & r_2^1 & r_3^1 & \dots & r_L^1 \\ r_1^2 & r_2^2 & r_3^2 & \dots & r_L^2 \\ \vdots & \vdots & \vdots & \ddots & \vdots \\ r_1^Z & r_2^Z & r_3^Z & \dots & r_L^Z \end{bmatrix}
\end{aligned}
\tag{4}
$$

where, $\mathbf{r_i}$ represents i^{th} band of hyperspectral image and $\mathbf{r^j}$ represents j^{th} mixed sample vector pixel of hyperspectral image as defined in LHU model. In (4), r_i^j is j^{th} pixel intensity value of ith band.

The proposed algorithm is divided into four parts. The first part normalizes each band which is very common in image processing applications. The second part finds covariance between each possible combination of two band data. Convex set points on highly covariance two bands are found in the third part. The final part removes extra points using well known clustering algorithm i.e. K-means if any.

3.1   Band Normalization

Band normalization is very useful for making all pixel values of band in similar range. Band normalization for pixel r_i^j is,

$$
\bar{r}_i^j = \frac{r_i^j - \mu_i}{\sigma_i}, \quad \forall r_i^j \in \mathbf{r_i}
\tag{5}
$$

The above Eq. (5) normalize each pixel value r_i^j of band $\mathbf{r_i} = [r_i^1, r_i^2, r_i^3, ..., r_i^Z]$.

3.2   Co-variance Between Bands

Variance is very useful statistical measure to measure the nature of the data. High variance data always contains variety of data. In this work, we use variance between bands. The variance between two bands $\mathbf{r_i}$ and $\mathbf{r_j}$ can be calculated as,

$$
cov(\bar{\mathbf{r}}_\mathbf{i}, \bar{\mathbf{r}}_\mathbf{j}) = E[(\bar{\mathbf{r}}_\mathbf{i} - E(\bar{\mathbf{r}}_\mathbf{i}))(\bar{\mathbf{r}}_\mathbf{j} - E(\bar{\mathbf{r}}_\mathbf{j}))]
\tag{6}
$$

where $E[.]$ denotes the expectation operator. In this work, objective is to find high covariance value bands. To find out these two bands, the optimization problem is defined as follows.

$$
\begin{aligned}
&\underset{i,j \in \{1,2,...,L\}}{\text{maximize}} \quad cov(\bar{\mathbf{r}}_\mathbf{i}, \bar{\mathbf{r}}_\mathbf{j}) \\
&\text{subject to} \quad i \neq j
\end{aligned}
\tag{7}
$$

The above optimization problem gives two values i and j. The bands ($\bar{\mathbf{r}}_i$ and $\bar{\mathbf{r}}_j$) related to i and j are used for further processing.

3.3 Convex Points of Two Points Data

Winter [22] firmly believes that convex geometry is the best suitable for LHU model (1). As per the literature [3,4,22], the convex hull is used to find vertex of the data. The convex hull is defined as,

$$CH(\mathbf{R}) = \left\{ \sum_{i=1}^{Q} \alpha_i r_i \Big| ANC, ASC, r_i \in \mathbf{R} \right\} \tag{8}$$

The above Eq. (8) gives N_R number of points for two band data $\mathbf{r_i}$ and $\mathbf{r_j}$.

3.4 Extra Points Removal Using Kmeans Clustering

It is necessary to find exactly Q points. But it is not always from the above three steps. There are two possibilities for N_R.

1. $N_R = Q$ is desirable from the algorithm. If it is true, no further processing is required.
2. $N_R > Q$ means the number of pure materials obtains from the previous step is more than the hyperspectral subspace dimension. It is necessary to remove extra $(N_R - Q)$ points when $N_R > Q$. These extra points are removed using a well-known clustering algorithm K-means [10]. K-means algorithm basically finds K clusters which are different from each other. A similar situation is here in this case. The algorithm desires only Q points out of N_R. K-means algorithm extracts exactly Q points.

After removing extra points, the algorithm fetch the spectral signature of the obtain points and make new matrix $\mathbf{A} = [\mathbf{a_1}, \mathbf{a_2}, ..., \mathbf{a_Q}]$. As defined in the problem statement, the proposed endmember extraction algorithm finds pure material matrix $\mathbf{A}$ for the given Q and $\mathbf{R}$.

4 Datasets and Evaluation Indices

In this section, a hyperspectral dataset used in the simulation is explained first and then evaluation indices are defined.

4.1 Datasets

Two types of datasets (simulated and real-world) are used in the simulation.

(a) Rational   (b) Spheric   (c) Matern   (d) Exponential   (e) Legendre

Fig. 2. Simulated data

Simulated Dataset. Computational Intelligence Group (CIG), Spain [9] has developed Hyperspectral Imagery Synthesis Toolbox (HIST) for scientific research in the hyperspectral image processing. In this simulation, simulated data is generated using HIST. Five endmembers from USGS spectral library [8] are used to generate simulated data. Five types of distributions (Rational, Spheric, Matern, Exponential and Legendre) are used as shown in Fig. 2. All five images are of size 128×128 of 431 bands.

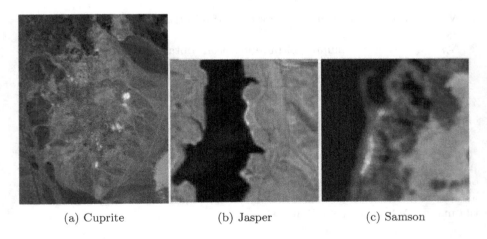

(a) Cuprite   (b) Jasper   (c) Samson

Fig. 3. Real-world data

Real-World Dataset. To evaluate the accuracy provided by the proposed work in a more realistic way, a widely used three benchmark datasets are used.

- **Cuprite**, as shown in Fig. 3a, is the benchmark dataset in the hyperspectral unmixing study. Only sub-part of size 250×191 from the original cuprite image is used. Only 188 channels are used in the simulation after removing low SNR and water absorption bands. Cuprite image consists of twelve endmembers as defined in [23].

- **Jasper**, as shown in Fig. 3b, is also a popular dataset used in the unmixing study. The original jasper image consists of 512×614 pixels with 224 channels in the electromagnetic spectrum of 380 nm to 2500 nm. As jasper image is highly complex, a part of 100×100 pixels are considered in the simulation. Only 196 bands are used in the simulation after removing high noise bands. There are 4 endmembers [23] in the image: Tree, Soil, Water and Road.
- **Samson**, as shown in Fig. 3c, is a popular dataset used in [23]. Samson image is of size 95×95 with 154 channels. This size is sub-image and after removing noisy bands. There are 3 endmembers [23] in the image: Tree, Soil and Water.

4.2 Evaluation Indices

Let the output of endmember extraction algorithm be $\mathbf{A} = [\mathbf{a_1}, \mathbf{a_2}, ..., \mathbf{a_Q}]$ and the each material of mixing matrix $\mathbf{A}$ be $\mathbf{a}_i = [a_i^1, a_i^2, ..., a_i^L]^T$. In this paper, Ground Truth (GT) endmember is noted as $\mathbf{b}_i = [b_i^1, b_i^2, ...b_i^L]^T$. Three standard evaluation indices [18–20] for Endmember extraction algorithms are defined as follows.

1. SAE: Spectral Angle Error (SAE) between two endmembers $\mathbf{a_i}$ and $\mathbf{b_i}$ is defined as,

$$\phi_i = arccos\left(\frac{\mathbf{a_i} \cdot \mathbf{b_i}}{|\mathbf{a_i}||\mathbf{b_i}|}\right) \tag{9}$$

SAE for all Q endmembers is defined as $\phi = [\phi_1, \phi_2, ...\phi_Q]^T$ of size $Q \times 1$. Parameters ϕ is defined between two endmembers. Root Mean Square (RMS) of all components of ϕ is generally used to consider all vectors.

$$RMSSAE = \left(\frac{1}{Q}E[\| \phi \|_2^2]\right)^{1/2} \tag{10}$$

Root Mean Square (RMS) value of SAE vector defined in (10) is RMSSAE [13].

2. SID: Spectral Information Divergence (SID) [13] is statistical parameter to evaluate spectral similarity between two spectral signatures. To define SID between two spectra $\mathbf{a}$ and $\mathbf{b}$, Probability vectors $\mathbf{p} = [p^1, p^2, ...p^L]^T$ and $\mathbf{q} = [q^1, q^2, ...q^L]^T$ of L-dimensional are necessary. Probability vector components are presented as,

$$p^i = \frac{a^i}{\sum_{i=1}^L a^i} \quad , \quad q^i = \frac{b^i}{\sum_{i=1}^L b^i} \tag{11}$$

SID parameter between two spectra $\mathbf{a_i}$ and $\bar{\mathbf{b}}_i$ is defined as,

$$\delta_i = \sum_{k=1}^L p^k \log\left(\frac{p^k}{q^k}\right) + \sum_{k=1}^L q^k \log\left(\frac{q^k}{p^k}\right) \tag{12}$$

Q-dimensional SID vector is defined as $\delta = [\delta_1, \delta_2, ...\delta_Q]^T$ for all Q endmembers. Root Mean Square (RMS) value of δ is defined as,

$$RMSSID = \left(\frac{1}{Q}E[\| \delta \|_2^2]\right)^{1/2} \tag{13}$$

3. NXC: Normalized Cross Correlation (NXC) between spectra a_i and b_i is defined as,

$$\psi = \frac{1}{(L-1)} \times \sqrt{\frac{\sum_{i=1}^{L}(a^i - m_a)(b^i - m_b)}{s_a \times s_b}} \tag{14}$$

Here, mean values of spectra $\mathbf{a}$ and $\mathbf{b}$ are denoted as m_a and m_b respectively. And standard deviation of spectra $\mathbf{a}$ and $\mathbf{b}$ are noted as s_a and s_b respectively. NXC vector is represented as ($\boldsymbol{\psi} = [\psi_1, \psi_2, ...\psi_Q]^T$). Root Mean Square (RMS) of $\boldsymbol{\psi}$ is defined as,

$$RMSNXC = \left(\frac{1}{Q}E[\| \boldsymbol{\psi} \|_2^2]\right)^{1/2} \tag{15}$$

5   Simulation Results

Comparative examines among several state-of-the-art endmember algorithms and our proposed algorithm was carried out on five simulated and three well defined real-world hyperspectral datasets (AVIRIS Cuprite, Jasper and Samson) to investigate their influences on endmember extraction accuracy. Eight endmember extraction algorithms (NFINDR, SGA, SVMAX, AVMAX, VCA, PPI, ICA, ATGP) are compared with our proposed algorithm based on evaluation indices.

Table 1. Cuprite dataset results

Parameter	NFINDR	SGA	SVMAX	AVMAX	VCA	PPI	ICA	ATGP	Proposed
RMSSAE	22.342	22.154	17.735	17.147	24.224	18.829	18.183	17.325	**17.120**
RMSSID	9.481	9.596	8.061	7.408	11.159	8.418	7.702	7.479	**7.159**
RMSNXC	0.819	0.823	0.839	0.836	0.815	0.836	0.839	0.845	**0.854**

Table 2. Jasper dataset results

Parameter	NFINDR	SGA	SVMAX	AVMAX	VCA	PPI	ICA	ATGP	Proposed
RMSSAE	26.424	26.491	28.645	28.430	20.250	37.236	31.946	32.805	**18.458**
RMSSID	24.940	24.944	33.560	33.429	16.710	42.743	45.330	35.232	**13.715**
RMSNXC	0.847	0.841	0.813	0.813	0.845	0.797	0.846	0.793	**0.852**

Table 3. Samson dataset results

Parameter	NFINDR	SGA	SVMAX	AVMAX	VCA	PPI	ICA	ATGP	Proposed
RMSSAE	39.398	36.240	21.807	30.746	30.448	21.239	29.223	35.565	**15.629**
RMSSID	76.455	61.083	22.311	36.873	35.693	22.214	29.718	55.368	**17.743**
RMSNXC	0.903	0.902	0.947	0.893	0.893	0.930	0.872	0.897	**0.958**

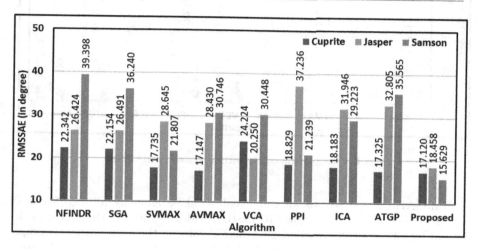

Fig. 4. Comparison of algorithms based on RMSSAE

5.1 Simulation with Simulated Data

Five types of distributions (Rational, Spheric, Matern, Exponential and Legendre) generated by HIST toolbox are applied to the proposed algorithm and state-of-art endmember extraction algorithms. All algorithms are working equally on all five images. RMSSAE and RMSSID values by all algorithms on all five images are zero. RMSNXC value is one for all algorithms. The ideal value of all three evaluation indices shows that the proposed algorithm is working well on all simulated images. The purpose of this simulation is to check the proposed algorithm is working properly or not.

5.2 Simulation with Real-World Data

The simulation with the real-world dataset is very essential to check the proposed algorithm effectiveness in the real situation. RMSSAE, RMSSID and RMSNXC values are noted in Table 1 for cuprite dataset by all algorithms. It has been observed from Table 1 that the proposed algorithm is working better than other algorithms for the most popular cuprite dataset. Table 2 shows three indices values for Jasper dataset by all algorithms. The results shown in Table 2 for Jasper shows that the proposed algorithm performs well. Three evaluation indices for Samson dataset by all algorithms are shown in Table 3. The proposed algorithm is seen to be effective in endmember extraction for samson dataset as per Table 3.

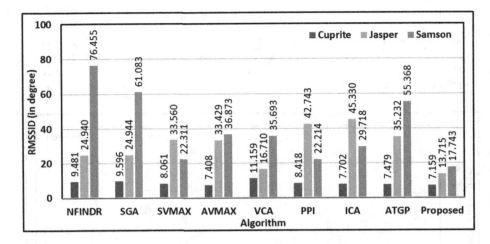

Fig. 5. Comparison of algorithms based on RMSSID

RMSSAE (in degree) for all three real-world datasets by all algorithms is shown in Fig. 4. Figure 5 shows RMSSID (in degree) for all three real-world dataset by all algorithm. Similarly, RMSNXC value in the form of the bar graph is shown in Fig. 6. It has been noticed from Fig. 4 and Fig. 5 that the proposed algorithm is giving the least value which is expected. RMSNXC value is maximum for all three real-world hyperspectral images as shown in Fig. 6 which shows the effectiveness of the proposed algorithm.

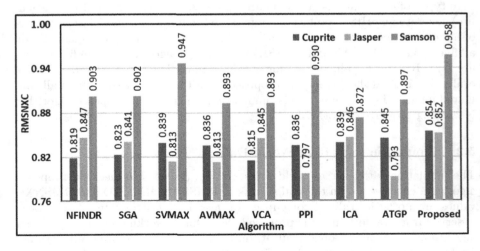

Fig. 6. Comparison of algorithms based on RMSNXC

6   Conclusion

The most challenging issue of hyperspectral unmixing chain i.e. endmember extraction is addressed in this paper. A novel algorithm based on convex geometry and K-means is proposed in this paper. The conventional endmember extraction algorithms only use convex geometry while the proposed algorithm adds K-means concept in addition to convex geometry which improves the accuracy. In the simulation, the proposed algorithm is applied to five simulated data and three real-world data. The proposed algorithm is compared with other state-of-art algorithms based on SAE, SID and NXC. Simulation results show that the proposed algorithm outperforms than other state-of-art algorithms.

Acknowledgement. This publication is an outcome of the Research and Development project funded by the Visvesvaraya PhD Scheme of Ministry of Electronics and Information Technology, Government of India, being implemented by Digital India Corporation and Institute of Technology, Nirma University.

References

1. Bhatt, J.S.: Novel approaches for spectral unmixing of hyperspectral data. Ph.D. thesis, Dhirubhai Ambani Institute of Information and Communication Technology (2014)
2. Bioucas-Dias, J.M., et al.: Hyperspectral unmixing overview: geometrical, statistical, and sparse regression-based approaches. IEEE J. Sel. Top. Appl. Earth Obs. Remote Sens. **5**(2), 354–379 (2012)
3. Chan, T., Ma, W., Ambikapathi, A., Chi, C.: A simplex volume maximization framework for hyperspectral endmember extraction. IEEE Trans. Geosci. Remote Sens. **49**(11), 4177–4193 (2011). https://doi.org/10.1109/TGRS.2011.2141672
4. Chang, C.I., Wu, C.C., Liu, W., Ouyang, Y.: A new growing method for simplex-based endmember extraction algorithm. IEEE Trans. Geosci. Remote Sens. **44**(10), 2804–2819 (2006). https://doi.org/10.1109/TGRS.2006.881803
5. Chang, C.I.: Hyperspectral Imaging: Techniques for Spectral Detection and Classification, vol. 1. Springer, Boston (2003). https://doi.org/10.1007/978-1-4419-9170-6
6. Chang, C.I.: A review of virtual dimensionality for hyperspectral imagery. IEEE J. Sel. Top. Appl. Earth Obs. Remote Sens. **11**(4), 1285–1305 (2018)
7. Chang, C.I., Plaza, A.: A fast iterative algorithm for implementation of pixel purity index. IEEE Geosci. Remote Sens. Lett. **3**(1), 63–67 (2006). https://doi.org/10.1109/LGRS.2005.856701
8. Clark, R.N., et al.: USGS digital spectral library splib06a. US geological survey, digital data series 231, 2007 (2007)
9. Computational Intelligence Group, University of the Basque Country/Euskal Herriko Unibertsitatea (UPV/EHU), S.: Hyperspectral imagery synthesis (EIAS) toolbox (2010)
10. Jain, A.K.: Data clustering: 50 years beyond k-means. Pattern Recogn. Lett. **31**(8), 651–666 (2010)
11. Li, J.: Wavelet-based feature extraction for improved endmember abundance estimation in linear unmixing of hyperspectral signals. IEEE Trans. Geosci. Remote Sens. **42**(3), 644–649 (2004)

12. Mishra, R., Shah, D., Zaveri, T., Ramakrishnan, R., Shah, P.: Separation of sewage water based on water quality parameters for South Karnataka coastal region. In: Asian Association on Remote Sensing, October, vol. 2017 (2017)

13. Nascimento, J.M., Dias, J.M.: Vertex component analysis: a fast algorithm to unmix hyperspectral data. IEEE Trans. Geosci. Remote Sens. **43**(4), 898–910 (2005)

14. Ren, H., Chang, C.I.: Automatic spectral target recognition in hyperspectral imagery. IEEE Trans. Aerosp. Electron. Syst. **39**(4), 1232–1249 (2003)

15. Shah, D., Tripathy, M., Zaveri, T.: Comparison of target detection techniques for hyperspectral images. In: 2019 4th International Conference on Information Systems and Computer Networks (ISCON), pp. 293–296, November 2019. https://doi.org/10.1109/ISCON47742.2019.9036193

16. Shah, D., Zaveri, T.: Fast hyperspectral subspace identification using eigenvalue based energy thresholding. In: 2019 4th International Conference on Information Systems and Computer Networks (ISCON), pp. 284–288, November 2019. https://doi.org/10.1109/ISCON47742.2019.9036190

17. Shah, D., Bera, K., Joshi, S.: Software implementation of ccsds recommended hyperspectral lossless image compression. Int. J. Image Graph. Sig. Process. **7**(4), 35 (2015). https://doi.org/10.5815/ijigsp.2015.04.04

18. Shah, D., Zaveri, T.: Hyperspectral endmember extraction using band quality. In: 2019 IEEE 16th India Council International Conference (INDICON), pp. 1–4. IEEE (2019)

19. Shah, D., Zaveri, T.: A novel geo-stat endmember extraction algorithm. In: TENCON 2019–2019 IEEE Region 10 Conference (TENCON), pp. 2685–2689. IEEE (2019)

20. Shah, D., Zaveri, T.: Energy based convex set hyperspectral endmember extraction algorithm. In: Nain, N., Vipparthi, S.K., Raman, B. (eds.) CVIP 2019. CCIS, vol. 1147, pp. 51–60. Springer, Singapore (2020). https://doi.org/10.1007/978-981-15-4015-8_5

21. Xia, W., Liu, X., Wang, B., Zhang, L.: Independent component analysis for blind unmixing of hyperspectral imagery with additional constraints. IEEE Trans. Geosci. Remote Sens. **49**(6), 2165–2179 (2011). https://doi.org/10.1109/TGRS.2010.2101609

22. Xiong, W., Chang, C., Wu, C., Kalpakis, K., Chen, H.M.: Fast algorithms to implement n-findr for hyperspectral endmember extraction. IEEE J. Sel. Top. Appl. Earth Obs. Remote Sens. **4**(3), 545–564 (2011). https://doi.org/10.1109/JSTARS.2011.2119466

23. Zhu, F.: Hyperspectral unmixing: ground truth labeling, datasets, benchmark performances and survey. arXiv preprint arXiv:1708.05125 (2017)

Automatic Melanoma Detection System (AMDS): A State-of-the-Art Review

Shakti Kumar[(⊠)] and Anuj Kumar

DCSA, Panjab University, Chandigarh, India
shaktikumarbajpai@gmail.com, anuj_gupta@pu.ac.in

Abstract. Melanoma is one of the most treacherous forms of skin cancer. An automatic melanoma detection system (AMDS) is an image based melanoma skin cancer detection system which detects the melanoma cancer from the captured image of the infected skin. AMDS is helpful in the early detection of skin cancer. The manual detection is time-consuming and depends upon factors like clinical tests, and knowledge of dermatologist. The detection of melanoma is an exigent task using manual processing. Therefore, an AMDS is needed. Macroscopic and dermoscopic images can be used for the analysis of melanocytic and non-melanocytic lesions. It is possible to detect melanoma in non-invasive manner using lesion characteristics like color, shape, and structure. In this paper, we present a comprehensive review of the state-of-the-art techniques for AMDS. We categorize different AMDS techniques according to features used for each stage, and compare them in terms of accuracy, sensitivity and working principle along with the suggestions for future scope for detection of melanoma.

Keywords: Melanoma · Preprocessing · Lesion segmentation · Feature extraction · Lesion classification

1 Introduction

Automatic Melanoma Detection System (AMDS) is an image processing and pattern recognition technique used to detect melanoma skin cancer from an image of the affected area. Melanoma is a type of skin cancer. It has the highest mortality rate of all dermatological cancers. It is one of the most common cancers in young and adults. The most inner layer of the epidermis as shown in Fig. 1, which is just above the dermis have cells that are known as melanocytes [1]. These cells are responsible for producing skin color or pigment. Due to melanoma, the healthy melanocytes cells change and their growth becomes uncontrollable, which forms a cancerous tumor.

Depletion in the ozone layer is the reason for diminished protection against the UV radiation which leads to more probability of melanoma cancer. More exposure to sun or solarium and tanning is a reason for infected skin as well. Skin cancer lesion may be benign which is found in the epidermis layer. Similar to that malignant lesion part of the epidermis is not life hazardous until it penetrates and reaches the dermis layer. Many challenges like lightning conditions, noise, hair and moisture present on the skin may occur while processing the image captured for melanoma detection. The melanoma detection system goes through four basic steps which are pre-processing,

© Springer Nature Singapore Pte Ltd. 2020
S. Gupta and J. N. Sarvaiya (Eds.): ET2ECN 2020, CCIS 1214, pp. 201–212, 2020.
https://doi.org/10.1007/978-981-15-7219-7_17

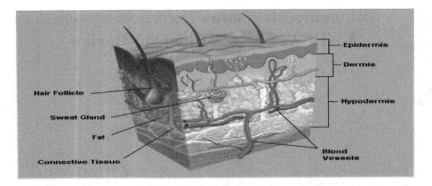

Fig. 1. Human skin anatomy [1]

segmentation, feature extraction, and classification. Captured image either by dermoscopic or by macroscopic method contains noise and preprocessing is performed for noise removal like hair removal from the skin, sharpening the lesion and resizing it for further use. Segmentation is the process of removing the lesion area from the surrounding skin image. Generally, it contains pixels with similar attributes. This phase provides input to the feature extraction phase to extract vital features of the segmented area of the skin. Feature extraction is the technique of finding parameters such as border, symmetry, and color. The extracted features control the performance of the classification phase directly.

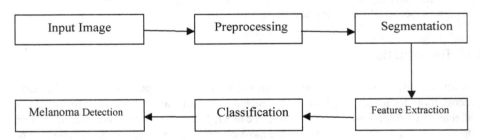

Fig. 2. Steps involved in automatic melanoma detection systems

Classification is done to distinguish melanoma from a benign or nevi. The process of AMDS is shown in Fig. 2. It can be done either on the local machine by the trained data set or further improvement can be done by sending the image to the server from where we receive classification results after processing in case of mobile devices where a limited number of resources are available. Classification results identify the lesion as melanoma or non-melanoma. The ensuing Sects. 2 to 5 present review based on preprocessing, segmentation, and feature extraction and classification phases respectively. Section 6 presents publically available datasets. Finally conclusion along with the future scope is discussed in Sect. 7.

2 Review Based on the Pre-processing Stage

This section represents the review of methods and techniques followed by the researchers in the preprocessing phase. The preprocessing is the first stage in the automatic melanoma detection system. First of all the data is acquired in the form of Image. As the images are captured in the real-time environment so images may have noise, uncontrolled illumination, and low contrast as shown in Fig. 3. Image captured for analysis don't have sufficient quality due to artifacts and different lightning condition. Therefore for complete analysis of lesion from pigmented skin noise removal is a necessary process. It is observed that problems such as hair [25, 26], skin line may affect lesion classification. These problems also result in a loss of accuracy.

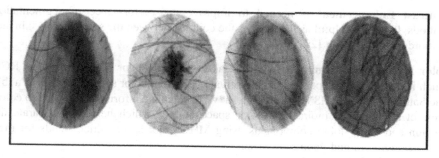

Fig. 3. Images with noise including hair, dust particles, blurry areas (Source: [48]).

Due to illumination conditions, unreliable color information becomes the part of the captured image which makes color normalization compulsory part of preprocessing. So preprocessing of the image is required, which ensures improved quality and hence better performance. Preprocessing methods are divided into two different groups as shown in Fig. 4. i) Image Enhancement ii) Artifact Removal.

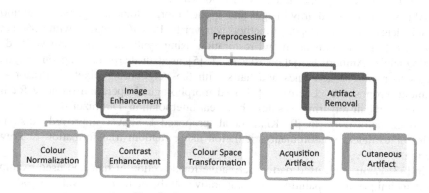

Fig. 4. Process of preprocessing

2.1 Image Enhancement includes processes like color normalization, color space transformation, and contrast enhancement. This step is necessary for easy retrieval of image properties. Images captured under different lighting conditions with variable illumination factors require enhancement.

Color Normalization. It is used for color information retrieval of lesion. It is done by hardware or software. In the hardware-based method, the color properties are dependent on device properties while in software-based method image properties are used for color normalization. If we don't have prior knowledge of acquisition setup then software-based techniques can be used to extract color information. If we have the knowledge of camera color gain, offset and aperture then hardware-based techniques can be used for the normalization process.

Contrast Enhancement is needed to improve the performance of segmentation methods. It is very helpful as it enhances the contrast between the surrounding skin and the border of the lesion [29].

Color Space Transformation is needed as the default color for the image is RGB which is not device independent so it motivated different color space like CIE L*a*b*, Hue Saturation Value (HSV), and CIE L*u*v* to calculate information related to color. Drew et al. proposed bioinspired color space in [24] which helped to separate the melanin and hemoglobin components using MHG color space which stands for melanin, hemoglobin, and geometric mean.

2.2 Artifact Removal. Different artifacts like reflection, ink, skin line, blood vessel, etc. are the elements that appear in the research but are of no use so their removal is required. According to [28] these artifacts are misleading for shape symmetry and color information of lesion. **Acquisition artifacts** include reflection, ink mark on skin. **Cutaneous artifacts** include skin line, blood vessel, hairs. Simplest solution for removing the artifact is a smoothening operator that can be applied using a median or mean filter. The two most basic steps which are involved in artifacts removal are Hair identification and inpainting. The inpainting process is necessary to replace the space covered by hair with proper intensity or color value.

Abbas et al. [2] used gray images and applied morphological edge based technique for hair detection. The proposed method was verified on 100 images with 93% accuracy. In [4] Hair identification and restoration using synthetic hairs were verified by Maglogiannis. Authors Korjakowaska et al. [5] used unsharp masking on grayscale images to repair broken lines and hairs with the neighboring pixel. Dullrazor – A technique proposed by Lee et al. [6] used morphological operation on edge for hair detection and hair repairing was done by linear interpolation. Dullrazor was compatible with thick hairs only. In [9] Kiani et al. proposed E-Shaver improved version of Dullrazor to detect predominant orientation using random transformation & Prewitt filtering.

In [33] Zhou et al. used partial derivative for detection of hair and used exampler based technique for inpainting. A comparative study of hair removal methods was given by Abbas [3]. For dermoscopic images, the authors [4] and [7] proposed an effective hair removal algorithm using PH^2 dataset.

Table 1. Comparison of preprocessing steps of melanoma detection

Hair detection technique	Hair repair technique	Results	Color space	Ref
Derivative of Gaussian and morphological techniques	Fast marching inpainting method	Hair detection error rate: 3.21 & Accuracy: 93%	CIE L*a*b* & grey scale	[2, 3]
Bothat, Laplasian, Logsobel	Interpolation	1) 92.68% 2) 84.80% 3) 88.36%	Grey scale	[4]
Unsharp masking and top-hat transformation	Values calculated by neighborhood pixels	Accuracy: 88.7%	HSL	[5]
Canny edge and morphological operation	Inpainting	Accuracy: 88.3%	Grey scale	[7]

Authors [7] applied the Wiener filter for noise removal from grayscale images. These techniques are summarized in Table 1 and the comparison are provided using PH^2 database from Pedro Hispano Hospital [46, 49].

3   Review Based on the Segmentation Stage

This section represents the review of methods and techniques followed by the researchers in the segmentation phase. Segmentation is the process of partitioning an image into unique and disjoint regions that are homogeneous with respect to attributes like color, shape, and textures [42]. Border detection of lesion is a crucial step [30]. In [43, 44] it is observed that the manual method of border detection is better than computer-based border detection (Fig. 5).

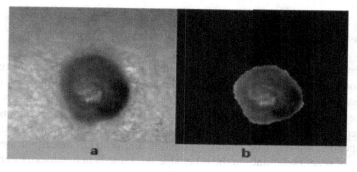

Fig. 5. (a) Original lesion image (b) segmented lesion image (Source: Nazia Hameed, Kamal Abu [46])

Therefore more focus is given to the automated segmentation algorithm. According to [10] in the threshold-based technique, we find threshold value and then group pixels according to the threshold value. In [12] authors used color based segmentation we use color bias for segmentation. Segmentation is done on the basis of active radial search or contour known as discontinuity based segmentation. In region-based segmentation, the image is divided into smaller parts and then merged according to the criteria like similarity [13]. Using PH^2, DermIS, ISIC and HAM10000 datasets the authors [45] summarized different segmentation techniques which are listed in Table 2.

Table 2. Comparison of segmentation techniques performance on input images

Technique	Working principle	Sensitivity	Specificity	Accuracy
Adaptive thresholding	Average thresholding and the standard deviation is used over the histogram area [10]	83.33	99.21	97.43
Neuro-fuzzy model	Color image is converted into device-independent color space and then textures like intensity and color are extracted to be analyzed for entropy and standard deviation [12]	77.84	97.59	96.66
Geometric deformable model	Geometric Curve evolution technique is used to find Coordinate distance (Normal skin lesser distance) [13]	91.78	94.47	87.58
Statistical region merging	Process Start from one region per pixel and then apply a statistical test using intensity differences in neighboring regions to merge similar values [13]	88.35	99.64	97.83

So we observed that lesion segmentation plays a vital role in the analysis and representation of image & segmentation algorithms are categorized according to the technique of Thresholding, region and cluster-based technique [45].

4   Review Based on the Feature Extraction Stage

This section represents the review of methods and techniques followed by the researchers in the feature extraction phase. Features of the lesion like shape, symmetry, color, and border are applied as an input to the classifier. Extracted features are very sensitive because they are measurable and result in a true positive or true negative responses. Based on extracted features different diagnostic models are used. Features to be extracted are problem-specific. On one side feature, extraction and problem descriptor are based on knowledge of practitioner and on the other side the same is automatically derived from datasets without requiring any prior knowledge of the problem.

Lesion is evaluated with respect to various features like Asymmetry, Border, Color and Different Structure. For this major and minor axis of one half are compared to the other half to find whether the lesion is fully symmetric or asymmetric on one axis or asymmetric on both axes. Asymmetric extraction is done mainly by using shape or color parameters. Pattern analysis methods try to identify the specification for global or local patterns. Texture Analysis work to observe fine rough and irregular textures and then utilizes their measurement and differences. In [28] Authors used ABCD rule to identify the lesion's features like Asymmetry, Border, Color, and Diameter. Advancement to ABCD rule was ABCDE which considered the Evaluation factor of the lesion. Authors [15] used a binary mask, area, compactness index, minor and major axis length of the lesion. In [16] color symmetry was computed using intensity value. For Border Extraction according to the authors [17] to identify the sharpness between skin and lesion semi-quantitative process can be used. In [18] authors used the statistical methods like average, standard deviation, mean, variance, entropy for extracting the color features. Menzies method was used for negative feature extraction by [19, 33]. Authors [35] used pigment network, blue-white veil, vascular pattern, irregular streaks, irregular blotches and regression structure for extracting features. Table 3 List various lesion feature extraction techniques.

Table 3. Comparison of feature extraction techniques using their working principle

Technique	Working principle
Asymmetric features	ABCD Rule (Asymmetry, Border, Color, and Diameter) Shape Symmetry [28] is computed using binary mask, area, perimeter, compactness index, rectangularity, major and minor axes length [15] Color Symmetry is computed using intensity value and color components of symmetric pixels [16]
Border features	A semi-quantitative process is used to identify the sharpness between lesion and skin because melanoma contains a higher border score than nevi Least square method can be used to quantify the blurriness of border Thinness ratio can be used to find the degree of irregularity using formula (4 a $\pi/p*p$) where a is area and p is perimeter [17]
Color features	Color distribution of lesion is studied using statistical method (average, SD, mean, variance, entropy, skewness, histogram & autocorrelogram) and color quantization based methods (reduce the colors in predefined values) pixels with similar properties are grouped into a single region using K-mean, Gaussian mixture model and multi-thresholding technique [18]
Dermoscopic feature	Dermoscopic structure is analyzed for visual patterns using pigment network with dark lines and light background, Gray Level Co-occurrence matrix GLCM, for higher-order computation we make use of Gray Level Run Length Matrix GLRLM, to extract gradient information Local Binary Patterns LBP is used [18, 32]
Single color detection	Menzies Method It seeks only negative features such as the presence of single color and symmetry of pattern [19, 33]
ELM-7	Pigment network, blue-white veil, vascular pattern, irregular streaks, irregular blotches, and regression structure [19, 35]

According to Catarina et al. [47], a feature extraction process can also be divided into four main classes. For global image descriptors like shape symmetry color and texture were defined to be the part of Hand Crafted Features Class while Dictionary-based features class covered local descriptors. To automatically learn from image (like CNN) features were classified under Deep Learning Class and clinically inspired Class described features attributing medical meaning.

5 Review Based on the Classification Stage

This section represents the review of methods and techniques followed by the researchers in the classification phase. Classification tells us whether the lesion is melanoma or not using features extracted from the lesion. The result of classification is based on the type of input from the previous phase that is extracted features. The classification is performed using Bayesian Classifier which uses color correlogram [37] and texture analysis and is used to detect the abnormal skin using color and SFTA features [38] or using KNN based classifier which is a linear classifier developed using receiver operating characteristic curve and compares the threshold against a fixed sensitivity or one may use Decision Tree Classifier involves pixel classification in which a simple shape descriptor is used for classification [39]. Comparison of various classification techniques is listed in Table 4.

Table 4. Comparison of various classification techniques for melanoma detection

Technique	Working principle
Neural network based diagnosis	Skin Lesion is considered for probability distribution over skin disease classes using Google Inception v3 CNN Architecture trained on ImageNet [20], Scratch Feature extractor Fine-tuning and Hybrid architecture using CNN can also be used [21]
Mobile automated skin lesion classification	The contour of the lesion is detected after converting image lesion to a monochrome image. After extracting all features, they are given as input to the KNN classifier. The experimental results show that this system is working efficiently well on test 1images, with accuracy of 66.7% [22]
Bayesian classifier	Bayesian classifier is used to detect the abnormal skin cells with feature vector SFTA and color correlogram [34]. Using given dermoscopic dataset system executed with 91.5% accuracy [23]
SVM classifier	Sequential minimal optimization uses iterative dilation method for noise removal and recognize melanoma using features like asymmetry border color [23]

Authors [20] used Google Inception v3 CNN architecture trained on ImageNet and [21] used hybrid architecture using CNN. In [23] SVM classifier made use of dilation method and sequential minimal optimization techniques. KNN classifier was used by

[22] and resulted in 66.7% accuracy with test data. Bayesian classifier used by [23, 34] for abnormal skin cell identification. According to [39] classification models used for melanoma, detection can be grouped into Global, semi-global, local or hybrid categories. Global Models contain Linear, polynomial models, and SVM. The semi-global model includes Multivariate Adaptive Regression Spline, Decision trees, and radial basis functions. Local model includes K-nearest neighbors, while projection-based radial basis functions are part of Hybrid Models [37–39].

6   Publically Available Datasets

Datasets which are publically available for various researchers are as follows:

6.1 ISIC Challenge Dataset. The International Skin Imaging Collaboration (ISIC) is an international repository of dermoscopic images to improve the diagnosis of melanoma. This challenge provides 25331 images under 8 different categories [50].

6.2 DermIS dataset is available for educational purpose and is available for educational purpose [51].

6.3 PH^2. This dermoscopic dataset is provided by Hospital Pedro Hispano and contains 200 images available for educational use [49].

7   Conclusion

Early detection of melanoma is essential therefore a meticulous review of the steps used in the Automatic Melanoma Detection System is required. The objective of this paper is to discuss and review the i) preprocessing for noise removal; ii) segmentation for extracting lesion from the skin; iii) feature extraction for accessing color, shape, symmetry and other features related to nevi; and iv) classification for melanoma detection used in automatic melanoma detection system. Each relevant techniques and associated features which provided a comprehensive explanation are discussed. Various steps, techniques, and methods are analyzed and compared with each other using various parameters like accuracy and working principle. There is still room for improvement and relevant contributions to the automatic melanoma detection system. Instead of using stable images we may capture the video of the infected area for the detection of melanoma. The rate for false detection of melanoma from a lesion may be minimized by developing the system with more accuracy by combining two or more classification techniques together. Work done so far in melanoma detection will be a valuable guide for researchers. Also, the well-designed automated melanoma detection system can substitute the invasive manual diagnosis system. It is observed from state-of-art literature in this research field that AMDS needs to overcome the challenges in the extraction of the lesion from the image of the skin and its segmentation with more accuracy to implement in real-life situations under different environments.

References

1. WebMD: Better information better health. The skin (Human Anatomy). http://www.webmd. com/skin-problems-andtreatments/picture-of-the-skin
2. Celebi, M.E., Fondon, I., Abbas, Q.: Hair removal method: a comparative study for dermoscopy images. BSP Control **6**(6), 395–404 (2011)
3. Abbas, Q., Ahmad, W., Garcia, I., Celebi, M.E.: A feature-preserving hair removal algorithm for dermoscopy images. Skin Res. Technol. **19**(1), 27–36 (2013)
4. Maglogiannis, I., Delibasis K.: Hair removal on dermoscopy images. In: IEEE (EMBC), pp. 2960–2963 (2015)
5. Korjakowska, T.: Hair removal from dermoscopic color images. Bio-Algorithms Med-Syst. **9**(2), 53–58 (2013)
6. Lee, T., Ng, V., Gallagher, R., Coldman, R., Dullrazor: a software approach to hair removal from images. Comput. Biol. Med. **27**(6), 533–543, 1799 (2013)
7. Toossi, M.T.B., Pourreza, H., Zare, H., Sigari, M., Azimi, A., Layegh, P.: An effective hair removal algorithm for dermoscopy images. Skin Rese. Technol. **19**(3), 230–235 (2013)
8. Celebi, M.E., et al.: A state-of-the-art survey on lesion border detection in dermoscopy images. Dermoscopy Image Analysis **10**, 97–129 (2015)
9. Kiani, K., Sharafat, A.: E-shaver an improved dullrazor for digitally removing dark and light-colored hairs in dermoscopic images. Comput. Biol. Med. **41**(3), 139–145 (2011)
10. Sforza, G., Castellano, G., Arika, S.K., Robert, W.: Using adaptive thresholding and skewness correction to detect gray areas in melanoma in situ images. IEEE Trans. Instrum. **61**(7), 1839–1847 (2012)
11. Lee, G., et al.: Quantitative color assessment of dermoscopy images using perceptible color regions. Skin Res. Technol. **18**, 462–470 (2012)
12. Baral, B., Gonnade, S., Verma, T.: Lesion segmentation in dermoscopic images using decision-based neuro-fuzzy model. Int. J. Comput. Sci. Inf. Technol. (IJCSIT) **5**(2), 2546–2552 (2014)
13. Ma, Z., Tavares, J.M.R.: A novel approach to segment skin lesions in dermoscopic images based on a deformable model. IEEE J. Biomed. **20**, 615–623 (2015)
14. Garnavi, R., Aldeen, M., Bailey, J.: Computer-aided diagnosis of melanoma using border and wavelet-based texture analysis. IEEE Trans. Inform. Technol. Biomed. **16**(6), 1239–1252 (2012)
15. Katapadi, A.B., et al.: Evolving strategies for the development and evaluation of a computerized melanoma image analysis system. Comput. Methods Biomech. Biomed. Eng. Imaging Vis. **6**, 465–472 (2018)
16. Møllersen, K., et al.: Improved skin lesion diagnostics for general practice by computer-aided diagnostics. In: Proceedings of Dermoscopy Image Analysis, pp. 247–292 (2015)
17. Abbas, Q., Celebi, M.E., Fondon, I.: Computer-aided pattern classification system for dermoscopy images. Skin Res. Technol. **18**, 278–289 (2012)
18. Giotis, I., Petkov, N.: Cluster-based adaptive metric classification. Neurocomputing **81**, 33–40 (2012)
19. Maier, T., Kulichova, D., Schotten, K., Astrid, R., Ruzicka, T., Berking, C., Udrea, A.: Accuracy of a smartphone application using fractal image analysis of pigmented moles compared to clinical diagnosis and histological result. J. Eur. Acad. Dermatol. Venereol. **29**, 663–667 (2015)
20. Esteva, A., et al.: Dermatologist-level classification of skin cancer with deep neural networks. Nature **542**, 115–118 (2017)

21. Murphree, D.H., Ngufor, C.: Transfer learning for melanoma detection participation in ISIC 2017 skin lesion classification challenge, vision and pattern recognition (cs.CV). arXiv:1703. 05235 (2017)

22. Stikic, M., Schiele, B.: A mobile automated skin lesion classification system. In: IEEE International Conference on Tools with Artificial Intelligence, pp. 138 – 141(2011)

23. Soumya, R.S., Neethu, S., Niju, T.S., Renjini, A., Aneesh, R.P: Advanced earlier melanoma detection algorithm using color correlogram. In: 2016 International Conference on Communication Systems and Networks (ComNet), pp. 190–194. IEEE (2013)

24. Madooei, D.: A bioinspired color representation for dermoscopy image analysis. In: Proceedings of Dermoscopy Image Analysis, pp. 23–66 (2015)

25. Do, T.T., Hoang, T., Pomponiu, V.: Accessible melanoma detection using smartphones and mobile image analysis. IEEE Trans. Multimedia **20**, 2849–2864 (2018)

26. Barata, C., Marques, J.S., Rozeira, J.: A system for the detection of pigment network in dermoscopy images using directional filters. IEEE Trans. Biomed. Eng. **59**(10), 2744–2754 (2012)

27. Shimizu, K., et al.: Four-class classification of skin lesions with task decomposition strategy. IEEE Trans. Biomed. Eng. **62**(1), 274–283 (2015)

28. Ruela, M., et al.: A system for the detection of melanomas in dermoscopy images using shape and symmetry features. Comput. Methods Biomech. Biomed. Eng. Imaging Vis. **5**, 127–137 (2017)

29. Jaworek-Korjakowska, J.: Novel method for border irregularity assessment in dermoscopic color images. Comput. Math. Methods Med. **2015** (2015). Art no. 496202

30. Kockara, S., et al.: Fractals for malignancy detection in dermoscopy images. In: Proceedings of IEEE International Conference on Healthcare Informatics, pp. 115–121 (2015)

31. Giotis, I., Molders, N., Land, S., Biehl, M., Jonkman, M.F., Petkov, N.: A computer-assisted melanoma diagnosis system using nondermoscopic images. Expert Syst. Appl. **42**(19), 6578–6585 (2015)

32. Do, T-T., Zhou, Y., Zheng, H., Cheung, N-M., Koh, D.: Early melanoma diagnosis with mobile imaging. In: 36th Annual International Conference of the IEEE Engineering in Medicine and Biology Society (2014)

33. Do, T-T., Zhou, Y., Pomponiu, V., Cheung, N-M., Koh, D.C.I.: Method and device for analyzing an image, Patent US 20 170 231 550 A1, 17 August 2017

34. Celebi, M.E., Wen, Q., Hwang, S., Schaefer, G.: Color quantization of dermoscopy images using the k-means clustering algorithm. In: Celebi, M., Schaefer, G. (eds.) Color Medical Image Analysis, pp. 87–107. Springer, Dordrecht (2013). https://doi.org/10.1007/978-94-007-5389-1_5

35. Lingala, M., Joe Stanley, R., Rader, R.K., Hagerty, J., Rabinovitz, H.S., Oliviero, M.: Stoecker: fuzzy logic color detection: blue areas in melanoma dermoscopy images. Comput. Med. Imaging Graph. **38**(5), 403–410 (2014)

36. Cudek, P., Hippe, Z.: Melanocytic skin lesions: a new approach to color assessment. In: 2015 8th International Conference on Human System Interaction (HSI), pp. 99–101 (2015)

37. Jain, S., Jagtap, V., Pise, N.: Computer-aided melanoma skin cancer detection using image processing. In: International Conference on Intelligent Computing, Communication Convergence, ELSEVIER, pp. 735–740 (2015)

38. Kasmi, R., Mokranii, K.: Classification of malignant melanoma and benign skin lesions: implementation of automatic ABCD rule. IET Image Process. **10**(6), 448–455 (2016)

39. Sujitha,S., LakshmiPriya, M., Premaladha, J., Ravichandran, K.S.: A combined segmentation approach for melanoma skin cancer diagnosis. In: 2015 IEEE Seventh National Conference on Computing, Communication and Information Systems (NCCCIS), pp. 11–16. IEEE (2015)

40. Hoshyar, A.N., AlJumailya, A., Hoshyar, A.N.: The beneficial techniques in preprocessing step of skin cancer detection system comparing. Procedia Comput. Sci. **42**, 25–31 (2014)

41. Urooj, S., Singh, S.: A novel computer assisted approach for diagnosis of skin disease. IEEE (2015)

42. Haseena Thasneem, A.A., Mehaboobathunnisa, R., Mohammed Sathik, M., Arumugam, S.: Comparison of different segmentation algorithms for dermoscopic images. ICTACT J. Image Video Process. **05**(04) (2015)

43. Revathi, V., Chithra, A.: A review on segmentation techniques in skin lesion images. Int. Res. J. Eng. Technol. (IRJET) **02**(09), 2598–2603 (2015)

44. Sadri, A.R., Zekri, M., Sadri, S., Gheissari, N., Mokhtari, M., Kolahdouzan, F.: Segmentation of dermoscopy images using wavelet networks. IEEE Trans. Biomed. Eng. **60**(4), 1134–1141 (2013)

45. Thompson, F.: Review of segmentation methods on malignant melanoma. In: International Conference on Circuit, Power and Computing Technologies (2016)

46. Hameed, N., Abu, K.: A comprehensive survey on image-based computer-aided diagnosis system for skin cancer. IEEE (2016)

47. Catarina, M.E., Jorge, S.: A survey of feature extraction in dermoscopy image analysis of skin cancer. IEEE J. Biomed. Health Inform. **23**, 1096–1109 (2018)

48. Prathamesh Somnathe, A., Gumaste, P.P.: A review of existing hair removal methods in dermoscopic images. IOSR-JECE **1**, 73–76 (2015)

49. PH^2 Database (2013). http://www.fc.up.pt

50. ISIC Database. https://www.isic-archive.com/#!/topWithHeader/tightContentTop/challenges

51. DermIS (2016). https://www.dermis.net/dermisroot/en/17697/image.htm

Comparative Study of Sentiment Analysis and Text Summarization for Commercial Social Networks

Hamza Abubakar Kheruwala(iD), Jimeet Viren Shah(iD),
and Jai Prakash Verma$^{(\boxtimes)}$(iD)

Institute of Technology, Nirma University, Ahmedabad, India
habubakar89@gmail.com, jimeet1999shah@gmail.com,
jaiprakash.verma@nirmauni.ac.in

Abstract. The rapid shift towards digitalization today has actually transferred the market to an entirely digitalized platform. The participation of such a large number of users has given rise to a huge amount of data over the internet, proving the need for proper structuring and removal of unwanted and redundant data. The presence of a system that gives them the complete overview of a product is a dire need for the public today. Diving deep, we nd technologies that help us in the analysis and modification of data found over the internet. Sentiment analysis helps us nd the opinions people have towards a variety of entities, through a series of processes. Along with this, we have text summarisation which aids in the attainment of meaningful information from the wide range of irrelevant and redundant data found online. Clubbing these two, we can obtain concise reviews in addition to the overall sentiment towards selected entities. Here, we propose a model where we convolve into a system that provides the user with the overall recommendation found on popular e-commerce websites (Amazon, Flipkart and TripAdvisor). Starting with the collection of data from given sources, we pre-process the data, we combine machine learning with a lexicon-based approach, obtain the summaries and sentiments and eventually provide the user with the popular opinion behind the product.

Keywords: Text summarization · Recommendation system · Sentiment analysis · Machine learning · Big data

1 Introduction

In recent years, the advancement in technology has led to big breakthroughs and most importantly, the emergence of social media in every corner of the world. Be it anything on the internet, people have had their say on everything they see. While this might not seem this big a deal, but the collection of tons of such reviews and comments, incorporated with the latest computing technologies, help people and organizations extract polarized opinion and relevant information.

On one hand, users can identify the popular opinion towards an entity; while on the other, companies can identify users' opinions on a large number of their products.

© Springer Nature Singapore Pte Ltd. 2020
S. Gupta and J. N. Sarvaiya (Eds.): ET2ECN 2020, CCIS 1214, pp. 213–224, 2020.
https://doi.org/10.1007/978-981-15-7219-7_18

A widely used technique is the Sentiment Analysis, one that helps formulate public opinions and attitudes towards a particular entity [1], removing redundant data and presenting it in the most succinct manner possible. In simple words, the main task of this technique is to identify the polarity in a given content.

As a result of the tremendous amount of data available [5], it is a necessity that we tackle the overloading of information, obtain data in the most efficient manner possible, extract the most relevant and vital information possible, in large volumes. To fulfill the requirements mentioned above, the one technology that comes into our minds is Sentiment Analysis, this has been attracting increasing attention in the recent years due to the tremendous increase in information and also because it is the best viable solution till date. While many people target the same technology, there are different approaches people adopt to fulfill their purpose.

In the last few years, the rise in the number of public opinions and their say on things on the internet has made it extremely difficult for individuals and corporations to read and analyze the required data available. As a result, it is important that such a vast amount of data is analyzed and presented in a properly understandable form. Sentiment Analysis is one mechanism that identifies and analyses the required data and presents users with a short and proper representation of the same. Not just for people, Sentiment Analysis also aids companies in knowing the public opinion on their products. Simply speaking, the polarity of a particular data set is classified as positive, negative and neutral [15].

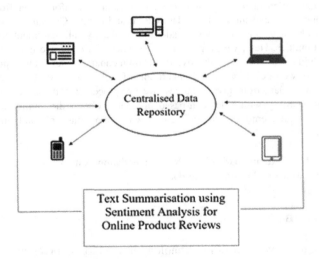

Fig. 1. Simplied overview of the system.

Furthermore, summarisation can be of two types: Abstractive Summarisation and Extractive Summarisation. Abstractive Summarisation involves the regeneration of content after the interpretation and examination of the passage while Extractive

Summarisation identifies the important sections from the text (The focus in this model) and produces a subset of sentences from the same. While both of these are better in their own applications, an Abstractive Summary will be more coherent and polished than its counterpart. [8] As given in Fig. 1, we come up with a system that analyses reviews and recommendations on online platforms, and generates sentiments and summaries behind the entire sets of available information. Any product that can be found such websites can be analyzed for public opinions.

2   Related Work

In this section, we present a brief overview of the work carried out earlier in the context of proposed methods and algorithms for sentiment analysis, followed by the revised proposal for the system. Since the inception of this technology, the wide network of the internet has brought people together. Millions come together to discuss their ideas, opinions, and sentiments over this technology. It is, therefore, a dire need to analyze these and go about the different processes that help us do the same. For the same, an expert system that goes about storing this data and detects sentiments behind such documents must be built [10].

Text Summarisation goes about creating a generative summary of a given piece, removing the redundant data [16] and can be of different types. An Abstractive Summary conveys the idea behind the entire text, but may not use the words or sentences there, while an Extractive Summary uses parts of the text to create the summary of the text piece [3]. Again, in a Query Based Summary, the user's query must be answered through the summary generated while a Generic Summary gives the general idea behind the text. Sentiment Analysis is one such technology that helps us formulate the opinion someone has towards a particular entity [11]. Combining it with Text Summarisation, there is a wide range of applications we can solve: Formulate the overall attitude of a group regarding the entity we wish to look upon. It can be of Document Level, Sentence Level, and Aspect Level [11].

Here, we go about fusing Sentiment Analysis with Text summarisation to accomplish our goal of formulating the overall opinion of people towards the entity we are targeting. While there a variety of approaches to this, there are three basic steps to fulfill this goal: Interpretation - Transformation - Generation. The approaches to this are mainly three: Machine Learning, Lexicon Based and the Hybrid Approach, which is a combination of the other two. While the Lexicon based approach gives scores to different words based on the dictionary, it fails to address the semantic analysis of the text, sentiment shifters and additionally fails outside the specified set of words. To tackle this problem, the deep learning approach initially trains on given sets and then tests the provided cases efficiently. Here, greater the cases trained upon, higher is the efficiency obtained in the results.

While the other two have features of their own, a hybrid of both can provide a better, more comprehensive summary with contextual polarity and word variations taken care of [3]. An example of the Lexicon Based Approach is the usage of the RSentiment Package, which involves thousands of words that are assigned individual scores based on their meanings. Again, the Machine Learning Approach involves a technique like Word2vec, which gives a vector representation of a given word, helping the user easily store as well as interpret the connections among words [2, 4] CoRank helps to create an unsupervised graph model for the word-sentence relationship, where the words are the vertices and the edges are the connectors [9]. The words are assigned weights as per their occurrences and importance in the passage. In fact, the higher the number of keywords, the higher the weight of the sentence in the graph model.

Once the data is collected, there comes the time to have an apt representation for further processes. Word Cloud provides a suitable approach where different words are displayed as a cloud as per their occurrence. Furthermore, depending on their sentiment (Positive, Negative or Neutral), they are assigned colors for ease of usage. Again, care is taken that the redundancy is removed, sentences are rid of unnecessary connectors and words that alter the polarity of the sentence are necessarily kept in the radar. These help in efficiently going with the process. The use of RNN for the same involves the incorporation of a number of strategies to cope with problems like contextual polarity, sentiment shifter, etc. [6]. The Naïve Bayes algorithm proves to be better when opposed to other ML approaches in terms of sentiment and emotion detection from the text [14].

In order to eliminate the features under consideration and obtain the best model, two approaches are used [7]: Feature Selection selects a subset of the most relevant features. Apart of this, filter methods select the most important features through statistical measures, wrapper methods use trained models and embedded methods select the features during model training. Feature Extraction reduces the variables by transforming a large number of attributes into a reduced set of features [17].

With the continuous development in the eld of E-Commerce and related fields, it is now a norm and for people to buy most products online. With attracting costumers being a big priority for all sellers in the market, there is a big competition among them to emerge out on the top. Amidst this, costumers search for the best methods that get them the best-suited products for the price they pay. Online reviews play an important role in influencing their decision for the same. It is shown that 92% of costumers read online reviews before making a purchase and most of them base their entire opinions on these reviews [13]. From the thousands of reviews available for each product online, it is important that people get to know what the vast majority supports, not just base their decision on a few reviews. Here comes the dire need for a system that does the work for them, one that combines all these and gives them a sum of all reviews and the sentiment behind these. Table 1 also shows a comparative analysis of different data analytic and approaches with their pros and cons in the area of text data analytics.

Table 1. Comparative analysis of work in the area of sentiment analysis and text summarisation

Approach	Year	Objective	Methodology	Pros	Cons
Sentiment infusion [6]	2016	Abstractive text summarisation using sentiment infusion	Sentiment infusion	An improvement on the existing extractive techniques, it outperforms related works in the field	Unable to combine sentences that are semantically related but not syntactically related
Graph-based technique [16]	2016	Abstractive text summarization using sentiment infusion	AMR graphs	Concise summaries are obtained from leveraging of sentence word order to form coherent sentences	Less precise when compared against to results of techniques that generate Abstractive summaries
Hybrid approach [3]	2017	Summarization of multiple short online reviews	NLP machine learning neural network extended biterm topic model	Concurrence patterns are explicitly generated using midterms	The collection of documents only has one shared topic distribution
Deep learning [4]	2017	Enhancing deep learning-based sentiment analysis	Generic and sentiment trained word embedding (NLP)	Improved performance with the ensemble of word embeddings & manually crafter features	Higher cost in terms of computational resources
Machine Learning [9]	2018	Automatic extractive text summarisation	CoRank model for co-ranking	Concise with guaranteed convergence	Can be replaced by a redundancy elimination technique
Topic and sentiment joint modeling [18]	2018	Short sentiment topic model for product reviews	World sentiment topic model	Performs better with the increased topics	Fluctuates lightly when there is a scarcity in data
Deep learning [6]	2019	Sentiment classification of evaluative text based on multifeature fusion	RNN	Overcomes word and contextual polarity, word sense variations, word coverage limit	Lack of a greater sentiment lexicon hinders the performance of the implementation
Text mining [19]	2018	Use of text mining to analyze the Syrian refugee crisis	NLP (lexicon based approach)	The lexicon contained a lot of subject-specific terms	Limit of Lexicons for analyzing languages further Emojis not analyzed
Machine learning [14]	2018	Analysis of sentiments and emotions from Twitter text	NLP, Naïve Bayes Theorem	All six emotions were analyzed from multiple dimensions	Full-text sentiment showed greater accuracy than others like Naive Bayes Theorem
Machine learning [10]	2018	Semi-supervised dimensionality reduction using feature weighting	Not discussed	Uses enhanced dimensionality reduction features	Applicable only for single label binary classification

3   Proposed Work

Categorisation of thousands of reviews into meaningful conclusions is of importance to costumers buying products online. Given the number of systems available that do the same, it is a necessity that we have an approach that takes into account the maximum parameters possible to provide the user with the best possible conclusion to support their decision. What many others have failed to solve is the inclusion of more factors, other than just reviews on products. Here, we include parameters like ratings, recommendations based on these, compound sentiment scoring, lemmatization and stemming to produce the most promising results. Furthermore, we test our model with parameters like accuracy, precision, F score, recall. The proposed architecture is given in Fig. 2, where we proceed to list the various steps involved in the process.

We begin with the collection of data from specific E-Commerce Websites, followed by the pre-processing of data, where we correct the spellings of words, remove stop words which create redundancy and perform lemmatization and stemming. Next, we summarise the text from the reviews and utilize the summarised text clubbed with ratings to provide the sentiments behind all the reviews. We utilize several parameters to provide an optimal recommendation system to the user. Text summarization is done using the NLTK package in python; we begin by the removal of unnecessary stop words, links, followed by the reduction of all data to root-base words. This is an open-source Python library that aids in text processing in the form of parsing, tokenization, semantics, tagging, stemming, etc. Next, tokenization is followed by the calculation of weighted frequency of occurrence, and the words appearing the most are plotted in a table in the order of their occurrence, as given in Fig. 2. TextBlob is a large library that provides a variety of text-related applications; one of which is sentiment analysis. Using this, we assign sentiment on a score of $[-1, 1]$ to all the product reviews and obtain resulting charts and graphs to present the overall sentiment behind the selected product. One issue that might generally occur would be due to the active and the passive style of sentences. TextBlob succeeds in this since it divides the words, performs tokenization and extracts only the required, meaningful words. This way, only the words behind the actual sentiments are captures, leaving behind the worry of how the sentence is spoken.

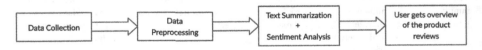

Fig. 2. Flow of the proposed architecture

4   Methodology and Concepts

The articles published in the table state the objectives and the methodology adopted for different models, where each of them has different efficiency; with their own advantages and disadvantages. Some use the lexicon-based approach, some go for the machine learning approach (Fig. 3), while there are others who implement their model as a hybrid of the two. While the lexicon-based approach directs the scores based on predefined sentiments for the bag of words, the machine learning approach is a more

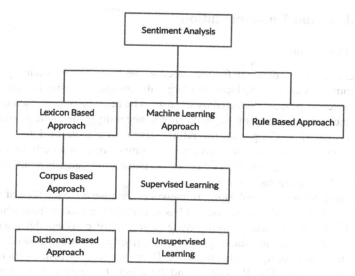

Fig. 3. Techniques for sentiment analysis

widely adopted method, using algorithms that give the idea behind the positive, negative and neutral sentiments of texts. Some approaches are specific with their applications while most of them focus on general applications that can have a wide range of uses. Initially, we used the Scrapy Framework to crawl on the amazon website and obtain recommendations, reviews and other parameters using specific CSS Selectors. Through the same framework, we obtain the data in the form of CSV files, which are easy to be worked upon. Next, to obtain the data in a precise form, we use the NLTK package (Stemming and Lemmatization) from python to remove unnecessary tags, links, stop words, etc. which unnecessarily increase the redundancy of the data. Once the root-based words are obtained, and concise reviews obtained, we perform the next step, where we obtain the corresponding frequencies. Their frequencies are obtained and we get the table as shown in Fig. 5. Using TextBlob and Sentiment Intensity Analyser, the sentiments for the reviews are obtained and the corresponding graphs and pie charts are obtained. Furthermore, the ratings which are obtained are used to either "Recommend" or "Not Recommend" the product given. The percentage of reviews in each category are obtained through the equation shows in Eq. 1.

$$category\% = \frac{number\ of\ reviews\ in\ selected\ category}{total\ number\ of\ tweets\ in\ all\ catergories\ (positive + negative + neutral)}$$

(1)

Once the results are obtained, we test the model for Accuracy, Precision, Recall, F1 Score and we obtain the corresponding Confusion Matrix. This is done using the Random Forest Classier and the pandas library from python.

5 Execution and Implementation

5.1 Data Extraction

For the selection of the data set for the process, we focused on obtaining the same ourselves from relevant places. Here, we target the amazon website for the data with regards to particular products selected by the user. The relevant data to each product, as taken here include the name of the user (not a necessity), the review given to the product, title of review along with the ratings given on a scale of 1 to 5. Since the recommendations for an individual product can range from hundreds to even thousands, it is necessary that a reliable tool is used to extract the same. For our application, we use the web-scraping tool: Scrapy.

A fairly straightforward application framework, once we have the idea of what data to extract from desired web pages, one just has to specify the classes from which it is to be extracted. Though we have varying reviews for every product, the selectors that specify these for each are the same, giving us the liberty of getting desired results for varying products specifying similar selectors. Here, we use the Inspect Element tool, which gives the CSS and HTML code behind the selected web page. Once the selectors are selected, they are entered into scrappy with desired selectors, which give us the output as required. The spider crawls on the basis of specified selectors and extracts the data from each of them. Again, the information is extracted to a CSV file where it can be used accordingly for further processing. Once the CSV file is generated, we obtain our data, properly bifurcated and divided into various categories, with each column specifying a feature and row specifying one particular review.

5.2 Data Pre-processing

Once the data is obtained and exported as readable les, it is necessary to preprocess the data before we perform the execution. The data has to be in proper form so that it can be worked upon for text summarisation and sentiment analysis. We need to have root based words which can be directly used to provide the sentiments behind the reviews and can be used in the summarisation. First, we apply segmentation followed by tokenization, where we split the long strings of text to paragraphs, and eventually obtain words as tokens. We take the individual words and perform stemming and lemmatization, which is in charge of eliminating axes, and obtaining the root word, thereby giving us the canonical forms of processed words. Next, we remove unnecessary stop words that fail to contribute towards the sentiment of the review. Noise removal is done next, where unnecessary tags are removed. For these purposes, we use the NLTK library which enables us to perform the different applications stated above.

5.3 Execution

We have the data in the base form, with the elimination of unnecessary words that are of no use to us. Initially, we use the Term Frequency-Inverse Document Frequency to tokenize the documents, and obtain weights for individual words. As given above in Table 2, we have the weights assigned to different words, arising out of their weight in the dataset in totality. We apply the TextBlob library in Python, where we perform the sentiment analysis behind the reviews, assigning the sentiment score on from [−1, 1]. To add to this, we take the rating, and assign the recommendation on the basis of those ratings, where the range from [3, 5] amounts to "True" and those from [0, 2] subject to "False" where the user does not recommend the product.

Again, based on the sentiment score calculated for each review, we bifurcate the reviews as \Positive, Neutral and Negative". The total reviews for each category are calculated, the reviews are categorized into respective categories. To make it easier for the user to comprehend, we prepare a user-friendly graph, with the total reviews divided into batches and divided into the two sentimental categories. In fact, as given in Fig. 4, we represent our accumulated data in the form of various representations that eventually make the user identify the results through a variety of approaches.

Table 2. Weights of words + breakdown of weights - Amazon Kindle

rating	recommend	sentiment	length
5.0	True	0.8910	52
5.0	True	0.9800	110
3.0	True	0.9678	168
2.0	False	0.6829	170
5.0	True	0.9715	132
2.0	False	0.5540	174

word	frequency
qualiti	56.084501
good	0.287370
even	2.321587
read	1.714336
2	0.485983
3	0.131513
hour	0.094560
stress	0.333211
eye	0.108215
batteri	0217953

6   Results and Discussions

We performed this project keeping in mind the need for an optimal system for the analysis and overall study of the reviews. While there are many others that target the same and obtain similar results (please refer Fig. 4), we combine various parameters ranging from text summarization, sentiment analysis to recommendations, where the average user gets to completely know the opinion and say of people who have reviewed the specific product(Amazon Kindle). To analyze the extent and the performance of this project, we apply the Random Forest Classier algorithm. We combine the various parameters in order to obtain the confusion matrix, which helps us evaluate the entire model proposed. Through results, we get a matrix as shown in Fig. 5. We obtain promising results with respect to sentiment analysis, used with the generated recommendation system to give the average user and optimal system to identify the take of public on social E-commerce platforms.

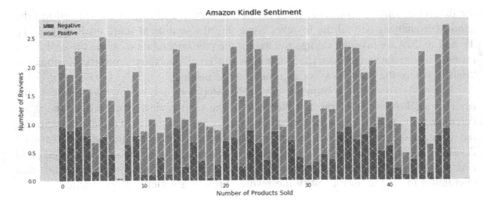

Fig. 4. Numeric categorization of reviews - Amazon Kindle

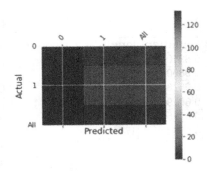

Fig. 5. Confusion matrix - Amazon Kindle

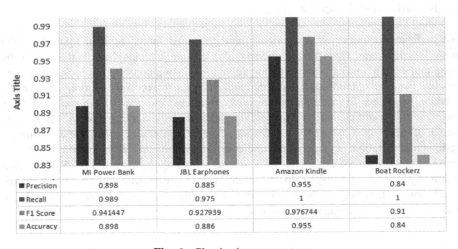

	MI Power Bank	JBL Earphones	Amazon Kindle	Boat Rockerz
Precision	0.898	0.885	0.955	0.84
Recall	0.989	0.975	1	1
F1 Score	0.941447	0.927939	0.976744	0.91
Accuracy	0.898	0.886	0.955	0.84

Fig. 6. Classication parameters

Figure 6 shows different products' calculated parameters for evaluation picked up from websites like Amazon (MI Power Bank, JBL Earphones and Amazon Kindle) and Flipkart (Boat Rockerz), in addition to Trip Advisor. Upon repeated evaluation, we compared the evaluation parameters and found out that the model performed best in the case of Amazon products, giving promising results. Our average Accuracy of 0.89 (approx.) is found to perform better than SVM and Linguistic approaches used by [12]. In addition to this, we include recommendations to give the user an added feature.

7 Conclusion

The presence of a large amount of data on the internet has made it necessary as well as advantageous to perform analysis for a variety of applications; say monitoring, research, commercialization, etc. Given the large pool of this data, the removal of unwanted and redundant information leaves us with precise data sets which can be worked upon for text mining purposes. This model is limited to specific E commerce websites currently, where the user gets the result upon entering the URL of the specific product which is to be analyzed. In this paper, we primarily targeted Amazon, Trip Advisor and Flipkart. In this paper, we presented sentiment analysis and summarization based on different products from different platforms. Our project is still limited to the point where the link of the product page on the website is to be given for further processing. In the future scope of this project, we look to incorporate a bigger system that takes in the product name searches for the product over the website, a variety of reviews and automatically obtains a detailed summarization of reviews for the thousands of reviews. Once implemented, this can prove to be a very useful system where an average user will have to just give their desired product and obtain the direct the sentiment of the public over the entire internet, and not go through hundreds of reviews on different websites and still, make a wrong decision based on just a few reviews.

References

1. The evolution of sentiment analysis-a review of research topics, venues, and top cited papers. Comput. Sci. Rev. **27**, 16–32 (2018). https://doi.org/10.1016/j.cosrev.2017.10.002
2. Abdi, A., Shamsuddin, S.M., Hasan, S., Piran, J.: Deep learning-based sentiment classification of evaluative text based on multi-feature fusion. Inf. Process. Manage. **56** (4), 1245–1259 (2019)
3. Amplayo, R.K., Song, M.: An adaptable ne-grained sentiment analysis for summarization of multiple short online reviews. Data Knowl. Eng. **110**, 54–67 (2017)
4. Araque, O., Corcuera-Platas, I., Sánchez-Rada, J.F., Iglesias, C.A.: Enhancing deep learning sentiment analysis with ensemble techniques in social applications. Expert Syst. Appl. **77**, 236–246 (2017)
5. Babar, S., Tech-Cse, M.: Rit: text summarization: an overview (2013)
6. Bhargava, R., Sharma, Y., Sharma, G.: ATSSI: abstractive text summarization using sentiment infusion. Procedia Comput. Sci. **89**, 404–411 (2016). Twelfth International Conference on Communication Networks, ICCN 2016, Bangalore, India, 19–21 August 2016, Twelfth International Conference on Data Mining and Warehousing, ICDMW 2016, Bangalore, India, 19–21 August 2016, Twelfth International Conference on Image and Signal Processing, ICISP 2016, Bangalore, India, 19–21 August 2016

7. Chan, S.W., Chong, M.W.: Sentiment analysis in financial texts. Decis. Support Syst. **94**, 53–64 (2017)
8. Collins, E., Augenstein, I., Riedel, S.: A supervised approach to extractive summarisation of scientific papers. In: Proceedings of the 21st Conference on Computational Natural Language Learning (CoNLL 2017), Vancouver, Canada, August 2017, pp. 195–205. Association for Computational Linguistics (2017)
9. Fang, C., Mu, D., Deng, Z., Wu, Z.: Word-sentence co-ranking for automatic extractive text summarization. Expert Syst. Appl. **72**, 189–195 (2017)
10. Kim, K.: An improved semi-supervised dimensionality reduction using feature weighting: application to sentiment analysis. Expert Syst. Appl. **109**, 49–65 (2018). https://doi.org/10.1016/j.eswa.2018.05.023
11. Medhat, W., Hassan, A., Korashy, H.: Sentiment analysis algorithms and applications: a survey. Ain Shams Eng. J. **5**(4), 1093–1113 (2014)
12. Na, J.C., Kyaing, W.: Sentiment analysis of user-generated content on drug review websites. J. Inf. Sci. Theory Pract. **3**, 6–23 (2015). https://doi.org/10.1633/JISTaP.2015.3.1.1
13. Perzynska, K.: Top 28 product review websites for online marketers (2018). https://partners.livechatinc.com/blog/best-product-reviews-websites/
14. Sailunaz, K., Alhajj, R.: Emotion and sentiment analysis from twitter text. J. Comput. Sci. **36**, 101003 (2019)
15. Verma, J.P., Patel, B., Patel, A.: Big data analysis: recommendation sys-tem with hadoop framework. In: 2015 IEEE International Conference on Computational Intelligence Communication Technology, pp. 92–97, February 2015. https://doi.org/10.1109/CICT.2015.86
16. Verma, J.P., Patel, A.: Evaluation of unsupervised learning based extractive text summarization technique for large scale review and feedback data. Indian J. Sci. Technol. **10**(17), 1–6 (2017)
17. Wu, P., Li, X., Shen, S., He, D.: Social media opinion summarization using emotion cognition and convolutional neural networks. Int. J. Inf. Manage. **51**, 101978 (2019)
18. Xiong, S., Wang, K., Ji, D., Wang, B.: A short text sentiment-topic model for product reviews. Neurocomputing **297**, 94–102 (2018)
19. Ã-ztÃrk, N., Ayvaz, S.: Sentiment analysis on twitter: a text mining approach to the Syrian refugee crisis. Telematics Inform. **35**(1), 136–147 (2018)

An Approach for Fusion of Thermal and Visible Images

Heena Patel, Kalpesh Prajapati, Vishal Chudasama, and Kishor P. Upla[✉]

Electronics Engineering Department, Sardar Vallabhbhai National Institute
of Technology, Surat, Gujarat, India
hpatel1323@gmail.com, kalpesh.jp89@gmail.com,
vishalchudasama2188@gmail.com, kishorupla@gmail.com

Abstract. We present a novel architecture to fuse thermal and visible images using deep learning algorithms. As infrared images contain higher information, an object can be distinguished from its background due to radiation difference and work well in all conditions such as bad weather and night time. Contrast to that, visible images provide texture information with high spatial resolution or visual context of the objects. Therefore, it is advisable to fuse infrared and visible images which can combine the advantages of thermal radiation information and detailed texture information. Compared to traditional methods of convolutional networks, our proposed network extracts more salient features from individual images by introducing depthwise convolution in the network which reduces more number of parameters. Then after, features from two different sources are fused and an image is reconstructed by decoder network. We compare our proposed method with other state-of-the-art methods, which outperforms on qualitative and quantitative assessment.

Keywords: Deep learning · Depthwise convolution · Image fusion · Infrared images · Visible images

1 Introduction

Image fusion is the process of combining multiple images to generate the single image having all meaningful information. The input/source images are captured through various sensing devices under different parameter setting. It is impossible to focus on all information or all small objects in single image. Hence, image fusion methods provide the composite image known as fused image with complementary information. Fused image should be more suitable for human as well as machine perception. Therefore, several methods have been developing to improve the quality of images [1,2]. The aim is to integrate the images of different features into single image, which can include more information in the source image without any distortion. As we know that, visible image provides better spatial resolution, but it easily affects by disguise and illumination. Where, thermal image is not affected by any disguise or different illumination.

© Springer Nature Singapore Pte Ltd. 2020
S. Gupta and J. N. Sarvaiya (Eds.): ET2ECN 2020, CCIS 1214, pp. 225–234, 2020.
https://doi.org/10.1007/978-981-15-7219-7_19

Image fusion techniques demonstrate great impact in the number of applications such as image enhancement, detection, video surveillance and military applications. Therefore, fusing these two types of images can be more useful for number of applications [3, 4].

Many image processing methods have been proposed to fuse more salient features such as multi-scale decomposition, sparse representation, neural network based methods and other methods [5, 6]. Multi-scale decomposition based methods extract salient features by decomposing images at different level which include pyramid [7, 8], wavelet [9], curvelet [10], shearlet [11] and other revised methods [12, 13]. Then after, appropriate fusion method is applied to obtain final image. Moreover, the representation learning based methods such as sparse representation (SR) [14], co-sparse representation [15] and joint sparse representation(JSR) [16] also offer attracting performance based on the possible representation of images with linear combinations of sparse bases with different fusion strategies. Furthermore, Li et al. [17] presented fusion method by utilizing the concept of low-rank representation(LRR) instead of SR to extract features. Then after, final fused image is obtained by applying max strategy and l_1 norm.

Recently, the concept of deep learning (DL) has enlarged to enhance the development in image processing and computer vision problems. Therefore, an investigation in the field of fusion using the concept of deep learning has become the active hot topic. Deep learning algorithms such as convolutional neural network (CNN), deep autoencoder(DAE), deep belief networks (DBN) with various architectures have been proposed for image fusion [18, 19]. As it is proved that CNN is used for feature extraction as well as reconstruction of the image, it is most recently used algorithm and more efficient for image fusion task. Liu et al. [20] in 2016 presented image fusion algorithm with convolutional sparse representation (CSR). They utilize single decomposition model in which source/input images are decomposed into base and detail layers with different scales to extract multi-features and final image is obtained by integrating these feature maps. In 2017 [5], they also presented CNN based image fusion method on multi-focus images. In which, they train the network by taking different patches of source images and generates the decision map and image is reconstructed by using decision map and source image.

Moreover, Prabhakar et al. in ICCV 2017 [6], performed exposure fusion based on CNN. They presented CNN framework with encoding and decoding network in which encoder and decoder consist of two and three CNN layers, respectively. Siamese network is used in encoder and tied the weights. It encodes two images and generates feature maps. Then, feature maps are fused by simple addition strategy. Decoding network reconstructs the final image by utilizing CNN layers. This method performs better but suffers from some drawbacks, i.e. network architecture does not extract salient features properly, utilize only the results from last layer as the image features, due to this, that approach fails to obtain a lot of useful information which can be extracted from middle layers. Therefore, Hui et al. in [3] proposed an architecture which also consists of encoding and decoding network. Encoding network is used to extract image features by convolutional layers and dense block [5], in which the output of each layer is used as the input to the next layer. Features generated at last layer of encoder are fused using addition and l_1 norm fusion strategy. Finally, the image is reconstructed by decoding network. In this architecture, the results of each layer in encoding network are utilized to construct fused map. Main drawback of this method is that, the dense layers increase the complexity of architecture which can be incredibly computationally expensive for deeper architecture of real time applications. To solve this problem, We propose a novel architecture which utilize the newly emerged depthwise convolution. As compared to CNN, it has less number of parameters to adjust, which reduces the problem of overfitting. Unlike standard CNN, convolution applied to single channel at a time, hence, it is computationally cheaper [21].

In this paper, we present a novel architecture for infrared and visible image fusion based on deep learning framework. The architecture is constructed with encoder and decoder module [3]. Encoding module consists of convolutional and depthwise convolutional layers in which each layer processes features from all previous layers. Hence, encoding module extracts salient features by taking feature maps from all connected layers and final fused image is reconstructed by decoder module which consists of inverse module of encoder. Structure of this paper is as following: Sect. 2 describes the proposed deep learning based image fusion framework in detail. Experimental evaluation is presented in Sect. 3. Finally, Sect. 4 conclude the paper.

2   Proposed Network

In Fig. 1, we display the framework of proposed method for thermal and visible image fusion. Proposed approach consists of two module namely, encoder and decoder. Encoder is utilized to extract more meaningful features. Therefore, it is applied on pair of source images to extract salient features. Encoder module consists of simple convolution and depthwise convolution (DC) layers. It could not possible to apply depthwise convolution at initial layer because of gray scale image. Hence, simple CNN is used to obtain multiple channels. Then after, depthwise convolution is introduced in the network which is inspired from [22]. In architecture, $3 \times 1 \times 3$ denotes filter size (f), input channels (m) and output channels (n) (i.e. $f \times m \times n$ for all layers). Leaky ReLU (LReLU) is used as an activation function at each layer, which is described as,

$$[y_i] = LReLU(W[x_i] + b) \tag{1}$$

Where, W, b, y_i and x_i denote the weight, bias, output and input to the particular layer, respectively. $LReLU$ is mathematically calculated as,

$$f(x = W[x_i] + b) = \begin{cases} x, & if \ \ x > 0; \\ 0.01x, & otherwise. \end{cases} \tag{2}$$

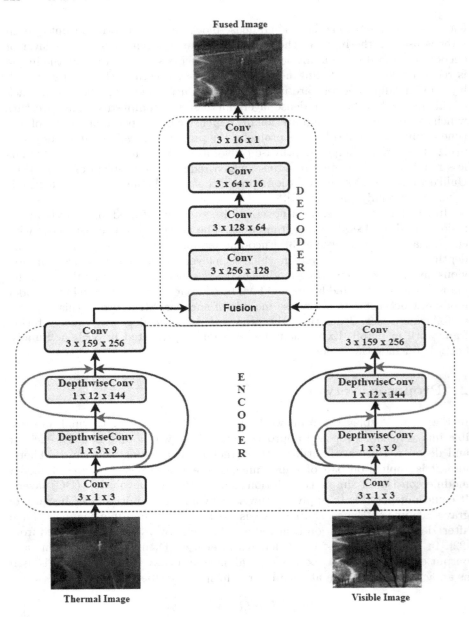

Fig. 1. Proposed architecture for infrared and visible image fusion

In DC, convolution is applied to single channel at a time, hence, it is computationally cheaper and it has less number of parameters to adjust, which reduces the problem of overfitting[1]. Channel multiplier at each layer of DC is set to 1. We use 1×1 filter in DC, hence, same number of channels are generated as input channels on layers of DC. Moreover, we utilize all features generated at previous layers in encoder module. Therefore, feature maps from all previous layers are concatenated at each layer as shown in Fig. 1. Hence, proposed encoder module helps to extract more meaningful features.

After extracting features, various fusion strategies are adopted to fuse features from different source images. We adopted three fusion strategies (i.e. addition, l_1 norm and weighted sum). Addition and l_1 norm are calculated as [3] and weighted sum is considered to fuse images according to different illumination condition (i.e. night/day vision) by applying different weights (e.g. for night vision, thermal images include more information than visible, hence, weight of thermal image would be greater than visible image and vice versa for day vision images). Weights are selected based on finding mean brightness value of images. If mean brightness is exceeded threshold value of 0.6 then higher weight is assigned to thermal image and vice versa. Image fusion using weighted sum is calculated as,

$$f(x,y) = \alpha_1 * I_1(x,y) + (1 - \alpha_2) * I_2(x,y) \tag{3}$$

where, α indicates the weight associated with individual image (I). Finally, fused image is reconstructed using decoder network which consists of multiple convolutional layers as shown in Fig. 1. In training phase, fusion module is not included, network is trained with encoder and decoder module. In order to reconstruct the image efficiently, we find structural similarity loss and pixel loss during training which is calculated as,

$$Loss(\ell) = w * \ell_{ssim} + \ell_p \tag{4}$$

where, w is weight which is taken 100 by observing performance of [3]. Structural similarity loss (ℓ_{ssim}) is calculated as,

$$\ell_{ssim} = 1 - SSIM(O_d, I_e) \tag{5}$$

where, $SSIM()$ represents structural similarity presented in [23], O_d and I_e indicate the output map from decoder and input map to encoder, respectively. Pixel loss (ℓ_p) is calculated by finding Euclidean distance between O_d and I_e. Hence,

$$\ell_p = \|O_d - I_e\|_2 \tag{6}$$

We evaluated our network with different fusion strategies and it is observed that fused image using proposed architecture contains more structural information.

---

[1] https://www.geeksforgeeks.org/depth-wise-separable-convolutional-neural-networks/.

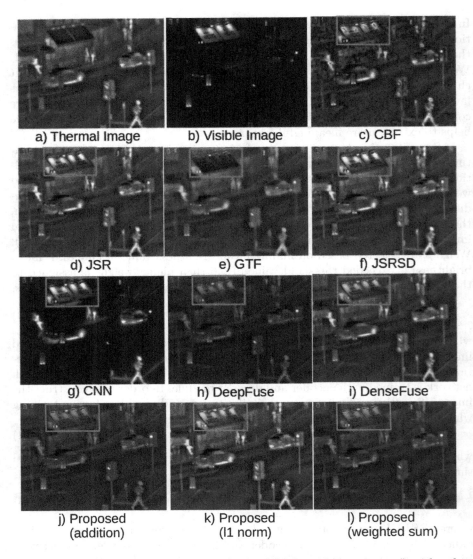

a) Thermal Image   b) Visible Image   c) CBF

d) JSR   e) GTF   f) JSRSD

g) CNN   h) DeepFuse   i) DenseFuse

j) Proposed (addition)   k) Proposed (l1 norm)   l) Proposed (weighted sum)

Fig. 2. Qualitative comparison of proposed method on "street images" with other existing methods

3   Experimental Evaluation

In order to evaluate the potential of proposed method, we utilize the hardware environment 7th Generation Intel Core $i7 - 7700K$ processor with $8M$ up to 3.60 GHz, a GPU NVIDIA GeForce GTX 1070 with 8-GB GDDR5. The tensor-flow libraries are utilized as a backend to the network architecture. Instead of

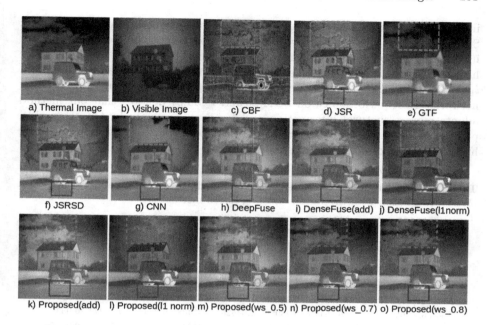

a) Thermal Image   b) Visible Image   c) CBF   d) JSR   e) GTF

f) JSRSD   g) CNN   h) DeepFuse   i) DenseFuse(add)   j) DenseFuse(l1norm)

k) Proposed(add)   l) Proposed(l1 norm)   m) Proposed(ws_0.5)   n) Proposed(ws_0.7)   o) Proposed(ws_0.8)

Fig. 3. Qualitative comparison of proposed method on "car images" with other existing methods

COCO dataset in [3], We use FLIR dataset[2] to train our proposed network. We also evaluated [3] on FLIR dataset and compared results with proposed network which is shown in Table 1. Dataset consists of 10,228 images, from which 8,862 images are used for training and 1,366 images are used for validation. Batch size and epochs values are set to 4. In single epoch, number of steps are considered as $\frac{no.\ of\ training\ images}{batch\ size}$. Learning rate is set to 1×10^{-4} and an adam optimizer is used to optimize the training process. In testing, pair of images (i.e. thermal and visible) are applied to the network which is collected from image fusion dataset[3]. We compare our proposed approach with various state-of-the-art methods which include cross bilateral filter (CBF) [24], joint sparse representation (JSR) [16], gradient transfer (GTF) [25], JSR with saliency detection (JSRSD) [26], CNN [27], deepfuse [6] and densefuse [3]. To evaluate the performance of proposed method by qualitative assessment, a common region from all figures is highlighted as shown in Fig. 2. Moreover, in Fig. 3, two regions are highlighted, one for cloud and another for tiles and proposed method showing the quality of images in last row along with different weights to infrared image. Weights are normalize in (0, 1). Quantitative assessment with various metrics (i.e. entropy (E_n), Qabf [28], SCD [29], FMI_w and FMI_{dct} [30], $SSIM_a$ and $MS\_SSIM)$ [31] is shown in Table 1. As it is observed in testing that, higher the weight of

---

[2] https://www.flir.in/oem/adas/adas-dataset-form/.
[3] https://figshare.com/articles/TNImageFusionDataset/1008029.

infrared image of night time, provides more details than addition and l_1 norm. Similarly, higher the weight of visible image of day time, provides more meaningful information in final reconstructed image. This concept could be more helpful in application of surveillance. Proposed network which adopts addition, l_1 norm, and weighted sum strategies has better performance than other existing networks. Best performance on $SSIM_a$ and FMI_{dct} denotes that our method adopts more structural information and features, respectively. On other side, performance on E_n, Qabf and SCD metrics shows that obtained fused image has less contain of noise and it is more natural.

Table 1. Comparison of the proposed method on addition, l1 norm and weighted sum (WS) based fusion with the various existing fusion methods.

Methods		E_n	Qabf	SCD	FMI_w	FMI_{dct}	$SSIM_a$	MS_SSIM
CBF [24]		6.81494	0.44119	1.38963	0.32012	0.26619	0.60304	0.70879
JSR [16]		6.78576	0.32572	1.59136	0.18506	0.14184	0.53906	0.75523
GTF [25]		6.63597	0.40992	1.00488	0.41004	0.39384	0.70369	0.80844
JSRSD [26]		6.78441	0.32553	1.59124	0.18502	0.14201	0.53963	0.75517
CNN [27]		6.80593	0.29451	1.48060	0.43954	0.35746	0.71109	0.80772
DeepFuse [6]		6.68170	0.43989	1.84525	0.42438	0.41357	0.72949	0.93353
DenseFuse [3]	Addition	6.74556	0.42693	1.84189	0.41341	0.39330	0.72108	0.92276
	$l_1 norm$	6.82926	0.45504	1.68922	0.42634	0.37488	0.71048	0.85689
Proposed	Addition	6.74252	0.44961	1.85923	0.42965	0.39924	0.75450	0.93430
	$l_1 norm$	**6.86922**	0.47163	1.69380	0.43101	0.38027	0.72124	0.86133
	WS_0.5	6.74736	0.45554	**1.88925**	0.42954	0.39906	0.76451	**0.94425**
	WS_0.7	6.27999	0.49713	1.76970	0.47154	0.44427	**0.80894**	0.93905
	WS_0.8	6.15654	**0.51739**	1.69109	**0.47693**	**0.46875**	0.79502	0.90780

4 Conclusion

In this paper, we present effective architecture for thermal and visible image fusion. Proposed network utilizes the concept of depthwise convolution to extract more salient features from given input images. After extracting features, fusion strategy is applied to fuse various features. We adopted three fusion strategies (i.e. addition, l_1 norm and weighted sum). Weighted sum performs better with higher structural information and it is considered to fuse night/day vision images by applying different weights to source images (e.g. for night vision, thermal images include more information than visible, hence, weight of thermal image would be greater than visible image and vice versa, for day vision images). Finally, fused image is reconstructed carefully by decoder module. It is observed that proposed architecture outperforms qualitatively and quantitatively than other existing methods.

References

1. Ma, J., Ma, Y., Li, C.: Infrared and visible image fusion methods and applications: a survey. Inf. Fusion **45**, 153–178 (2019)
2. Li, S., Kang, X., Fang, L., Jianwen, H., Yin, H.: Pixel-level image fusion: a survey of the state of the art. Inf. Fusion **33**, 100–112 (2017)
3. Li, H., Wu, X.: DenseFuse: a fusion approach to infrared and visible images. IEEE Trans. Image Process. **28**, 2614–2623 (2019)
4. Li, H., Wu, X., Kittler, J.: Infrared and visible image fusion using a deep learning framework, pp. 2705–2710 (2018)
5. Huang, G., Liu, Z., Van Der Maaten, L., Weinberger, K.Q.: Densely connected convolutional networks. In: 2017 IEEE Conference on Computer Vision and Pattern Recognition (CVPR), pp. 2261–2269. IEEE (2017)
6. Prabhakar, K.R., Srikar, V.S., Babu, R.V.: DeepFuse: a deep unsupervised approach for exposure fusion with extreme exposure image pairs. In: 2017 IEEE International Conference on Computer Vision (ICCV), pp. 4724–4732. IEEE (2017)
7. Durga Prasad Bavirisetti and Ravindra Dhuli: Two-scale image fusion of visible and infrared images using saliency detection. Infrared Phys. Technol. **76**, 52–64 (2016)
8. Wang, X., Nie, R., Guo, X.: Two-scale image fusion of visible and infrared images using guided filter. In: Proceedings of the 7th International Conference on Informatics, Environment, Energy and Applications, pp. 217–221. ACM (2018)
9. Pang, H., Zhu, M., Guo, L.: Multifocus color image fusion using quaternion wavelet transform. In: 2012 5th International Congress on Image and Signal Processing (CISP), pp. 543–546. IEEE (2012)
10. Yang, S., Wang, M., Jiao, L., Ruixia, W., Wang, Z.: Image fusion based on a new contourlet packet. Inf. Fusion **11**(2), 78–84 (2010)
11. Wang, L., Li, B., Tian, L.-F.: EGGDD: an explicit dependency model for multimodal medical image fusion in shift-invariant shearlet transform domain. Inf. Fusion **19**, 29–37 (2014)
12. Hamza, A.B., He, Y., Krim, H., Willsky, A.: A multiscale approach to pixel-level image fusion. Integr. Comput.-Aided Eng. **12**(2), 135–146 (2005)
13. Li, S., Kang, X., Jianwen, H.: Image fusion with guided filtering. IEEE Trans. Image Process. **22**(7), 2864–2875 (2013)
14. Zong, J., Qiu, T.: Medical image fusion based on sparse representation of classified image patches. Biomed. Signal Process. Control **34**, 195–205 (2017)
15. Gao, R., Vorobyov, S.A., Zhao, H.: Image fusion with cosparse analysis operator. IEEE Signal Process. Lett. **24**(7), 943–947 (2017)
16. Zhang, Q., Yuli, F., Li, H., Zou, J.: Dictionary learning method for joint sparse representation-based image fusion. Opt. Eng. **52**(5), 057006 (2013)
17. Li, H., Wu, X.-J.: Multi-focus image fusion using dictionary learning and low-rank representation. In: Zhao, Y., Kong, X., Taubman, D. (eds.) ICIG 2017. LNCS, vol. 10666, pp. 675–686. Springer, Cham (2017). https://doi.org/10.1007/978-3-319-71607-7_59
18. Ma, G., Yang, X., Zhang, B., Shi, Z.: Multi-feature fusion deep networks. Neurocomputing **218**, 164–171 (2016)
19. Li, K., Zou, C., Shuhui, B., Liang, Y., Zhang, J., Gong, M.: Multi-modal feature fusion for geographic image annotation. Pattern Recogn. **73**, 1–14 (2017)
20. Liu, Y., Chen, X., Ward, R.K., Wang, Z.J.: Image fusion with convolutional sparse representation. IEEE Signal Process. Lett. **23**(12), 1882–1886 (2016)

21. Ye, R., Liu, F., Zhang, L.: 3D depthwise convolution: Reducing model parameters in 3d vision tasks. arXiv preprint arXiv:1808.01556 (2018)
22. Chen, L.-C., Zhu, Y., Apandreou, G., Schroff, F., Adam, H.: Encoder-decoder with Atrous separable convolution for semantic image segmentation. arXiv preprint arXiv:1802.02611 (2018)
23. Wang, Z., Bovik, A.C., Sheikh, H.R., Simoncelli, E.P.: Image quality assessment: from error visibility to structural similarity. IEEE Trans. Image Process. 13(4), 600–612 (2004)
24. Shreyamsha Kumar, B.K.: Image fusion based on pixel significance using cross bilateral filter. SIViP 9(5), 1193–1204 (2013). https://doi.org/10.1007/s11760-013-0556-9
25. Ma, J., Chen, C., Li, C., Huang, J.: Infrared and visible image fusion via gradient transfer and total variation minimization. Inf. Fusion 31, 100–109 (2016)
26. Liu, C.H., Qi, Y., Ding, W.R.: Infrared and visible image fusion method based on saliency detection in sparse domain. Infrared Phys. Technol. 83, 94–102 (2017)
27. Liu, Y., Chen, X., Peng, H., Wang, Z.: Multi-focus image fusion with a deep convolutional neural network. Inf. Fusion 36, 191–207 (2017)
28. Xydeas, C.S., Petrovic, V.: Objective image fusion performance measure. Electron. Lett. 36(4), 308–309 (2000)
29. Aslantas, V., Bendes, E.: A new image quality metric for image fusion: the sum of the correlations of differences. AEU Int. J. Electron. Commun. 69(12), 1890–1896 (2015)
30. Haghighat, M.B.A., Aghagolzadeh, A., Seyedarabi, H.: A non-reference image fusion metric based on mutual information of image features. Comput. Electr. Eng. 37(5), 744–756 (2011)
31. Ma, K., Zeng, K., Wang, Z.: Perceptual quality assessment for multi-exposure image fusion. IEEE Trans. Image Process. 24(11), 3345–3356 (2015)

Indian Sign Language Recognition Using Framework of Skin Color Detection, Viola-Jones Algorithm, Correlation-Coefficient Technique and Distance Based Neuro-Fuzzy Classification Approach

Hemina Bhavsar$^{(\boxtimes)}$ and Jeegar Trivedi

Sardar Patel University, Vallabh Vidyanagar, India
heminabhavsar@gmail.com, jeegar.trivedi@gmail.com

Abstract. Sign language recognition is exceptionally a vast in the research field where one can utilize a few procedures like glove based method, image based method, sensors and so on, to acquire the signs. In this paper we have undertaken an image based technique to recognize sign language. In this paper we have proposed a framework which is comprised of 4 phases: in first phase we have applied various image processing techniques to smooth the image. Further we have used skin color detection and Viola-Jones algorithm, which are used to segment a face part and hand part from the image. Second phase consist of a distance count method and Correlation-Coefficient method to extract distance and similarity index features respectively. These features continue to 3rd phase to classify and identify the sign using Neuro-Fuzzy classification algorithm. Finally in the 4th phase we have used Natural Language Processing (NLP) to display the final word. Presented framework has been implemented on MATLAB. We have tested 20 videos (total 100 images) of different family relation signs and our experimental result is 95% accuracy.

Keywords: Natural Language Processing · Sign language recognition · Neuro-Fuzzy

1 Introduction

Huge amount of research has been done in the field of Artificial Intelligence and Image Processing in all over world. To prepare the model for recognize the object is exceptionally well known idea. Combination of image processing and machine learning algorithms is valuable for building up the recognition model.

In this paper we displayed our proposed framework which is implemented and tested for dynamic sign language recognition (SLR) model. Our proposed structure joins the techniques of machine learning and image processing. Dynamic SLR model is extremely valuable in the public eyes as for individuals who are incapable to talk or unfit to hear. They can without much of difficulties express their musings in public area like shopping center, Hospitals and other organization with the assistance of SLR framework.

S. Gupta and J. N. Sarvaiya (Eds.): ET2ECN 2020, CCIS 1214, pp. 235–243, 2020.
https://doi.org/10.1007/978-981-15-7219-7_20

As studied literature survey which we have described in this paper, different techniques can be utilized for acquire gesture data, like Glove based method, Image based methods, Sensor based methods etc. To avoid the use of sensor or glove we have used image based methods to acquired gestures. Simple Smart mobile camera with high quality mega pixel accuracy is used for collect the data. Videos will be used as input. When it will display, the recognize word will be displayed as an output.

2   Objective

- To create dynamic sign language recognition system, this can be recognizing family connection words from video.
- Example of Family relation words (Fig. 1):

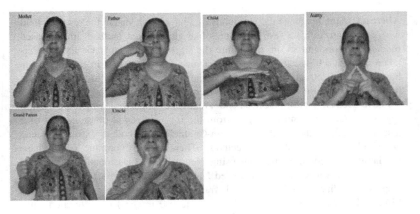

Fig. 1. Sign of family relation words

3   Related Study

Athira, Sruthi, Lijiya [1], presented on "Signer independent novel vision-based gesture recognition system" which is fit for perceiving single handed static and dynamic gestures, double-handed static gestures and finger spelling words of Indian Sign Language (ISL) from live video. The gesture recognition model includes essentially three stages – Preprocessing, Feature Extraction, and Classification. During the pre-processing phase, they extract the signs from continues video recording by utilize the skin color segmentation algorithm. Further during the co-articulation elimination phase. A proper feature vector is founded from the sequence of gestures. Then Support Vector Machine (SVM) is utilizing for classification of gated features. The framework effectively perceived finger spelling letters in order with 91% precision and courageous unique words with 89% exactness.

Shreyashi Narayan Sawant [2], presented on "Sign Language Recognition System to aid Deaf-dumb People Using PCA", in which she describe plan and usage of ongoing Sign Language Recognition framework to perceive 26 signals from the Indian Sign Language utilizing MATLAB. The signs are caught by utilizing web cam. Image processing has been applied on signs to filter the images by utilize of HSV color model. The acquired features are matched with testing dataset by using Principle Component Analysis algorithm. This comparison calculated the Euclidean distance for sign recognition.

Hartanto, Susanto, and Santosa [3], introduced on "Real Time Static Hand Gesture Recognition System Prototype for Indonesian Sign Language", they present a model framework that can perceive the dynamic hand gesture sign language. They utilized HSV (Hue Saturation Value) shading space joined with skin location to evacuate the intricate foundation and make divided pictures. At that point a contour detection is applied to confine and spare hand region. Further, they utilized SURF algorithm to extract features and recognize each hand gesture sign alphabet by matching with training database. In light of the analyses, the framework is proficient to perceive hand motion sign and mean Alphabets, with perceive rate 63% in normal.

Korean Sign Language Recognition framework had the option to accomplish 85% of acknowledgment rate out of 25 Korean Sign Language words [4]. The framework utilized Fuzzy Min-Max to perceive the contribution from a Data-glove. The information got was the situation of hand (x, y, z position) framing 10 essential developments and 14 fundamental hand shapes.

Sarkar, Gade [5], present their methodology on "Vision Based Hand Gesture Recognition Using Skin Detection and Morphological Operations". Their methodology comprises ventures for applying pre-handling procedures, portioning the hand region and finally classifying the gesture using MATLAB. The framework distinguishes skin locales dependent on a lot of skin identification criteria which sift through the non-skin areas and concentrate the hand shape utilizing morphological activities.

Singha, Das [6], exhibited their strategy on "Indian Sign Language Recognition Using Eigen Value Weighted Euclidean Distance Based Classification Technique". They proposed a framework utilizing Eigen worth weighted Euclidean separation as a characterization strategy for acknowledgment of different Sign Languages of India. The framework contains four sections: Skincolor identification, Segment Handpart, Feature Extraction and Recgoniton. 24 signs were considered in this paper, each having 10 examples, along these lines an aggregate of 240 pictures was considered for which acknowledgment rate acquired was 97%.

Rahman, Salam, Islam, and Sarker [7], have proposed a method to find the distance between objects in a same image. They have found a method that first find the object height by identify pixels then find distance between two objects by mapping the pixels height and physical distance. They justify this method with the accuracy of 98.76%.

Saqib, Kazmi [8] presented on "Recognition of static gestures using correlation and cross-correlation". They use correlation-coefficient technique. Correlation technique is being used for image registration between input image and images from the database to find the closest match. For identification of words and sentences they implemented image acquisition, image preprocessing, and use of correlation and labeling of an identified symbol. Normalized correlation is used to find the nearest match.

Dynamic hand movement affirmation of Arabic Sign Language made by Abdalla and Hemayed [9], using Hand Motion Trajectory Features. The system recognizes the hand mass using YCbCr concealing space to perceive skin shade of hand. The structure bunches the data model reliant on relationship coefficients coordinating framework.

Novel and consistent technique for hand signal acknowledgment framework is displayed by Azad, Azad and kazerooni [10], They used component extraction compose the Cross-association coefficient is associated on the movement to recollect it.

4 Research Methodology

The proposed research is based on framework which is developed in four phases. First phase segment the gesture part of both hand and face. Second phase extracted the features and pass to the third phase. Third phase utilized the extracted features into classification algorithm to identify gesture. Fourth phase use the Natural language processing technique to identify word. Basic model of framework is as following Fig. 2:

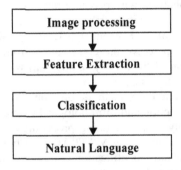

Fig. 2. Proposed framework

Presented framework is connected with Matlab. Framework is used by both training and testing datasets. Training dataset consists of trained static images. These images contain sign of family connection words. Trained images consist of only sign part which is cropped explicitly. Testing dataset contain multiple videos of family relation sign. Images and videos are taken by normal smart mobile camera.

4.1 Image Processing

Video has been taken as contribution into propose algorithm. During the primary stage, videos are extracted into frames. Next frames changed over into isolated images. After that various methods have been applied to pre-process those images. Hand article and face have been segmented by utilizing skin identification algorithm [11] from processed images.

First period of proposed system comprise following advances:

   i. Input video
  ii. Covert video into frames
 iii. Frames converted into RGB images
 iv. Extract the face and hand part using skin color detection algorithm (Fig. 3)

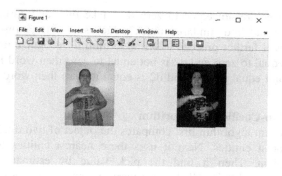

Fig. 3. Skin color detection

Images of segmented objects proceed to next phase of propose framework and that is feature extraction. Face recognition, nose discovery, mouth identification and hand part segmentation [12] have been done using viola-jones algorithm. We have used vision.cascade object detector function of vision toolbox in matlab to the separate face, nose, and mouth and hand object from the image (Fig. 4).

Fig. 4. Face, Mouth, Nose detection

4.2 Feature Extraction and Classification

There are two features; distance and similarity index value, which have been extracted using distance method and correlation-coefficient [13] method respectively. Further these features will be proceeding to neuro-fuzzy (NF) classification algorithm to recognize the word.

Steps of 2nd & 3rd period of proposed framework:

i. Find two distances d1 and d2 where d1 is distance from hands to nose and d2 is distance from hands to mouth.
ii. Compare the distances d1 and d2.

a. If both distances are not equal to zero then take the hand part and match with training model and find similarity index value using correlation-coefficient algorithm which will further proceed to NF algorithm to recognize the word.
b. Else if d1 is equal to zero and d2 is not equal to zero then word is she or mother.
c. Else if d1 is not equal to zero and d2 is equal to zero then word is he or father.

4.2.1   Correlation-Coefficient Algorithm

Correlation-coefficient algorithm first compares the object of two different images and identifies the nearest entities. Next it uses these nearest entities to normalize the correlation-coefficient. Then it find the pick value by estimate the correlation-coefficient. This pick value is called as similarity index value. Correlation-coefficient algorithm is work based on following equation [14].

$$y(u, v) = \frac{\sum_{x,y} \left[f(x, y) - \bar{f}_{u,v} \right] \left[t(x - y, y - v) - \bar{t} \right]}{\left\{ \sum_{x,y} \left[f(x, y) - \bar{f}_{u,v} \right]^2 \sum_{x,y} \left[t(x - y, y - v) - \bar{t} \right]^2 \right\}^{0.5}}$$

Where,

- f is the image.
- $\bar{t}$ is the mean of the template
- $\bar{f}_{u,v}$ is the mean of f(x,y) in the region under the template.
- x & y are the dataset (Here, x & y dataset are the training and testing data respectively)

4.2.2   Neuro-Fuzzy (NF) Algorithm

Here in NF algorithm, fuzzy logic and inference rules are used where rules compare the values of extracted features to classify the particular word [15]. NF work as following (Fig. 5):

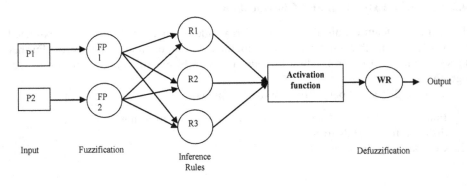

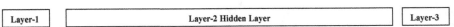

Fig. 5. Neuro-Fuzzy classification algorithm

Above figure comprise of three layers where Pi is feature, Ri is inference rule and WR is consider as identified word. Features are contribution as neuron continue to hidden layer (Fuzzification layer) and convert into crisp value. These crisp values are analyzing by inference rules and return the derived value that further transfer to activation function for optimization. Optimal crisp value then converts to original value and displayed as output. Here Pi is the similarity index value features. Further Pi is multiply by weight Wi and this PiWi convert into FPi (Crisp value).

4.3   Natural Language Processing

Language processing performs on ordered words. Limited processing is performed on the system. If the first word is "she" and second word is "child" then recognized word is "daughter". In the event that first word is "he" and second word is "child" at that point the word is "Son" and so forth.

Following figure shows how framework will be work (Fig. 6):

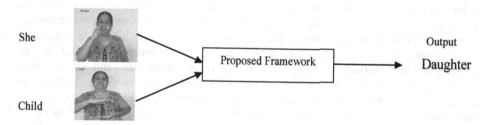

Fig. 6. Output of proposed framework

5   Result and Discussion

Training database contain 12 family relation words in .jpeg structured pictures of hand gesture. Additionally, testing database contain 20 videos which has been further extract into 100 pictures (frames), of different family relation words. Pictures & Videos are taken by versatile camera. Proposed Image Processing techniques and Recognition algorithm executed and took a stab at Matlab. Following Table 1 shows average outcome of attempted pictures. Overall result of the proposed research system is 95%.

Table 1. Evaluation result

Hand gesture types	Total testing images	Total correct images after evaluation	Total incorrect images after evaluation	Evaluation rate in %
He	10	10	0	100%
She	10	10	0	100%
Father	10	9	1	90%
Mother	10	10	0	100%
Son	10	10	0	100%

(*continued*)

Table 1. (*continued*)

Hand gesture types	Total testing images	Total correct images after evaluation	Total incorrect images after evaluation	Evaluation rate in %
Daughter	10	8	2	80%
Grand father	5	5	0	90%
Grand mother	5	5	0	90%
Brother	5	5	0	100%
Sister	5	5	0	100%
Uncle	10	9	1	100%
Aunty	10	9	1	100%
	100	**95**	**5**	**95%**

6 Conclusion and Future Work

It has been conclude, from our paper that the proposed framework is used to build up the dynamic gesture based recognition model which can be perceive family connection words and is very useful application in the society for the specially able people for easily communication. We have reviewed many existing techniques based on our presented work, through it many feature extraction techniques, and classification techniques were studied. Our main focus is on skin detection algorithm, Viola-Jones algorithm, correlation-coefficient technique and Neuro-fuzzy algorithm for classification. Our system have been described with 95% accuracy rate with the utilization of preparing dataset of 12 genuine static pictures and testing dataset of 20 recordings (Each with various family signals). The structure is worked on matlab. One can build up a similar framework for more expressions of sign language with use of different image processing techniques and classification algorithms. In future we will focus on more words and sentences with the use of different algorithms.

References

1. Athira, P., Sruthi, C., Lijiya, A.: Signer independent sign language recognition with co-articulation elimination from live videos: an Indian scenario. J. King Saud Univ. Comput. Inf. Sci. 1319–1578 (2019). Production and hosting by Elsevier B.V. on behalf of King Saud University
2. Sawant, S.: Sign language recognition system to aid deaf-dumb people using PCA. Int. J. Comput. Sci. Eng. Technol. (IJCSET), 5(05) (2014). ISSN: 2229–3345
3. Hartanto, R., Susanto, A., Santosa, P.: Real time static hand gesture recognition system prototype for Indonesian sign language. In: 6th International Conference on Information Technology and Electrical Engineering (ICITEE), Yogyakarta, Indonesia, 978-1-4799-5303-5. IEEE (2014)
4. Kim, S., Jang, W., Bien, Z.: A dynamic gesture recognition system for the Korean Sign Language (KSL). IEEE Trans. Syst. Man Cybern. Part B (Cybern.) **26**(2), 354–359 (1996)

5. Sarkar, S., Gade, A.: Vision based hand gesture recognition using skin detection and morphological operations. Int. J. Innov. Res. Sci. Eng. Technol. (An ISO 3297: 2007 Certified Organization) 5(3) (2016)
6. Singha, J., Das, K.: Indian sign language recognition using eigen value weighted euclidean distance based classification technique. (IJACSA) Int. J. Adv. Comput. Sci. Appl. 4(2) (2013)
7. Rahman, A., Salam, A., Islam, M., Sarker, P.: An image based approach to compute object distance. Int. J. Comput. Intell. Syst. 1(4) (2008)
8. Saqib, S., Kazmi, A.: Recognition of static gestures using correlation and cross-correlation. Int. J. Adv. Appl. Sci. 5(6), 11–18 (2018)
9. Abdalla, M., Hemayed, E.: Dynamic hand gesture recognition of Arabic sign language using hand motion trajectory features. Global J. Comput. Sci. Technol. Graph. Vision, 13(5). Version 1.0, Online ISSN: 0975-4172 & Print ISSN: 0975-4350 (2013)
10. Azad, R., Azad, B., kazerooni, I.: Real-time and robust method for hand gesture recognition system based on cross-correlation coefficient. ACSIJ Adv. Comput. Sci. Int. J. 2(5), 6 (2013). ISSN: 2322-5157
11. Singha, J., Das, K.: Indian sign language recognition using eigen value weighted euclidean distance based classification technique. Int. J. Adv. Comput. Sci. Appl. 4(2), 188–195 (2013)
12. Maghraby, A., Abdalla, M., Enany, O., El, Y.: Detect and analyze face parts information using Viola- Jones and geometric approaches. Int. J. Comput. Appl. 101(3) (2014). (0975 – 8887)
13. Bhavsar, H., Trivedi, J.: Indian sign language alphabets recognition from static images using correlation-coefficient algorithm with neuro-fuzzy approach. In: International Conference on Communication and Information Processing (ICCIP-2019). https://ssrn.com/abstract= 3421685
14. Haralick, M., Shapiro, L.: Computer and Robot Vision, vol. II, pp. 316–317. Addison-Wesley, Boston (1992)
15. Binh, N., Ejima, T.: Hand gesture recognition using fuzzy neural network. In: ICGST Conference Graphics, Vision and Image Process (Cairo 2005), pp. 1–6 (2005)

Stroke Extraction of Handwritten Gujarati Consonant Using Structural Features

Preeti P. Bhatt[✉] and Jitendra V. Nasriwala

Babu Madhav Institute of Information Technology, Uka Tarsadia University,
Bardoli, India
preeti.patel2929@gmail.com, jvnasriwala@utu.ac.in

Abstract. Handwriting synthesis aims to generate the artificial font that exactly mimics the writing style of the individual user. It has several applications such as improvement of text recognition, font personalization, writer identification and it spreading as the technology becomes popular. For font synthesis of handwritten Gujarati script using structural features of character, the detailed analysis of the shape and characteristic of Gujarati characters is required. Gujarati characters classified according to different features such as vertical lines, horizontal lines, close region (loop), endpoints, cross points, concave curve, and convex curve. Moreover, Gujarati characters are structured symbols, each of which is composed of more than one basic structured components called a stroke. Stroke is the most popular way to analyze and describe the character structure. Therefore, this document proposed a methodology for extracting stroke from the thinned binary image and separate the stroke based on the endpoint and junction point. This methodology uses 3×3 pattern mask to detect the junction point and endpoint by considering all its orientation. Removal of these points from thin character splits skeleton into different strokes. The process continue until each stroke have only two endpoints. The stroke from Character having a minimum number of junction point extracted easily. Still, it expected to improve results for a character having multiple junction points.

Keywords: Handwriting synthesis · Stroke extraction · Component segmentation

1 Introduction

In education and culture, the primary mean of communication served by handwritten text and it considered as a form of art. It have been very useful in the task such as note-taking, reading with writing, may have great impact on short term and long term memory. Handwriting is normally indication of individual personality represented by neurological patterns in the brain. Handwriting synthesis is an automatic process of converting input data in to handwriting style text, which exactly mimic the human writing style. Handwriting synthesis not only help to give personal touch or user style preservation, but it has several applications and spreading as the technology becomes popular. Some of the principal applications are. Synthesis in Information retrieval, Synthesis in biometric security, handwriting recognition by dataset generation and

© Springer Nature Singapore Pte Ltd. 2020
S. Gupta and J. N. Sarvaiya (Eds.): ET2ECN 2020, CCIS 1214, pp. 244–253, 2020.
https://doi.org/10.1007/978-981-15-7219-7_21

performance improvement, writer identification and forgery detection, historical documents repairing, font graphics [1] and many more.

Handwriting can be synthesize by imitating author's writing by analyzing its features. There were two approaches to model the handwriting. One is by Movement simulation [2], where neuro muscular moment of hand is used to simulate the writing. Another is shape simulation [2] where handwriting can be synthesized by learning features of writing style and without imitating human hand movement. Handwriting synthesis had been developed for many languages such as Chines, English, Arabic and Bangla, Korean, Japanese, Indian (Hindi, Tamil, Malayalam, and Telugu) scripts [1]. Form the survey, it has been notice that, the generation based on Indian language script under done. Objective of proposed work is to synthesize the handwritten font for Gujarati script based on learning the features of handwriting like stroke.

In machine version, many researchers work on the handwritten Gujarati script such as handwritten character recognition, handwriting generation, writer identification and many more. This paper aims to extract the stroke from the Gujarati character based in its structural features of character. To extract the structural features of character, it requires critical analysis of the shape and characteristic of characters. So features of consonants of Gujarati characters are analyzed as Connected Components and disconnected components, Vertical Lines, Horizontal lines, Negative/positive slope lines, Close Region (Loop), Endpoints, Cross points, C-curve, D-curve, U-curve [3].

In this paper, stroke extraction carried out by its directional features like endpoints, cross points and stroke has based features. For the endpoint detection, total beginning and ending of the character is defines by endpoints. Total six classification is taken in to account based on considering every subcomponent of character having disconnected component like character having one endpoint, two-endpoints up to six endpoints. Classification shown in Fig. 1(a). Here the Junction point or cross points is consider where the component intersect known as cross point. Figure 1(b) shows three-group categorization based on number of cross points like character having one cross point, two cross points and three cross points [2]. The rest of paper organized as follows. Next section describes the stroke-based analysis of Gujarati characters followed by proposed methodology for stroke extraction. Finally, conclusion and future work given in last section.

No. of End Point	
One	Two
છ ય ડ ઈ	ટ ડ ષ ર ળ
Three	Four
ખ ધ ચ ત ધ ન પ બ ભ મ ચ વ શ ષ હ ક્ષ જ્ઞ	ક ઝ ૐ ઙ સ
Five	Six
લ	જ્ઞ

No. of Cross Point	
One	Two
ક ડ ઙ ત દ ૬ ૫ ર ળ વ	ખ ઘ ઝ છ જ ૐ ઙ ઘ ધ ન ફ બ ભ મ
Three	શ ૫ ૬ ષ
સ શ	

(a)   (b)

Fig. 1. a) Set of characters based on variation in end points b) Set of characters based on variation in cross points

2   Stroke Based Analysis of Gujarati Characters

Gujarati characters are structured symbols, each of which is composed of more than one basic structured components called stroke. Any characters made up of set of strokes arranged in specific order as shown in Fig. 2. Many stroke are present in multiple characters. Therefore, study of stroke segmentation can be highly beneficial for processing of Gujarati characters.

If the Gujarati handwritten characters could be decomposed into multiple stroke then it could decrease the difficulties of character recognition [4]. It is also used to evaluating the representation of characters [5]. In addition, stroke extraction and reassembling can helps the construction of Gujarati handwritten font library by reusing the strokes from very few characters.

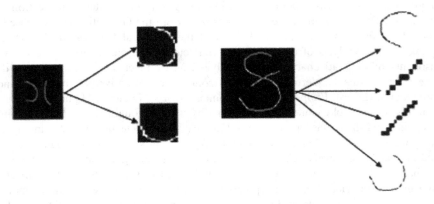

Fig. 2. Character representation by multiple stroke

The majority of the work have been reported for handwriting generation for the script like Chinese, English, Tamil [6–10]. Stoke extraction approach is normally used in Chinese script [6, 11]. Even In Gujarati script some work using stroke segmentation are reported for improving result of character recognition [4, 5, 12, 13].

In [12], Structural feature based classification of printed Gujarati characters would be carried out. They applied 3×3 mask to detect primitive strokes from the thinned image. Characters generated from set of order set strokes and further classified to improved recognition rate of Gujarati character. However, their work gave best result if the number of stroke presented in characters are less. In [3–5, 13], They presented well-designed techniques to extract the low level stroke such as end Point, junction point, line element, curve element from printed Gujarati text using template matching approach. The features extracted are quite reasonable against other work. However, work are not as robust as of handwritten Gujarati characters. In [11], they presented radical segmentation techniques to synthesize Chinese character. However, their results aimed for creating single characters at a time.

This study aim to create Gujarati font in personal handwriting style using stroke based synthesis. So characters segmented in to multiple stroke using structural features of characters like junction point and endpoint, so it could use to construct other characters.

3 Proposed Architecture

The fundamental idea for the construction of Gujarati characters is to consider each character as a set of multiple stroke that connected in specific order. So main aim to break up the preprocess characters in to different stroke based on the junction point and endpoint. The complete system of stroke segmentation from characters is mention in Fig. 3.

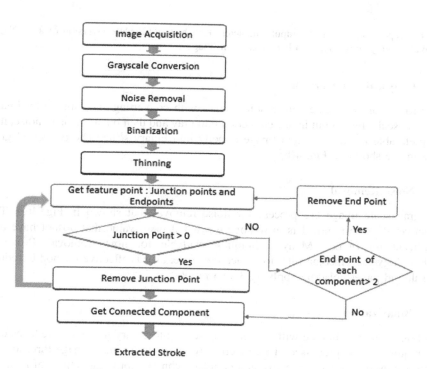

Fig. 3. Proposed architecture of stroke extraction

3.1 Image Acquisition

Image acquisition is a first step in stroke segmentation. For that the dataset chosen is TDIL (Data set of handwritten Gujarati characters) [14]. Dataset comprises two sub-parts: isolated handwritten characters and isolated handwritten words and phrases.

Isolated handwritten characters from dataset that collected from 360 different writers considered for experimentation. These sample characters scanned at 300 dots per inch resolution. The original character 'Ka' image shown in Fig. 4 (a).

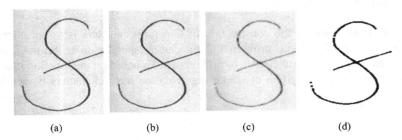

(a)	(b)	(c)	(d)

Fig. 4. Prepossessing steps a) Input Character 'Ka', b) Gray Scale conversion of a. c) Noise removal on gray scale image d) Binarization of image c.

3.2   Grayscale Conversion

The process of gray scale conversion is deals with converting and input color image into gray scale. First input image converted into gray and then binary. Due to noise, it is not preferable to convert input image directly into binary scale. The converted gray scale image shown in Fig. 4(b).

3.3   Noise Removal

The gray scale image are process for noise removal that shown in Fig. 4(c). The objective of noise removal is to remove unwanted pixel value that do not have any significant for output. Many techniques available for noise removal. Proposed methodology used median filter to reduce the noise, as it is effective method to reduce the salt and paper noise by applying 3 × 3 mask.

3.4   Binarization

The binarization technique will convert gray scale into binary image and reduces data that required to be processed. To convert gray image into binary image thresholding technique used. The most effective and popular technique for binarizations of image is Otsu's thresholding method [15]. In which optimum threshold is chosen and therefore all the pixel intensities are converted to 1 i.e. Background and 0 i.e. Foreground. The out of binarization shown in Fig. 4(d).

3.5   Thinning

Thinning is process of converting input image into one pixel-wide thinned image that maintain the original structure of image. Various thinning algorithms were implemented on Gujarati handwritten character such as Zhang [16], Stentiford [17], Lu.

Wang [18] by considering parameter like unit width skeleton, connectivity, spurious branches and processing time. Based on observations made and results obtained, it could concluded that ZhangSuen algorithm provides better thinning process for handwritten Gujarati character as it gives unit width skeleton image. The result of output image and image matrix of thinned image shown in Fig. 5. Thinning is very important stage as shape of the stroke described well by the unit width skeleton image and more effective while detecting junction and endpoint of characters.

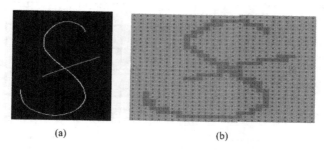

(a)   (b)

Fig. 5. Results of Thinning Algorithm a) Thinning by Zhang [16], b) Image Matrix of thinned image.

3.6 Endpoint and Junction Point Detection

Endpoint of the character identified as a point where stroke start and end. At this point, the character pixel have only one connecting neighbor that represented in Fig. 6(A). The hit-or-miss transformation is a morphological operation which used to process bit pattern of corner pixel [15]. Here if the 3 × 3 structuring element is completely match with 1 or 0 element of pixel then it is set to 1, if not match it set to 0. Total eight structuring elements have used to detect the endpoint which shown in Fig. 6(B).

Junction Point is a point where the one pixel connected with more than two neighbors that shown in Fig. 7(A). To represent the junction point, again the hit or miss transformation used with different 3 × 3 structuring element. There are three possible types of junction point: T-Junction, Y-Junction and Cross-Junction (+ , ×) in Gujarati consonant. Here all orientation of T, Y and Cross- Junction is taken in to account by taking 3 × 3 structuring element, which shown in Fig. 7(B) also the graphical view of all 18 junction point were shown in Fig. 7(C).

In [3–5, 13], They presented well-designed techniques to detect junction point from printed Gujarati text using total 14 structuring element as direction was fixed for printed character. However, work are not as robust as of handwritten Gujarati characters. For handwritten Gujarati character, the junction point position and glyph are very according to user-to-user. So existing method was not applicable for handwritten Gujarati characters. Proposed mathematical model for junction point detection includes four 3 × 3 structuring element set for T-Junction, Y-Junction and Cross-Junction (+ , ×). Total seven different orientation of T and Y junction by 45 angle was consider. Then after hit or miss morphological operation applied on all 18 corresponding

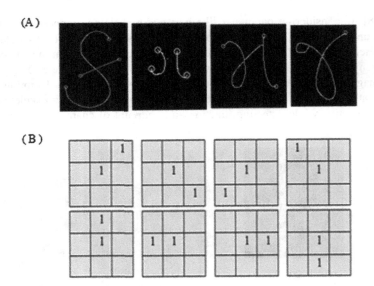

Fig. 6. A) End Points detected in different Gujarati character B) 3 × 3 Structuring Element for different End Point Orientation.

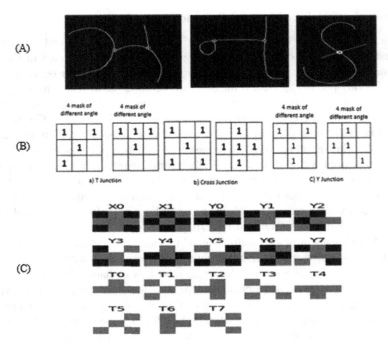

Fig. 7. (A) Junction point detected in different Gujarati character. (B) 3 × 3 Structuring Element for different Junction Point Orientation. (C) Graphical Layout of 18 structuring element.

element. Finally, logical OR between each resultant operation forms an image having junction point. The complete mathematical model is describe below.

Let H is set of eighteen structuring element which is composed of

$X\_0 = \{(-1,0),(0,-1),(0,0),(0,1),(1,0)\}$, For cross junction $+$

$X\_1 = \{(-1,-1),(-1,1),(0,0),(1,-1),(1,1)\}$, For cross junction $\times$

$Y = \{(-1,-1),(1,1),(0,0),(1,0)\}$, and seven rotation by 45 angle orientation (45, 90, 135, 180, 225, 270, 315).

$T = \{(-1,0),(0,-1),(0,0),(0,1)\}$, and seven rotation by 45 angle orientation (45, 90, 135, 180, 225, 270, 315).

The corresponding 18 structuring element denoted by B_1 to B_{18}.

For all i between 1 to 18 and any binary skeleton image X, The morphological hit-or-miss operation defined on B_i as

$$H_i = X \odot B_i$$

Junction point of binary skeleton image X defined by

$$\mathbf{H} = \mathbf{B}_1 + \mathbf{B}_2 + \ldots \ldots \mathbf{B}_{18}, \quad \text{where} + \text{is logical OR operator}$$

3.7 Stroke Extraction

Once the endpoint and junction points detected, it proceed for disjoint operation on characters. Disjoint operation create one list of junction point and endpoint where strokes are connected. This procedure was carried out by finding position of junction point p(x,y) to disconnect the object.

For the same first Identified 3×3 neighboring element of junction point p(x,y) and set 3×3 neighboring element pixel of p(x,y) as 0 likewise preprocessed image become disconnect image which is shown in Fig. 8. Afterwards the disjoint image is pass to connected component method. Thereafter, create junction and endpoint list of each extracted component. This procedure is continue until the each stroke have only two endpoint and no more junction point. Finally, image decomposed into strokes, and extracted stroke from the image shown in Fig. 9. Following steps, describe procedure for stroke extraction.

Fig. 8. Result of disjoint image based on junction points of different Gujarati character.

1. Get list of object pixel of junction point and endpoint as p(x,y).
2. For each element in p(x,y), identified 3×3 neighboring element of object pixel and set it to 0.
3. Find connected component of disjoint image.
4. Continue until the each stroke have only two endpoint and no more junction point.

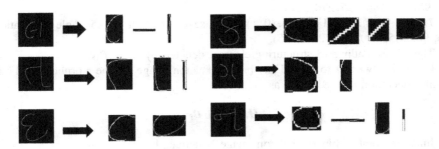

Fig. 9. Result of Proposed method on few characters in the form of stroke segmentation.

4   Conclusion

This article presents and complete procedure of stroke extraction of Gujarati handwritten consonant with the help of junction point and endpoint from thin binary image. Also proposed a mathematical model for junction point detection. Then after, the systematic procedure of stroke extraction were also proposed. Proposed work have certain limitation like Character having minimum number of junction point easily extracted. Still it expected to improve results for multiple junction point. In addition, Weird handwritten character not extracted properly and we have considered only character that have at least one junction point.

5   Future Work

The future direction of this work is to improve the stroke segmentation of handwritten characters for all Gujarati characters. Also expected to classify stroke and create stroke bank for Gujarati character.

References

1. Bhatt, P., Nasriwala, J.: Aspects of handwriting synthesis and its applications. Int. J. Adv. Innov. Res. **6**(3), 36–43 (2019)
2. Elarian, Y., Abdel-Aal, R., Ahmad, I., Parvez, M.T., Zidouri, A.: Handwriting synthesis: classifications and techniques. Int. J. Document Anal. Recogn. (IJDAR) **17**(4), 455–469 (2014)
3. Thaker, H., Kumbharana, C.: Analysis of structural features and classification of Gujarati consonant for offline character recognition. Int. J. Sci. Res. Publ. **4**, 8 (2014)

4. Goswami, M.M., Mitra, S.K.: Printed Gujarati character classification using high-level strokes. In: Chaudhuri, B..B., Kankanhalli, M.S., Raman, B. (eds.) Proceedings of 2nd International Conference on Computer Vision & Image Processing. AISC, vol. 704, pp. 197–209. Springer, Singapore (2018). https://doi.org/10.1007/978-981-10-7898-9_16

5. Goswami, M. M., Mitra, S.K.: High level shape representation in printed Gujarati character. In: Proceedings of the 6th International Conference on Pattern Recognition Applications and Methods: ICPRAM, pp. 418–425 (2017)

6. Lin, J.-W., Hong, C.-Y., Chang, R.-I., Wang, Y.-C., Lin, S.-Y., Ho, J.-M.: Complete font generation of Chinese characters in personal handwriting style. In: 2015 IEEE 34th International Performance Computing and Communications Conference (IPCCC), pp. 1–5. IEEE (2015)

7. Lian, Z., Zhao, B., Xiao, J.: Automatic generation of large-scale handwriting fonts via style learning. In: SIGGRAPH ASIA 2016 Technical Briefs, p. 12. ACM (2016)

8. Helmers, M., Bunke, H.: Generation and use of synthetic training data in cursive handwriting recognition. In: Perales, F.J., Campilho, Aurélio J.C., de la Blanca, N.P., Sanfeliu, A. (eds.) IbPRIA 2003. LNCS, vol. 2652, pp. 336–345. Springer, Heidelberg (2003). https://doi.org/10.1007/978-3-540-44871-6_39

9. Haines, T.S.F., Aodha, O.M., Brostow, G.J.: My text in your handwriting. ACM Trans. Graphics (TOG) **35**(3), 26 (2016)

10. Balreira, D.G., Walter, M.: Handwriting synthesis from Public Fonts. In: 2017 30th SIBGRAPI Conference on Graphics, Patterns and Images (SIBGRAPI), pp. 246–253. IEEE (2017)

11. Chen, Z., Zhou, B.: Effective radical segmentation of offline handwritten Chinese characters towards constructing personal handwritten fonts. In: Proceedings of the 2012 ACM symposium on Document engineering, pp. 107–116. ACM (2012)

12. Goswami, M., Mitra, S.: Structural Feature Based Classification of Printed Gujarati Characters. In: Maji, P., Ghosh, A., Murty, M.N., Ghosh, K., Pal, Sankar K. (eds.) PReMI 2013. LNCS, vol. 8251, pp. 82–87. Springer, Heidelberg (2013). https://doi.org/10.1007/978-3-642-45062-4_10

13. Goswami, M.M., Mitra, S.K.: Classification of printed Gujarati characters using low-level stroke features. ACM Transactions on Asian and Low-Resource Language Information Processing (TALLIP) **15**(4), 25 (2016)

14. Prasad, M.J.R.: Data set of handwritten Gujrati characters. Technol. Dev. Indian Lang. (2013)

15. Gonzalez, R.C., Woods, R.E.: Digital Image Processing (3rd Edition) (2007)

16. Zhang, T.Y., Suen, C.Y.: A fast parallel algorithm for thinning digital patterns. Commun. ACM **27**(3), 236–239 (1984)

17. Stentiford, F.W.M., Mortimer, R.G.: Some new heuristics for thinning binary handprinted characters for OCR. IEEE Trans. Syst. Man cybern. **1**, 81–84 (1983)

18. Sossa, J.H.: An improved parallel algorithm for thinning digital patterns. Pattern Recogn. Lett. **10**(2), 77–80 (1989)

Convolutional Neural Network Based Chest X-Ray Image Classification for Pneumonia Diagnosis

Rushi Bhatt[✉], Sudhanshusinh Yadav[✉],
and Jignesh N. Sarvaiya[✉]

Electronics Engineering Department, SVNIT, Surat 395007, India
rybhatt27@gmail.com, sudhanshusingh8570@gmail.com,
jns@eced.svnit.ac.in

Abstract. Pneumonia is one of the most chronic diseases, and therefore, its timely diagnosis is of utmost importance. Traditionally, clinical decisions have been considered as a gold standard for diagnosis, but it is not a practical option in all scenarios. Therefore, several methods have been explored to make the process of diagnosis faster, efficient and as accurate as clinical decisions. In this paper, we have described and proposed a Convolutional Neural Network (CNN) based deep learning technique for the classification of chest X-ray images for the diagnosis of Pneumonia. The proposed model is trained on 4099 images and tested on 1757 images resulting in an accuracy of 96.18%. The evaluation and training are conducted on *'Labeled Optical Coherence Tomography (OCT) and Chest X-Ray Images for Classification'* dataset which is one of the largest labeled datasets which is publicly available. Also, a comparison of the proposed model with various other popular models is discussed. The results indicate that our model despite having simpler architecture and without any pre-training outperforms many of the popular models on several different performance parameters.

Keywords: Pneumonia · Deep learning · CNN · Chest X-Ray · Diagnosis

1 Introduction

Chest diseases are one of the major health problems in particular pneumonia is extremely dangerous for people already suffering from other diseases, infants, and older adults. According to WHO evaluation, 450 million cases of pneumonia are registered every year that is 7% of the total world population. Moreover, nearly 4 million people die because of it. This ratio is even higher for infants and older adults [1]. That is why Pneumonia requires proper diagnosis at the initial stages for recovery treatment.

Traditionally, diagnosis of pneumonia has been done by medical specialists using chest X-rays and sophisticated radiological investigation on them. However, this approach, for appropriate analysis, would require radiologists. For instance, the laboratory diagnosis of these ailments involves the detection of pathogens such as a virus in the upper and lower respiratory by the use of microscopy techniques [1]. World Health Organization (WHO) has estimated that approximately only one-third of the world

© Springer Nature Singapore Pte Ltd. 2020
S. Gupta and J. N. Sarvaiya (Eds.): ET2ECN 2020, CCIS 1214, pp. 254–266, 2020.
https://doi.org/10.1007/978-981-15-7219-7_22

population has access to a radiologist for the diagnosis of their disease. Therefore, to bring about a solution to these challenges, various computerized systems have been developed to analyze these X-ray images for medical diagnosis [2].

The computerized technique has been adopted because they give more precise results and are easily accessible for diagnosis. The image processing technique has a powerful ability to detect various objects together, extract deep features and classifying them [3] and therefore it is popularly the initial step achieved by convolutional layers of CNN. Traditionally in the interpretation of pneumonia, a radiologist looks for a white spot in the lung, which represents infection. This step of observing patterns, similarities and dissimilarities is achieved by the kernels of CNN and is a crucial step in classification problems.

The major problem in the medical domain is the lack of availability of large image datasets. Particularly for pneumonia detection, the task is very tedious because of the multiple and diverse nature of the disease. This leads to the development of transfer-learning based pre-trained models for medical imaging-based classification problems. The Deep Convolutional Neural Network shows the potential for highly variable tasks across many object categories [4] and therefore selecting appropriate hyperparameters is of utmost importance. However, in this paper, we have outperformed transfer-learning based models using a simpler architecture purely by precisely tuning hyper-parameters of the model.

2 Literature Review

In this work [5], General Regression Neural Network proposed for the prediction of active pulmonary TB. Input parameters are divided into three groups: demographic variables, constitutional symptoms, and radiographic findings. The model consists of three layers: input, hidden, and output layer, where the hidden layer is used to extract higher-order features, and the output layer gives the probability of active pulmonary TB. This model achieved the specificity of 69% on the validation dataset.

This paper [6], focuses on chest disease diagnosis using several neural network architectures. The analysis was done for six different chest diseases, out of which the best accuracy was obtained for Pneumonia diagnosis using a Multi-Layer NN (MLNN) model. The model achieves an accuracy of 91.67% for a single hidden layer and 90.00% for two hidden layers.

Because of inefficiency in working with high-dimensional image datasets, various deep learning models have been developed for the diagnosis of various diseases. CheXNet [7] uses a 121-layer pre-trained CNN and was extended to detect 14 diseases from ChestX-ray14 [8] dataset. The accuracy achieved for the binary classification problem of pneumonia detection is 76.80%.

Another deep learning model called ChetNet [9] was developed for the diagnosis of 14 thorax diseases. The proposed model comprises of classification and attention branch, where the classification branch implements feature extraction and attention branch calculates the correlation between class label and location of abnormalities. The final diagnosis is achieved by averaging the output of both branches. This proposed method achieves an accuracy for pneumonia detection is 69.75%, while the average per-class accuracy encountering all the thorax diseases is 78.10%.

The availability of pre-trained models led to the development of various transfer-learning based models for diagnosis of Pneumonia. The paper [10] describes a generalized model primarily capable of performing diagnosis through OCT image analysis. It was further extended to diagnose pneumonia based on chest X-ray images. The model was pre-trained on the ImageNet dataset and then was fine-tuned for the desired application. This model achieved an accuracy of 92.8% with a sensitivity of 93.2% and a specificity of 90.1%.

Recently, various CNN based models have been developed for the detection of pneumonia from a chest X-ray image. The work [11] proposes a model consisting of feature extraction and classification. The feature extractor consists of four convolution layers, and the classifier is a simple feed-forward network. The best performing validation accuracy by this model is 93.73%.

Another CNN based binary classifier [12] uses Chest X-Ray Images for diagnosis of Pneumonia. It uses k-fold cross-validation for evaluation of the performance of the model, obtaining an average accuracy of 95.30%.

Before this paper, a lot of work has been done in the field of diagnosis of Pneumonia by using chest X-ray images. The ANN-based architectures [5, 6] fail to produce high accuracy results because of the lack of ANNs to deal with high-dimensional features from images for better generalizability. Later, various CNN based models [11, 12] have been developed to tackle the challenges of overfitting due to the huge number of training parameters resulting in problems of overfitting. Moreover, even some transfer-learning based models [10] have been utilized due to the availability of pre-trained models. In this paper, we propose a 9-layer CNN based model that is trained on the same dataset as several of the models, as mentioned earlier, achieving a 96.18% validation accuracy with minimum trainable parameters.

3   Methodology

3.1   Proposed Model

Figure 1 shows the proposed CNN architecture for the two-class problem of pneumonia diagnosis. The proposed model consists of nine layers out of which there are two 2D-Convolutional layers, two Pooling layers, one layer each for Batch Normalization, Dropout, and Flatten and then finally two Dense (Fully Connected) layers leading to a SoftMax output.

3.2   Input Preprocessing

The first step involves resizing the input image to a 64 × 64 × 3-dimensional matrix. Then, the 8-bit representation of each image is normalized to a scale of 0 to 1 by dividing each pixel value by 255.

For an input image 'X', each pixel at position (i, j), the zero-centered standardization is expressed in terms of the mean '$\bar{X}$' and standard deviation 'σ_X' as shown in the Eq. (1)

$$X_{stand}(i,j) = \frac{X(i,j) - \bar{X}}{\sigma_X} \qquad (1)$$

These input scaling methods remove the biases that might have been introduced due to abnormal deformities in the X-ray images.

3.3   Description of the Architecture

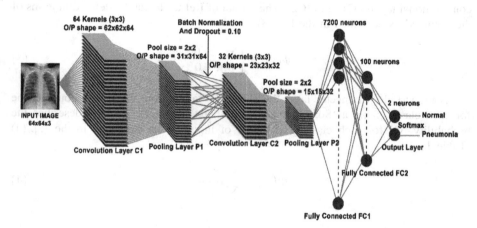

Fig. 1. Proposed CNN architecture

As shown in Fig. 1, the first convolutional layer 'C1' comprises of 64 kernels, each of size 3 × 3. Moreover, the kernel is initialized by the 'glorot uniform' distribution function, which unlike random initialization, helps in achieving the global minimum of the loss function faster with relatively less training.

The initial weight values 'W' for the jth layer is dependent on the number of weights in j^{th} layer 'n_j' as well as the next layer 'n_{j+1}' according to the Uniform Distribution function 'U' as shown in Eq. (2).

$$W \sim U\left[-\frac{\sqrt{6}}{\sqrt{n_j + n_{j+1}}}, +\frac{\sqrt{6}}{\sqrt{n_j + n_{j+1}}}\right] \qquad (2)$$

The layer immediately after 'C1' is the first 2D-pooling layer 'P1' implementing maxpool with a pool size of 2 × 2. Including 'P1' helps in the reduction of dimension as well as the complexity of the network and also avoids overfitting, thereby making the model generalized.

Following the 'P1' layer is the Batch Normalization layer, which normalizes the entire batch of inputs from the previous layer in a slightly modified way, as described in Eq. (1) for the input image. This layer helps in speeding up convergence and accelerating the training by reducing the internal covariate shift [13]. Moreover, a dropout layer is also added, which is set to drop 10% of the connection to the next layer to prevent overfitting [14].

The next layers consisting of a convolutional layer 'C2' with 32 kernels each of size 3×3, and following it is the pooling layer 'P2'. The output of 'P2' is flattened and then fed as input to the fully connected neural network layers and finally classifying the image into two classes: Normal and Pneumonia. The first Fully Connected layer 'FC1' has 7200 input neurons and 100 output neurons, each a 'ReLu' activation.

'ReLu' stands for the Rectified Linear Unit and is also used as activation for the convolutional layers 'C1' and 'C2'. The output of ReLu 'Φ' can be defined in terms of the input 'x' as described in the Eq. (3)

$$\Phi(x) = \begin{cases} x; x > 0 \\ 0; x \leq 0 \end{cases} \tag{3}$$

The next Fully Connected layer 'FC2' has 100 inputs from 'FC1' and 2 output, one for each class having a 'SoftMax' activation. The output of SoftMax describes the probability 'Φ' for each class 'j' in terms of input 'x' as described in the Eq. (4) (Table 1).

$$\Phi(x_j) = \frac{e^{x_j}}{\sum_{i=1}^{2} e^{x_i}} \tag{4}$$

Table 1. Description of the proposed CNN architecture comprising of a total of 740,714 trainable parameters and 128 non-trainable parameters

Layer (Type)	Output shape	No. of parameters
conv2d_1 (Conv2D)	(None, 62, 62, 64)	1792
max_pooling2d_1 (MaxPooling2)	(None, 31, 31, 64)	0
batch_normalization_1 (Batch Normalization)	(None, 31, 31, 64)	256
dropout_1 (Dropout)	(None, 31, 31, 64)	0
conv2d_2 (Conv2D)	(None, 29, 29, 32)	18464
max_pooling2d_2 (MaxPooling2)	(None, 15, 15, 32)	0
flatten_1 (Flatten)	(None, 7200)	0
dense_1 (Dense)	(None, 100)	720000
dense_2 (Dense)	(None, 2)	202

3.4   Dataset

The dataset [15] used for training, testing, and validating the model contains a total of 5863 chest X-ray Images (JPEG file format) belonging to two categories: Normal and

Pneumonia. Pneumonia class further has two subclasses of Pneumonia, which are Bacterial and Viral.

The labeling of these chest X-ray radiographs was carried out by two expert physicians, followed by a third expert to avoid discrepancies due to grading errors. Some of the sample images of chest X-ray from the dataset [15] have been shown in Fig. 2 and Fig. 3.

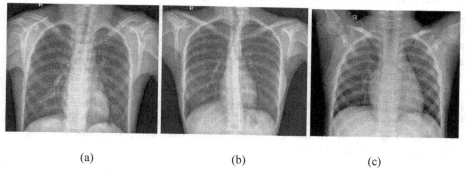

(a)   (b)   (c)

Fig. 2. (a), (b) and (c): Sample images without pneumonia (Normal)

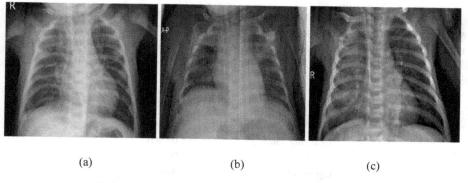

(a)   (b)   (c)

Fig. 3. (a), (b) and (c): Sample images with pneumonia

3.5 Computational Logistics

All the simulation was performed on 'Spyder IDE' with all codebase written in 'Python3'. The primary deep learning frameworks that have been used are 'Keras 2.2.4' and 'Tensorflow 1.13.1' to build and train the convolutional neural network model. All the experiments were run on a standard PC with Nvidia GeForce 1050 Ti GPU card of 4 GB (DDR5) with a DDR4 RAM of 16 GB.

3.6   Training and Testing

The entire database [15] on which the model training, as well as model evaluation, is performed consists of 1583 Normal Images and 4273 Pneumonia Images. Out of these, the model is trained on 70% of the dataset, and the remaining 30% is reserved for testing and validation.

The proposed CNN based architecture consists of several parameters (or weights) distributed throughout the layers which are optimized and used for constructing the classification model. Out of all the layers shown in Fig. 1, the layer 'C1', Batch Normalization, 'C2', 'FC1', and 'FC2' contribute to the weight parameters. Out of all these layers, 'C2' contributes the most with 720,000 parameters. The entire proposed architecture has a total of 7,40,714 parameters, out of which 7,40,586 are trainable, and 128 are non-trainable parameters.

The training process uses categorical cross-entropy as the loss function. The reason for using this loss function is its robustness against noisy labels [16].

The categorical cross-entropy loss 'H' can be calculated based on the predicted categorical output by the model 'Q' and the ground-truth categorical labels 'P' for 'N' classes as shown in the Eq. (5).

$$H(P, Q) = -\sum_{i=1}^{N} P(i) \cdot \log(Q(i)) \tag{5}$$

Furthermore, a stochastic optimizer - 'Adam' is used because of its ability to work well in a sparse setting with low-resource requirements [17] with a stepsize α of 0.01 and exponential decay rate for moment estimates β_1 and β_2 of 0.9 and 0.999 respectively. The hyperparameters chosen for developing the model are summarized in Table 2.

Table 2. Hyperparameters used in training the model

Parameter name	Value
Learning rate	0.0001
Dropout rate	0.1
Optimizer used	Adam
Convolutional layer activation	ReLu
'FC1' Activation	ReLu
'FC2' Activation	SoftMax
Batch size	32

4   Results

4.1   Confusion Matrix

The confusion matrix is an 'N' × 'N' size matrix, where 'N' is the total number of classes, representing the number of correct as well as misclassifications. In our binary classifier, the confusion matrix is a 2 × 2 matrix consisting of each of the following parameters as defined below:

- True Positive (TP) is defined as the number of true pneumonia X-ray images correctly predicted by the classifier.
- True Negative (TN) is defined as the number of true normal X-ray images correctly predicted by the classifier.
- False Positive (FP) is defined as a number of true normal X-ray images wrongly predicted by the classifier.
- False Negative (FN) is defined as the number of true pneumonia X-ray images wrongly predicted by the classifier.

As shown in Fig. 4, the TP are 1225 contributing to the probability of 0.98 of correctly identifying Pneumonia, and the TN is 461 contributing to a probability of 0.91 to classify normal samples correctly.

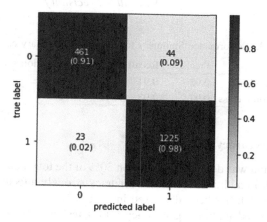

Fig. 4. Confusion Matrix evaluation on the testing dataset (Class 0 represents Normal X-ray Chest Images, and Class 1 represents Pneumonia X-ray Chest Images)

4.2   Fundamental Performance Parameters

Some of the fundamental parameters which are used for performance evaluation of a classifier are Sensitivity, Specificity, Precision, and F1 score.

Sensitivity is the probability of images that were classified as pneumonia out of the total number of pneumonia image samples and also known as the Recall parameter or TPR (True Positive Rate). Specificity is the ratio of the correctly classified normal images out of the total number of normal samples. Precision is defined as the ratio of the total number of correctly classified pneumonia samples out of total samples that were classified as pneumonia [18]. The mathematical equations of sensitivity, specificity, and precision are as shown in Eq. (6), Eq. (7) and Eq. (8) respectively.

$$Recall = TPR = Sensitivity = \frac{TP}{TP + FN} \qquad (6)$$

$$Specificity = \frac{TN}{TN + FP} \qquad (7)$$

$$Precision = \frac{TP}{TP + FP} \qquad (8)$$

F1 Score is a metric that takes into account recall as well as the precision and is the weighted average of precision and recall. F1 score gives more information than the ROC curve for binary classifiers [19]. The Performance Summary for the Binary Classifier is given in Table 3.

$$F1\ Score = 2\left(\frac{Recall \times Precision}{Recall + Precision}\right) \qquad (9)$$

Table 3. Performance Summary for the proposed binary classifier

	Precision	Recall	F1 score	Validation samples
Normal class	0.95	0.91	0.93	505
Pneumonia class	0.97	0.98	0.97	1248

4.3   Validation Accuracy and Loss

The model evaluation was done by testing it on 30% of the total dataset on which it had never been trained. In addition, the model accuracy strongly affected by the values of hyperparameters, which has been discussed in Sect. 5.1.

The results obtained are training accuracy = 1.00, testing accuracy = 0.9618 and the plots of accuracies and losses after each epoch are as shown in Fig. 5 (Table 4).

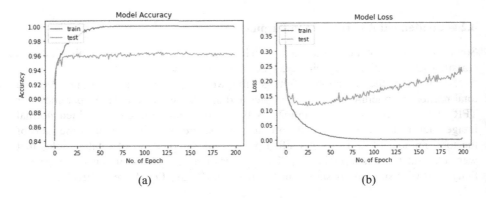

(a)   (b)

Fig. 5. Training and Testing accuracy and loss plots

Table 4. Performance comparison between [10] and our proposed model on the same dataset

Performance metric (%)	D. S. Kerman etc. [10]	Proposed model
Validation accuracy	92.8	96.18
Sensitivity	93.2	98.16
Specificity	90.1	91.29
Area under ROC	96.8	98.91

4.4 ROC Curve and AUC

ROC (Receiver Operating Characteristics) and AUC (Area Under the Curve) are some of the most crucial performance measurement parameters for classification models. ROC represents the classifier performance across the entire distribution of classes [20] and the AUC the area under ROC, which is the measure of separability or the model's capability to distinguish between classes. Higher the AUC, the better the model can identify the categories and therefore it is an essential parameter for characterizing the strength and weakness of diagnostic tests [21].

The area under the ROC curve or AUC, achieved by our model, is 0.9891. Figure 6 shows the ROC curve plotted between True Positive Rate and False Positive Rate on the testing data for our model.

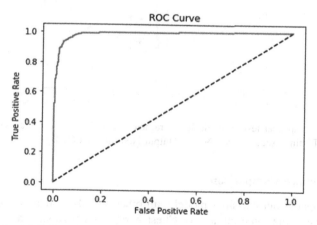

Fig. 6. ROC Curve between True Positive Rate and False Positive Rate.

5 Discussion

The proposed model has a relatively simpler architecture as compared to other architectures that have a relatively deeper network with a large number of training parameters. This is because of the careful design of various hyperparameters and design parameters, which play a vital role in determining the performance of the model. The next section discusses in detail various empirical testing methods used to select appropriate hypermeters and also a comparison of the performance of our proposed model with various other models developed using similar architecture on the same dataset.

5.1   Empirical Determination of Hyperparameters

The performance of deep learning classifiers is heavily dependent on hyperparameters, and therefore, to achieve the desired result for a particular application, customized models have to be designed.

The first design parameter is the number of CNN layers, in particular, the number of convolutional layers. When the number of convolution layers changes, the performance is significantly impacted because of the distribution of weights and kernels across several layers. The second design parameter is the number of outputs of the FC1 layer. The dense network essentially behaves like a neural network with a hidden layer, and therefore, the number of the output of the FC1 layer plays a vital role in model performance. Therefore, in this paper, we have performed two empirical analyses to select the best performing parameters and results have been plotted as shown in Fig. 7.

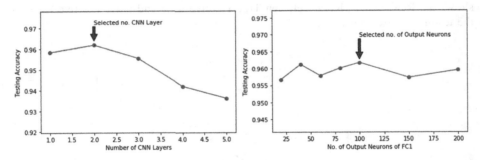

Fig. 7. Plot for empirical testing of design parameters. (a) Testing Accuracy v/s No. of CNN layers and (b) Testing Accuracy v/s No. of Output Neurons of FC1 layer

5.2   Performance Comparison

Next, we compared our classifier model with other models, which also uses the same dataset [15] using the same number of Chest X-ray images as shown in Table 5. The validation accuracy achieved of the proposed model, despite relatively simpler architecture without any pretraining, is 96.18%, which is higher than the accuracy achieved by various models developed using the same dataset.

Table 5. Performance Comparison of the model evaluated on the same dataset

Performance metric	No. of chest X-ray image used	Architecture	Validation accuracy (%)
D. S. Kerman etc. [10]	5856	Pretrained TensorFlow Inception V3 Architecture	92.8
O. Stephen etc. [11]	5856	4 Convolutional and 2 Dense layers	93.73
A. A. Saraiva etc. [12]	5856	7 Convolutional and 3 Dense layers	95.30
Proposed Model	**5856**	**2 Convolutional and 2 Dense layers**	**96.18**

6 Conclusion

In this paper, we proposed the model a nine-layer convolutional neural network for detecting pneumonia from chest X-ray images. The proposed model achieved a training accuracy of 100% (trained for 200 epochs) and a validation accuracy of 96.18% for this problem of binary classification. The result shows that the proposed approach offers a very high prediction accuracy on the chest X-ray images with minimum training parameters. The proposed method can be extended as a generalized technique to assist medical professionals for faster diagnosis of other diseases as well. The future research work will be focusing on to extend this classification model for multiple classes of diseases that are possible to be diagnosed from such similar chest X-ray image datasets.

Acknowledgment. The research work was supported by the Electronics Engineering Department, S. V. National Institute of Technology, Surat, India. We appreciate the effort kept to collect and share the labeled Chest X-ray image dataset [15]. We would also like to appreciate Apurva Randeria's (SVNIT, Surat) effort for developing an interpretable graphical model for the proposed CNN based classifier.

References

1. Ruuskanen, O., Lahti, E., Jennings, L.C., Murdoch, D.R.: Viral pneumonia. Lancet (2011)
2. Islam, S.R., Maity, S.P., Ray, A.K., Mandal, M.: Automatic detection of pneumonia on compressed sensing images using deep learning. In: IEEE Canadian Conference of Electrical and Computer Engineering (CCECE) (2019)
3. Kaiming, H., Xiangyu, Z., Shaoqing, R., Jian, S.: Deep residual learning for image recognition. In: IEEE Conference on Computer Vision and Pattern Recognition (CVPR) (2016)
4. Esteva, A., Kuprel, B., Roberto, A.N., Ko, J., Susan, M.S., Helen, M.B., Thrun, S.: Dermatologist-level classification of skin cancer. Nature (2017)
5. El-Solh, A.A., Hsiao, C.B., Goodnough, S., Serghani, J., Grant, B.J.: Predicting active pulmonary tuberculosis using an artificial neural network (1999)
6. Er, O., Yumusak, N., Temurtas, F.: Chest diseases diagnosis using artificial neural networks. Expert System with Application **37**(12), 7648–7655 (2010)

7. Rajpurkar, P., et al.: CheXNet: radiologist-level pneumonia detection on chest X-rays with deep learning, arXiv (2017)
8. Wang, X., Peng, Y., Lu, L., Lu, Z., Bagheri, M., Summers, R.M.: ChestX-ray8: hospital-scale chest X-ray database and benchmarks on weakly-supervised classification and localization of common thorax diseases. In: IEEE - Computer Vision and Pattern Recognition (2017)
9. Xia, Y., Wang, H.: ChestNet: a deep neural network for classification of thoracic diseases on chest radiography. ArXiv (2018)
10. Kermany, D.S., et al.: Identifying medical diagnoses and treatable diseases by image-based deep learning. Cell **72**(5), 1122–1131 (2018)
11. Stephen, O., Sain, M., Maduh, U.J., Jeong, D.-U.: An efficient deep learning approach to Pneumonia classification in healthcare. J. Healthcare Eng. **2019** (2019). Article ID 4180949
12. Saraiva, A.A., et al.: Classification of images of childhood pneumonia using convolutional neural networks. In: 6th International Conference on Bioimaging (2019)
13. Ioffe, S., Szegedy, C.: Batch normalization: accelerating deep network training by reducing internal covariate shift. In: International Conference on Machine Learning (2015)
14. Srivastava, N., Hinton, G., Krizhevsky, A., Sutskever, I., Salakhutdinov, R.: Dropout: a simple way to prevent neural networks from overfitting. J. Mach. Learn. Res. **15**(1), 1929–1958 (2014)
15. Kermany, D., Zhang, K., Goldbaum, M.: Labeled Optical Coherence Tomography (OCT) and chest X-Ray images for classification. Mendeley Data (2018)
16. Zhang, Z., Sabuncu, M.R.: Generalized cross entropy loss for training deep neural networks with noisy labels. In: NIPS 2018 Proceedings of the 32nd International Conference on Neural Information Processing Systems (2018)
17. Kingma, D.P., Ba, J.L.: Adam: a method for stochastic optimization. In: International Conference on Learning Representations (2015)
18. Zhu, W., Zeng, N., Wang, N.: Sensitivity, specificity, accuracy, associated confidence interval and ROC analysis with practical SAS implementations. Health Care and Life Science **19**, 67 (2010)
19. Saito, T., Rehmsmeier, M.: The precision-recall plot is more informative than the ROC plot when evaluating binary classifiers on imbalanced datasets. PLoS ONE **10**(3), e0118432 (2015)
20. Brzezinski, D., Stefanowski, J.: Prequential AUC: properties of the area under the ROC curve for data streams with concept drift. Knowledge and Information Systems, 52(2), 531–562 (2017)
21. Junge, M.R.J., Dettori, J.R.: ROC Solid: Receiver Operator Characteristic (ROC) curves as a foundation for better diagnostic tests. Global Spine J. **8**(4), 424–429 (2018)

Plant Leaf Disease Detection Using Machine Learning

Jay Trivedi$^{(\boxtimes)}$, Yash Shamnani, and Ruchi Gajjar

Department of Electronics and Communication Engineering, Institute of Technology,
Nirma University, Ahmedabad, Gujarat, India
jay.trivedi3141@gmail.com, shamnaniyash@gmail.com,
ruchi.gajjar@nirmauni.ac.in

Abstract. In this paper, a Convolutional Neural Network (CNN) architecture for plant leaf disease detection using techniques of Deep Learning is proposed. A CNN model is trained with the help of the Plant Village Dataset consisting of 54,305 images comprising of 38 different classes of both unhealthy and healthy leaves. The disease classification accuracy achieved by the proposed architecture is up to 95.81% and various observations were made with different hyperparameters of the CNN architecture. The experiment results achieved are comparable with other existing techniques in literature.

Keywords: Plant disease detection · Deep Learning · Convolutional Neural Network · Image classification

1 Introduction

Crop diseases, however, the small issue it may sound, holds an immense potential to bring famines and is the main reason for the world's food insecurity. Loss of 30 to 50% of yield for major crops due to disease is not uncommon. History in recent times has witnessed many severe crop disease outbreaks such as the late blight of potato in Ireland (1845–1860), Coffee rust in Sri Lanka (Ceylon then, 1870), and in Central and South America (1960, 2012 to present). The effects are worse for the underdeveloped countries where there are fewer facilities and access to plant-disease control methods [12].

Diagnosis of crop disease is done by analyzing a large number of samples by means of Microscopy, DNA sequencing-based methods that provide detailed information regarding disease-causing pathogens such as bacteria, viruses, fungi, etc. and many more [3]. However, the problem is, most of the farmers don't have access to these diagnosing methods. According to the research of the World Bank in 2016, 7 out of 10 of the poorest 20% of developing countries are exposed to mobile communication and 40% of the whole world has internet access [10].

Due to the recent advancement and heavy research being made in the field of deep learning and Artificial Intelligence (AI), applied to agriculture and vegetation, a lot of problems like yield detection, crop disease identification, intelligent

© Springer Nature Singapore Pte Ltd. 2020
S. Gupta and J. N. Sarvaiya (Eds.): ET2ECN 2020, CCIS 1214, pp. 267–276, 2020.
https://doi.org/10.1007/978-981-15-7219-7_23

farming are solved. To address the problem of poor yield and loss due to crop disease, if an automated system can identify the type of disease in the crop, timely aid can be provided in terms of pesticides or suitable measures can be taken, which will be beneficial for agricultural dependent countries like India, where the agricultural sector contributes 375.61 billion dollars towards the Gross Domestic Product of the country. Farmers can be provided with the technology in their hands through an application in their smartphones that can detect the health of the crop at an early stage and can alert them to proceed further to treat those crops.

A Convolutional Neural Network Architecture, followed by a fully connected network had been implemented which exhibits higher accuracy in the detection of plant disease as compared to other similar researches, and to begin with, correct identification of the type of disease in a crop is the first step. Once the disease in a crop is detected, corrective measures to reduce further damage can be taken. In this paper, Machine Learning approach is employed to detect the disease in crop. The main contributions of this paper are listed as below:

- A Convolutional Neural Network Architecture is proposed for the detection of disease in plants from leaf images.
- The proposed architecture gives a higher accuracy as compared to existing models.
- The classification accuracy is achieved and validated by using different combinations of hyperparameters.

Rest of the paper is organized as follows: Sect. 2 gives the Literature Survey and describes various techniques for plant disease detection. Section 3 describes the proposed CNN Architecture for disease classification. Section 4 presents the classification results and comparison with other method. Section 5 gives the conclusion.

2   Related Work

Crop Disease detection at an early stage can drastically reduce the economic losses caused by it. Several methods are used for the same and more research is being done in order to bring out the most accurate and economical way that can reach each and every farmer. So basically plant disease detection can be carried out by two methods: 1) Direct and 2) Indirect. The direct method includes analyzing a large number of samples through molecular and serological methods. Direct methods need to have a lot of samples to provide results and are time-consuming. However, they are accurate as well. Commonly used direct methods for plant disease detection are Polymerase Chain Reaction (PCR), Fluorescence In-Situ Hybridization (FISH), Enzyme-Linked Immunosorbent Assay (ELISA), Immunofluorescence (IF) and Flow Cytometry (FCM) [3].

The advancement in the field of image processing brought out several optical sensor-based solutions which we call indirect methods for plant disease detection. Detailed information is provided by these optical sensors in the form of different electromagnetic spectra which helps in determining the plant health. Commonly used indirect methods are thermography, fluorescence imaging, hyperspectral techniques, gas chromatography [3]. Hyperspectral techniques are used by farmers on a large scale and are one of the most robust and rapid methods to detect plant diseases [11].

Nanoparticles providing high electronic and optical properties are also under the research which can provide robust detection by means of biosensors, also it can be used to treat the diseases as well. These methods involve bio-recognition elements like DNA, enzymes, antibodies, etc. [3].

In recent times, researches in Artificial Intelligence and Deep Learning are also carried out to solve agriculture-related problems. A number of solutions are proposed for the plant disease detection that involves the use of Artificial Neural Networks (ANN), Support Vector Machines (SVM), K-means Clustering. A LeNet architecture is used by [1] to efficiently detect diseases of Banana such as Banana Sigatoka, Banana Speckle. [5] Disease detection in Tomato using three main detectors Faster Region-based Convolutional Neural Network (Faster R-CNN), Region-based Fully Convolutional Network (R-FCN), and Single Shot Multibox Detector (SSD) is explained by [5]. [8] shows the results of their two proposed architectures VGG-FCN-VD16 and VGG-FCN-S on the Wheat Disease Database 2017. They received an accuracy of 97.95% and 95.12% with those architectures respectively. A 9 layer CNN was trained with the help of the images from the Plant Village dataset in [6]. CNN is also used by [9] to detect diseases of the rice plants using 500 natural images collected from rice experimental field. Almost all of these papers have tried to solve the problem using a similar approach. This approach for disease detection is a four-step process. 1) Image Acquisition, 2) Image preprocessing, 3) Feature extraction and at last, passing the image through 4) Recognition and Identification techniques.

The performance of various CNN model on the database of 87,848 images of healthy and unhealthy plant leaves, consisting of 25 different plants in a set of 58 distinct classes was investigated by [4]. The various architectures such as AlexNet, AlexNetOWTBn, VGG, GoogLeNet, Over-feat with parameters such as batches, epochs, size, momentum, weight decay, and learning rate are examined. The most successful rates were 99.53% observed in VGG.

Deploying a convolution neural network on hardware was demonstrated by [2]. Two different deep learning architectures were used which were AlexNet and SqueezNet for detecting unhealthy leaves in tomato plants in fields. These architectures were trained and tested on the tomato images from the Plant Village dataset. The training and validation of both networks were done on hardware by Nvidia namely Nvidia Jetson Tx1. In this work trained models are tested on the validation set with using GPU.

A new model named INAR-SSD that uses deep CNN along with GoogLeNet Inception and Rainbow concatenation to detect apple leaf disease is proposed by [7]. The CNN model mentioned in the paper [7] was trained with 26,377 images of a plant leaf with different diseases. The results showed a high-performance solution with 78.80% mAP.

Optimising the algorithms by reducing the number of parameters and to improve the classification accuracy of maize leaf disease using improved GoogLeNet and Cifar10 models was aimed in [15]. These 2 models test and train nine kinds of maize leaf images by changing a few parameters such as adding dropouts to reduce overfitting, altering the pooling combination and some linear functions. In this process, both the models were able to give an average classification accuracy of 98.8%. It also shows that altering the parameters like the addition of activation function, dropout layers with proper parameters, and few pooling combinations can improve the accuracy of the model.

Convolutional Neural Network and Learning Vector Quantization (LVQ) on 500 images of tomato leaves classified in 4 different disease of tomato with major focus on the color of the leaf is used by [13]. The average accuracy that they achieved on tomato leaves dataset is around 86.0%. A few variations in the LeNet is implemented by [14] on a dateset of 18100 tomato images with 10 classes. The validation accuracy achieved here was 94.8%.

This paper address the issue of crop disease detection using similar approach and have employed a Convolutional Neural Network for the disease identification task with higher accuracy.

3   Methods and Materials

The proposed CNN architecture for crop disease detection using leaf images of different plants is discussed in detail here. The various stages included in the process are discussed in the subsections from collecting the images to the classification of the images.

3.1   Data Pre-processing

The images in the dataset comprises of the healthy and diseased plant leaf images from the Plantvillage Dataset. Few samples of the leaf images from the dataset are shown in Fig. 1. The dataset for classification consists of a total of 54,305 images which are divided into 38 different classes of healthy and diseased plant leaf images, which are identified by the given label for each class [6]. Table 1 lists the classes of the plants and related diseases with number of images in each category. The image transformation is done in order to decrease the size of the image to limit the parameters of the CNN network. The original images are of the size 256×256, which is reduced to a size of 64×64, both the sizes being in the RGB channel.

3.2   Training the CNN Network

The Convolutional Neural Network plays a significant role in feature extraction from the images which helps in the process of classification. Initially, the proposed CNN architecture is trained with images from the dataset mentioned in the above Sect. 3.1.

Table 1. Classes of plant leaf disease dataset

Class name	Number of images
Apple with scab	630
Apple with Black Rot	621
Apple with Cedar Apple Rust	275
Healthy Apple	1645
Healthy Blueberry	1502
Cherry with Powdery Mildew	1052
Healthy Cherry	854
Corn with grey leaf spot	513
Corn with common rust	1192
Corn with northern leaf blight	985
Healthy Corn	1162
Grape with black rot	1180
Grape with black measles	1383
Grape with leaf blight	1076
Healthy grape	423
Orange with Huanglongbing	5507
Peach with bacterial spot	2297
Healthy peach	360
Pepper with bacterial spot	997
Healthy pepper	1478
Potato with early blight	1000
Healthy potato	152
Potato with late blight	1000
Healthy raspberry	371
Healthy soybean	5090
Squash with powdery mildew	1835
Healthy strawberry	456
Strawberry with leaf scorch	1109
Tomato with bacterial spot	2127
Tomato with early blight	1000
Healthy tomato	1591
Tomato with late blight	1909
Tomato with leaf mold	952
Tomato with septoria leaf spot	1771
Tomato with two spotted spider mite	1676
Tomato with target spot	1404
Tomato with mosaic virus	373
Tomato with yellow leaf curl virus	5357

Fig. 1. Sample images of the dataset: (a) Apple with Black Rot. (b) Apple with Scab. (c) Corn with Leaf Blight. (d) Healthy Cherry. (e) Tomato Healthy. (f) Tomato Leaf with Yellow Curl Disease. (Color figure online)

The proposed convolutional network comprises of various layers in which different convolutions take place. The layers generate various forms of the training data which become deeper with the layers in the network. Initially, the convolutional layers work as feature extractors and the dimensionality of the image is reduced by the pooling layers. The convolutional layers being the fundamental building blocks of the network, they extract various lower level features into additional distinct features.

The pooling layer of the network is used to reduce the dimensions of the images, also known as down-sampling. The max-pooling is used in the proposed architecture for downsampling the input image. Another important layer used in architecture is the dropout layer. It used as a regularization technique to prevent overfitting. Finally, the dense layer classifies the image using the output of convolutional and pooling layers. There are other hyperparameters that determine the performance of the neural network like an epoch, which is a hyperparameter

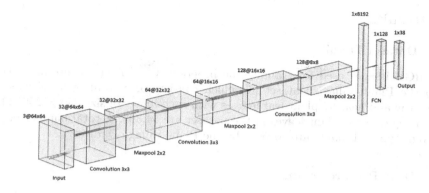

Fig. 2. Layers of proposed CNN architecture

in which all the images are once passed individually forward and backward to the network, Batch size, which is the number of training images in the forward or backward pass and the learning rate which determines the rate at which the weights of the parameters of the network get updated.

In the proposed CNN architecture for plant leaf disease classification, the RGB images of leaves of size 64 × 64 are given as an input. The first layer consists of a convolutional layer with 32 filters each of size 3 × 3 followed by a max-pool layer of size 2 × 2. The second layer is also a convolutional layer with 64 filters each of size 3 × 3 followed by a max-pool layer of filter size 2 × 2. The third layer is again a convloutional layer but with 128 filters each of size 3 × 3 and again followed by a max-pool layer of filter size 2 × 2. The 3D structure is then flattened to a 1D structure of 8192 parameters which is then followed by a fully connected layer of size 1 × 128 which classifies the input in one of the 38 categories. The visual representation of the layers is shown in Fig. 2.

The model was trained using the optimized hyperparameters which are mention in Table 2 and the dataset mentioned in the Sect. 3.1.

Table 2. Hyper parameters of the architecture

Name of the parameter	Value
Training Epochs	10
Batch size	64
Dropout after first layer	0.1
Dropout after second layer	0.3
Dropout after third layer	0.2
Learning Rate	0.1
Training set size	42,242
Validation set size	10,561

4   Results

4.1   Dataset Details

The RGB images used for training the proposed CNN Architecture are taken from the Plant Village Dataset [6] which consists of a total of 38 classes of unhealthy and healthy plant leaf images with each image of size 256 × 256. The total images of the plant leaves in the dataset are 54,305. A total number of 14 different types of plants are covered by the Plant Village Dataset.

4.2   Data Pre-processing

The data pre-processing plays a vital role in determining the accuracy of the proposed architecture and time of training. The size of an RGB image in the Plant Village Dataset is 256 × 256 which is then reduced to 64 × 64 before feeding the image into the architecture, to decrease the number of parameters of architecture and time of training of the architecture.

4.3   Simulation Results

The CNN architecture proposed in this paper was trained on a total of 42,242 plant leaf disease images and was validated on 10,561 images. Later the architecture was tested on 441 images unknown to the architecture. As mentioned the images are to be classified into 38 different classes of leaf diseases. The results we obtained were compared with the results of the architecture mentioned in [6]. Table 3 presents the comparison of classification accuracy by proposed CNN architecture and that by [6].

Table 3. Comparison of results

CNN architecture	Validation accuracy	Validation loss
Model mentioned in [6]	91.43%	0.4797
Our architecture	95.81%	0.1366

The validation loss observed in the first epoch was high at around 0.5665 and decreased to 0.1366 in the last epoch. The same issue was addressed by [6] who proposed a CNN architecture with different sets of parameters. The input it accepts is 128 × 128 × 32 which is large as compared to the size input image used in the proposed architecture. The validation accuracy obtained by [6] on the same dataset as used in the present paper came out to be 91.43% and the validation loss obtained is 0.4797, while the architecture proposed in this paper gave a validation accuracy of 95.81% and loss of 0.1366 for disease classification from leaf images.

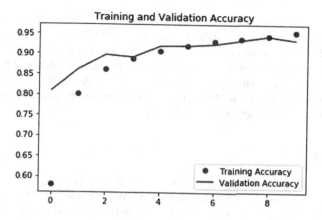

Fig. 3. Plot of validation accuracy v/s Epochs

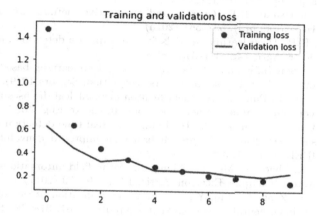

Fig. 4. Plot of validation loss v/s Epochs

Figure 3 gives the plot of Validation Accuracy vs number of Epochs and from this figure it is observed that accuracy increases with the epochs. Figure 4 presents the plot of Validation Loss vs number of Epochs and it is observed that the Validation Loss decreases with increase in number of epochs.

5   Conclusion

Today, most of the research work is focused on solving the common problems using various techniques of Machine Learning. In this paper, a solution to the most common problem of untimely or wrongly identified crop diseases faced by Indian farmers and the agricultural sector is discussed.

Deep Learning is widely used in the field of image classification and pattern recognition. The proposed CNN architecture helps to classify 38 different classes of healthy and diseased plant leaves effectively. The CNN architecture with optimized parameters gave us a validation accuracy of 95.81%. It can be seen that convolutional neural networks provides a high-end performance and hence they are highly suitable for automated detection of the plant diseases through simple plant leaf images. Also, the hyperparameters play a great deal of role in determining the accuracy of the architecture. Alteration in the parameters can bring up changes to the accuracy of the architecture.

References

1. Amara, J., Bouaziz, B., Algergawy, A., et al.: A deep learning-based approach for banana leaf diseases classification. In: BTW (Workshops), pp. 79–88 (2017)
2. Durmuş, H., Güneş, E.O., Kırcı, M.: Disease detection on the leaves of the tomato plants by using deep learning. In: 2017 6th International Conference on Agro-Geoinformatics, pp. 1–5. IEEE (2017)
3. Fang, Y., Ramasamy, R.P.: Current and prospective methods for plant disease detection. Biosensors 5(3), 537–561 (2015)
4. Ferentinos, K.P.: Deep learning models for plant disease detection and diagnosis. Comput. Electr. Agri. 145, 311–318 (2018)
5. Fuentes, A., Yoon, S., Kim, S., Park, D.: A robust deep-learning-based detector for real-time tomato plant diseases and pests recognition. Sensors 17(9), 2022 (2017)
6. Geetharamani, G., Pandian, A.: Identification of plant leaf diseases using a nine-layer deep convolutional neural network. Comput. Electr. Eng. 76, 323–338 (2019)
7. Jiang, P., Chen, Y., Liu, B., He, D., Liang, C.: Real-time detection of apple leaf diseases using deep learning approach based on improved convolutional neural networks. IEEE Access 7, 59069–59080 (2019)
8. Lu, J., Hu, J., Zhao, G., Mei, F., Zhang, C.: An in-field automatic wheat disease diagnosis system. Comput. Electron. Agric. 142, 369–379 (2017)
9. Lu, Y., Yi, S., Zeng, N., Liu, Y., Zhang, Y.: Identification of rice diseases using deep convolutional neural networks. Neurocomputing 267, 378–384 (2017)
10. Nikola, M., Trendov, S.V., Zeng, M.: Digital technologies in agriculture and rural areas briefing paper (2019). http://www.fao.org/3/ca4887en/ca4887en.pdf
11. Patil, J.K., Kumar, R.: Advances in image processing for detection of plant diseases. J. Adv. Bioinform. Appl. Res. 2(2), 135–141 (2011)
12. Shurtleff, M.C., Pelczar, M.J., Kelman, A., Pelczar, R.M.: Plant disease. Encyclopædia Britannica (2019). https://www.britannica.com/science/plant-disease
13. Sardogan, M., Tuncer, A., Ozen, Y.: Plant leaf disease detection and classification based on CNN with LVQ algorithm. In: 2018 3rd International Conference on Computer Science and Engineering (UBMK), pp. 382–385. IEEE (2018)
14. Tm, P., Pranathi, A., SaiAshritha, K., Chittaragi, N.B., Koolagudi, S.G.: Tomato leaf disease detection using convolutional neural networks. In: 2018 Eleventh International Conference on Contemporary Computing (IC3), pp. 1–5. IEEE (2018)
15. Zhang, X., Qiao, Y., Meng, F., Fan, C., Zhang, M.: Identification of maize leaf diseases using improved deep convolutional neural networks. IEEE Access 6, 30370–30377 (2018)

Author Index

Printed in the United States
By Bookmasters